LA VOZ DE M.A.Y.O.

TATA

RAMBO

™

La Voz De M.A.Y.O.: TATA RAMBO

Created by - Henry Barajas

published by

Top Cow Productions, Inc.

Los Angeles

LA VOZ D

TA

RA

FOR TOP COW PRODUCTIONS, INC. • **Marc Silvestri**: CEO • **Matt Hawkins** President & COO • **Elena Salcedo**: Vice President of Operations • **Vincent Valentine**: Production Manager • **Henry Barajas**: Director of Operations • **Dylan Gray**: Marketing Director

IMAGE COMICS, INC. • **Robert Kirkman**: Chief Operating Officer • **Erik Larsen**: Chief Financial Officer • **Todd McFarlane**: President • **Marc Silvestri**: Chief Executive Officer • **Jim Valentino**: Vice President • **Eric Stephenson**: Publisher / Chief Creative Officer • **Jeff Boison**: Director of Publishing Planning & Book Trade Sales • **Chris Ross**: Director of Digital Sales • **Jeff Stang**: Director of Direct Market Sales • **Kat Salazar**: Director of PR & Marketing • **Drew Gill**: Cover Editor • **Heather Doornink**: Production Director • **Nicole Lapalme**: Controller • **IMAGECOMICS.COM**

STORY . . . . Henry Barajas
ART. . . . . .J. Gonzo
EDITOR . . . . Claire Napier
ASSISTANT EDITOR . . . . Elena Salcedo
STORY EDITOR . . . . .El Anderson
EDITOR-IN-CHIEF . . . . Matt Hawkins
LETTER ART. . . . . Bernardo Brice
PROOFREADING. . . . . Kat Overland
LOGO & PRODUCTION DESIGN. .J. Gonzo

SPECIAL THANKS . . . . .Jann Jones
                                                           Chris Arrant
                                                           Danny Djeljosevic
                                                           Mike Macropoulos

Graphic Reclamations:
A Foreword

Frederick Luis Aldama

It's 2019, and mainstream narratives that put the capital H in History in all forms—from the big scholarly tomes and school textbooks to epic-dimensioned documentaries—continue to fail us Latinxs. Put simply, when I ask my college students if they know about the 1898 Spanish-American War, the Mexican or Cuban Revolution, and the Civil Rights Movement, they pause then frenetically grab at straws. I ask if they know anything about particular figures such as Pancho Villa, Emiliano Zapata, Simón Bolívar, Che Guevara, the Young Lords, Dolores Huerta, Elena Ochoa, and Cesar Chavez, and their eyes turn a shade of dull. Latinx and Latin American shapers of US history, culture, politics have been willfully dust-balled in K-12 education in this country.

> *"OVER THE DECADES, COMIC BOOKS BY AND ABOUT PEOPLE OF COLOR HAVE BECOME AN IMPORTANT SPACE AS CORRECTIVE TO AN OTHERWISE STRAIGHT MALE, ANGLO-BIASED HISTORICAL RECORD."*

Willful and *shameful* absenting of Latinxs from history continues to walk hand in hand with textbooks that turn Anglos into the A-list makers of history *and* that sugarcoat the violence and violation committed against Latinxs and people of color in the shaping of the US. As recent as 2018, *Prentice Hall Classics: A History of the United States* not only included a worksheet for 8th graders entitled, "The Life of Slaves: A Balanced View." They were asked to list the "positives" and "negatives" of slavery. The textbook itself described slavery as a "peculiar institution" that included "cruel masters who maimed or even killed their slaves [. . .] there were also

kind and generous owners." The textbook concludes how "many [slaves] may not have even been terribly unhappy with their lot, for they knew no other."
Shocked? Those of us pushed to the shadows of these egregious historical narratives aren't. We've been actively creating counternarrative correctives forever and eternity. I think readily of our borderland *corrido* tradition that used music, song, and performance to pass down from generation to generation our histories; we see kinetic iterations of this today in Latinx hip-hop, performance art, poetry, and poetry slams across the nation. To wit: grand shapers of history such as Villa, Zapata, Juan Seguín, Gregorio Cortez, Dolores Huerta, Cesar Chavez and so many others. I think readily of Luis Valdez and his teatro campesino whose actos dynamically blended theatre, music, ritual, and myth to make known the unwritten histories of everyday struggles and triumphs of Chicanxs. And, of course, I think readily of comic books.

Over the decades, comic books by and about people of color have become an important space as corrective to an otherwise straight male, Anglo-biased historical record. Think: Howard Cruse's hard-hitting *Stuck Rubber Baby* (1995). Ho Che Anderson's breathtaking *King: A Comic Biography* (2005). Howard Zinn, Mike Konopacki, and Paul Buhl's magisterial *A People's History of American Empire: The American Empire Project, A Graphic Adaptation* (2008). John Lewis's epic-dimensioned *March* (2013–2016). And, Pénélope Bagieu's globe-sweeping *Brazen: Rebel Ladies who Rocked the World* (2018). In these and many others, readers are asked to recover, remember, reclaim, and restore a complexly shaped historical record. As Jorge J. Santos remarks in *Graphic Memories of the Civil Rights Movement*, this is more than "historical supplementation" (3). This is a way to materialize erased, lost, and troubled histories through graphic means.

Comics has proved an important space for Latinx creators to reclaim and affirm our significant presence as shapers of politics, culture—society in the US. Indeed, the title that launched the now famous alternative comics publisher, Fantagraphics, was the graphic non-fiction history, *Los Tejanos* (1981). While created by a non-Latinx, the focus is. Spurred on by the racist maligning of Tejanos and African Americans in the *Texas History Movies*—a cartoon strip that ran in the *Dallas Daily News* from 1926–1928 and that was collected into a volume and circulated in classrooms till 1968—Jackson wanted *Los Tejanos*

> *"HENRY BARAJAS AND J GONZO JOIN THESE LATINX CREATORS IN RECLAIMING, RESTORING, AND AFFIRMING LATINXS AS SIGNIFICANT SHAPERS OF THE HISTORICAL RECORD."*

to make visible Tejano history makers such as Juan Seguin, a figure who should be remembered along with Austin, Travis, Crockett, and Bowie. Jackson not only chooses to filter all of the events of the Texas-Mexican conflict from 1835 to 1875 through the subjectivity of Juan Seguín, Jackson uses his pen & ink on 10-inch by 15-inch sheets of paper to critique the brutalities of Western Exceptionalism, Manifest Destiny, and imperial expansion. Since *Los Tejanos*, we can add many Latinx-created titles to the list, including Inverna Lockpez and Dean Haspiel's *Cuba My Revolution* (2010), Christine Redfern and Caro Caron's *Who is Ana Mendieta?* (2011), Lila Quintero Weaver's *Darkroom* (2012), Wilfred Santiago's *21: The Story of Roberto Clemente* (2013), Lalo Alcaraz and Ilan Stavans's *A Most Imperfect Union: A Contrarian History of the United States* (2014) Julian Voloj and Claudia Ahlering's *Ghetto Brothers: Warrior to Peacekeeper* (2015), and the many Latinx histories in my edited, *Tales from la Vida* (2018). Remarkably, with the recent publication of the multi-creator 52-page comic, *Alexandria Ocasio-Cortez and the Freshman Force* (2019), we see Latinx history recreated as history in the absolute present-tense, contemporary making.

With the publication of of *La Voz De M.A.Y.O: TATA RAMBO*, Henry Barajas and J Gonzo join these Latinx creators in reclaiming, restoring, and affirming Latinxs

as significant shapers of the historical record. Henry and Gonzo breathe vibrant life into the biography of Tucson-based activist and Henry's bisabuelo, Ramon Jaurigue. In chapter two we meet a white-haired Ramon living in ramshackle trailer. As readers learn of Ramon's PTSD, serving the US in the frontlines of WWII, along with his coming into a social-justice-warrior consciousness, fighting for the rights of the Pascua Yaqui tribe peoples. We step back in time to meet Dolores Huerta and Cesar Chavez, who spent time with Ramon in Tucson. Here we meet a strong and sturdy Ramon galvanizing resistance: "They're more afraid of you. They're afraid of your voice. They're afraid of our strength in numbers."

In *La Voz De M.A.Y.O: TATA RAMBO* Gonzo's trademark alert, vibrant, and kinetic visual storytelling skills powerfully place us in Ramon's consciousness and world. We stand aghast at the behind-closed-doors wheeling and dealing between city and government officials and greedy corporate capitalists who will do anything to turn a profit. We learn of the extreme poverty that plagues our brothers and sisters living in reservations. We experience the pain with the decimation of spiritual, ancestral lands. We stand with Ramon and his calls to action to hold ground against gun-wielding, violent police. With Ramon, we suffer defeat. We grow angry. We mobilize. We triumph.

I actively read, share with others, and teach comics like Henry and Gonzo's *TATA RAMBO*. They have the power to reclaim, restore, and affirm our place in the *real* complex histories that braid together in the shaping of our world today. As Jorge Santos so aptly states, "graphic novels and graphic memoirs present an opportunity to push against the consensus and create a more complete history."(9) I read, share, and teach these comics to make visible our otherwise *hidden figures*: the struggles, lives lost, and triumphs of our parents, abuelos, bisabuelos, tíos and tías who fought for a better tomorrow.

Frederick Luis Aldama is Distinguished University Professor at the Ohio State University. He is the award-winning author, co-author, and editor of 40 books, including the Eisner Award-winning, Latinx *Superheroes in Mainstream Comics.* He is editor of *Latinographix,* a trade-press series that publishes Latinx graphic fiction and nonfiction. He is creator of the first documentary on the history of Latinx superheroes in comics (Amazon Prime) and co-founder and director of SÕL-CON: Brown & Black Comix Expo. For more on Aldama visit: **professorlatinx.osu.edu**

This book is sincerely dedicated

Ramon H. Jaurigue

Padre Antonio Shanchez

Ted Valenzuela

Rosie Jimenez

Felipe Olivas

George Salgado

Joaquin Burruel

Felipe Gastelo

Gloria Tona

Ignacio Elenez

Cecilia Valencia

Rudy Romero

Dolores Sanchez

Pete Lopez

Agustina Gllardo

Juan Alvarez

Teodora Acuna

Basilio Olivas

Delfina Soto

Joaquin Bracamonte

Don Manuel Alvarez

Richard Flores

Natalia Cocio

Eddie Flores

Ralph Gomez

to the M.A.Y.O. Organization.

—— Early praise for *La Voz de M.A.Y.O. Tata Rambo* ——

66 BARAJAS' *TATA RAMBO* SHOWS US VIA HIS STORY THAT FAMILY IS TRULY WHAT GIVES LATINX SUPERPOWER. 99

—Edgardo Miranda-Rodriguez
La Borinqueña, Ricanstruction: Reminiscing & Rebuilding Puerto Rico

66 WITH THIS COLLECTION OF HISTORY, BIOGRAPHY, ART, POLITICS, AND DRAMA, BARAJAS, GONZO, NAPIER, BRICE, AND CABRERA ARE CHARTING GORGEOUSLY DEPICTED NEW TERRITORY— AND WE CAN'T GET ENOUGH. THE STORY GETS BETTER WITH EACH CHAPTER. I CANNOT WAIT TO ADD *LA VOZ DE M.A.Y.O.: TATA RAMBO* TO MY CLASSROOM TEXTS. 99

—Dr. Theresa Rojas,
Modesto College

66 IN *LA VOZ DE M.A.Y.O.: TATA RAMBO* GONZO'S TRADEMARK ALERT, VIBRANT AND KINETIC VISUAL STORYTELLING SKILLS POWERFULLY PLACE US IN RAMON'S CONSCIOUSNESS AND WORLD. 99

—Frederick Luis Aldama
Latinx Superheroes, Tales From la Vida: A Latinx Comics Anthology

66 UNLIKE MARVEL SUPERHEROES FIGHTING VILLAINS, BARAJAS WANTS THIS COMIC BOOK SERIES TO BE MORE ABOUT DOCUMENTING LATINO AND ARIZONA HISTORY—WHICH HE FEELS HAS ITS OWN SUPERPOWER. 99

—NPR's KJZZ
Phoenix, Arizona

66 *TATA RAMBO* IS A HEARTFELT STORY ABOUT HEARTBREAKING LOSS. BARAJAS, GONZO, NAPIER, AND BRICE GIVE A FACE AND A SOUL TO HISTORY LONG FORGOTTEN, BUT NOT SO LONG AGO. 99

—Erica Schultz
Daredevil, Xena

66 HENRY BARAJAS' POWERFUL TRUE STORY BLENDS PERFECTLY WITH J. GONZO'S STUNNING ART AND ELECTRIC COLORS MAKING *LA VOZ DE M.A.Y.O.: TATA RAMBO* A POWERFUL AND COMPELLING GRAPHIC BIOGRAPHY. 99

—Terence Dollard
host of PBS' *Comic Culture*

CHAPTER ONE:

BATTLE FOR THE BARRIO

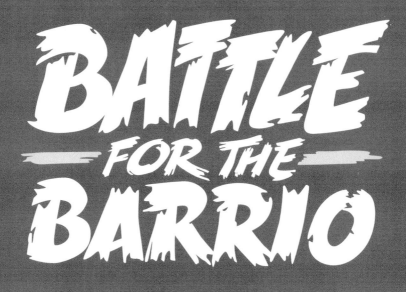

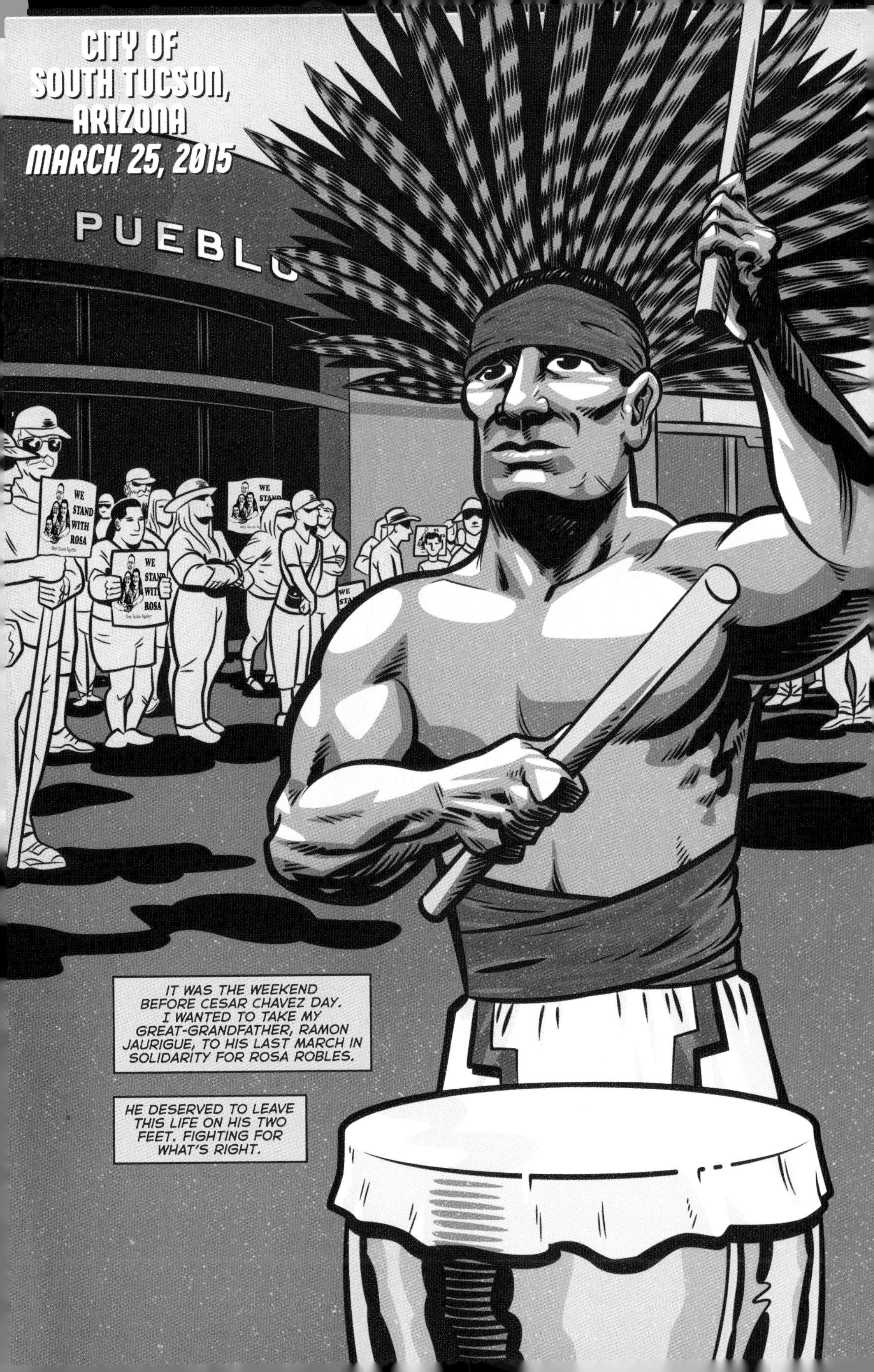
CITY OF SOUTH TUCSON, ARIZONA
MARCH 25, 2015
PUEBLO
WE STAND WITH ROSA
WE STAND WITH ROSA
IT WAS THE WEEKEND BEFORE CESAR CHAVEZ DAY. I WANTED TO TAKE MY GREAT-GRANDFATHER, RAMON JAURIGUE, TO HIS LAST MARCH IN SOLIDARITY FOR ROSA ROBLES.
HE DESERVED TO LEAVE THIS LIFE ON HIS TWO FEET. FIGHTING FOR WHAT'S RIGHT.

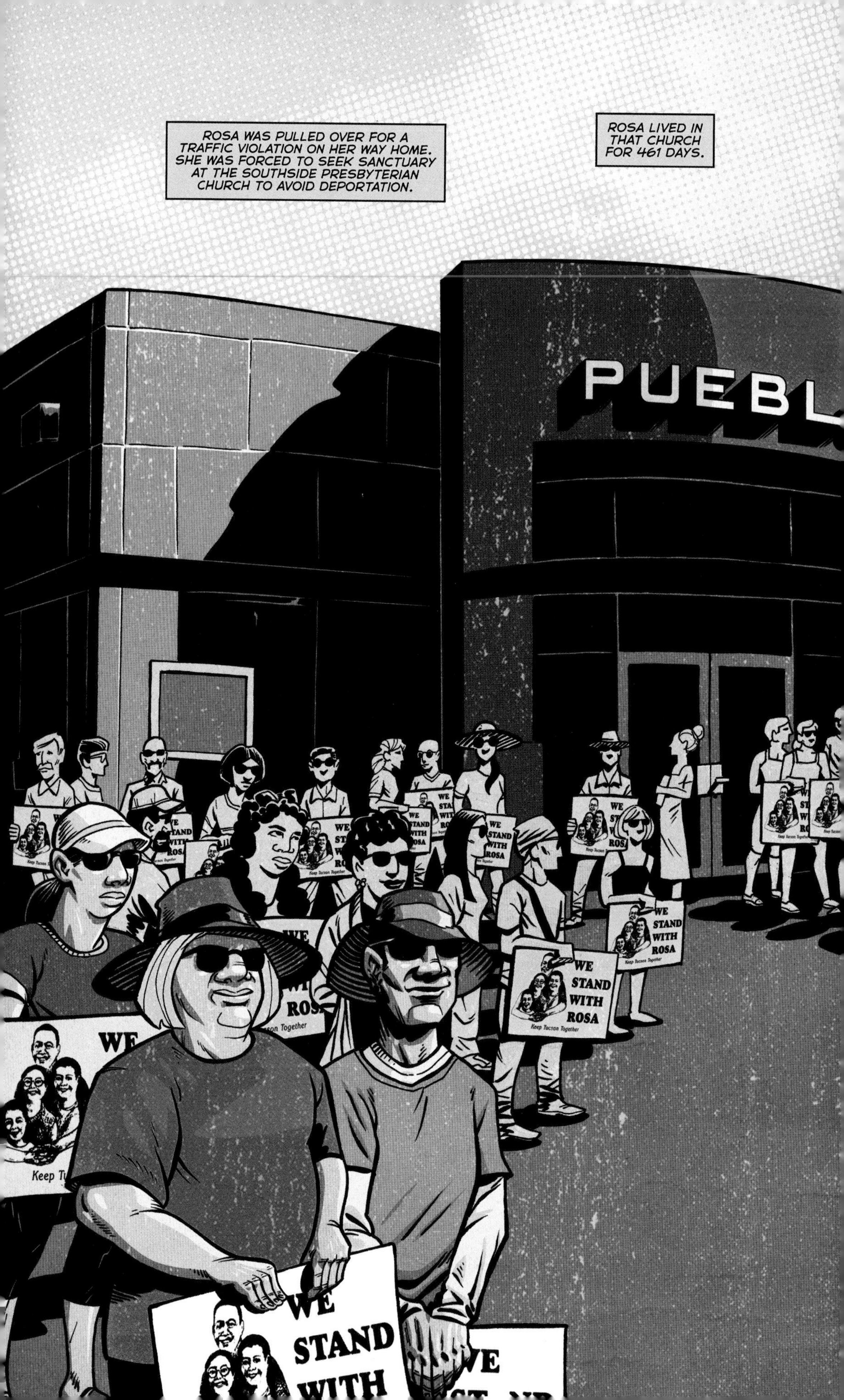
ROSA WAS PULLED OVER FOR A TRAFFIC VIOLATION ON HER WAY HOME. SHE WAS FORCED TO SEEK SANCTUARY AT THE SOUTHSIDE PRESBYTERIAN CHURCH TO AVOID DEPORTATION.
ROSA LIVED IN THAT CHURCH FOR 461 DAYS.
PUEBL
WE STAND WITH ROSA
Keep Tucson Together

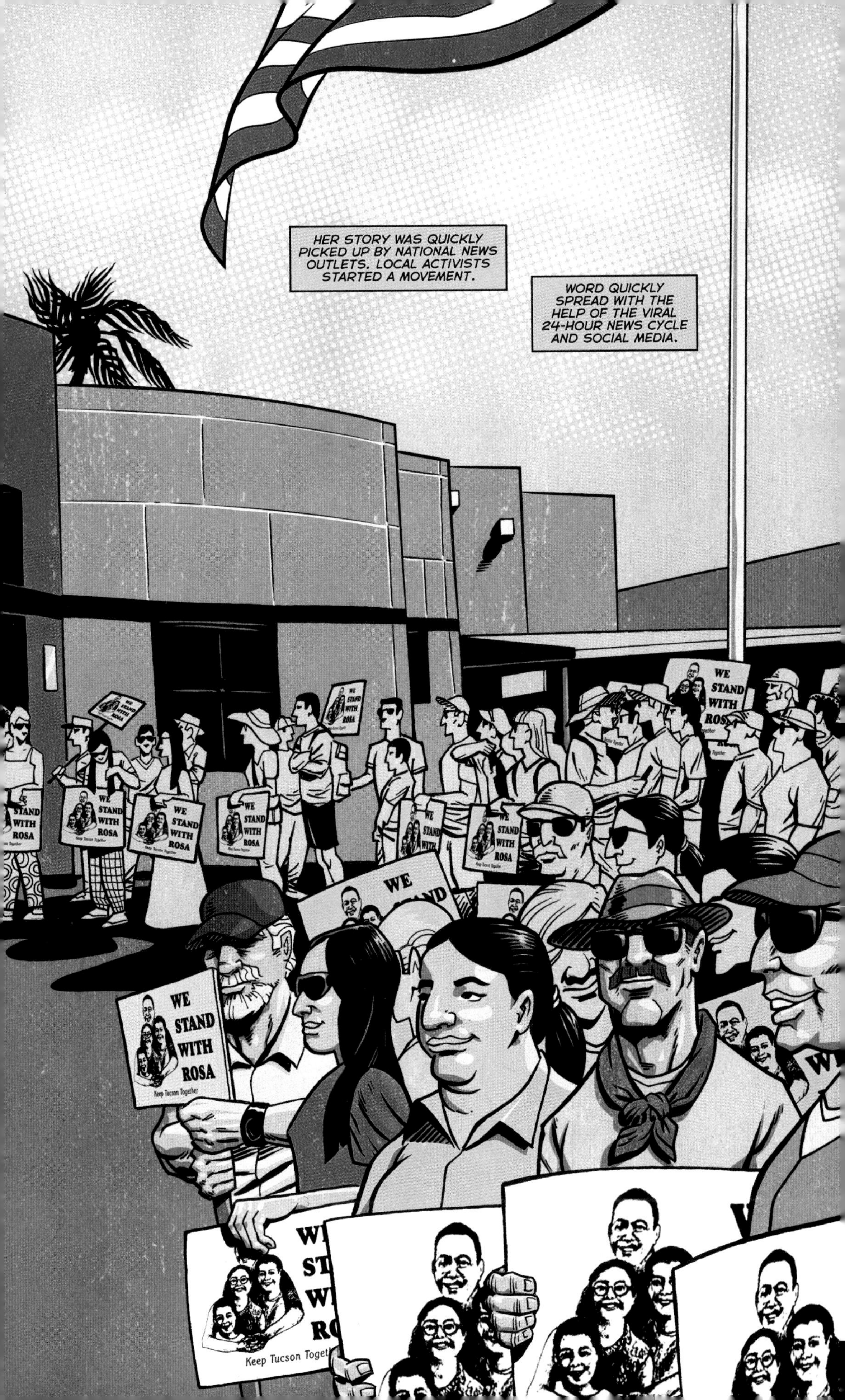
HER STORY WAS QUICKLY PICKED UP BY NATIONAL NEWS OUTLETS. LOCAL ACTIVISTS STARTED A MOVEMENT.
WORD QUICKLY SPREAD WITH THE HELP OF THE VIRAL 24-HOUR NEWS CYCLE AND SOCIAL MEDIA.
WE STAND WITH ROSA
Keep Tucson Together

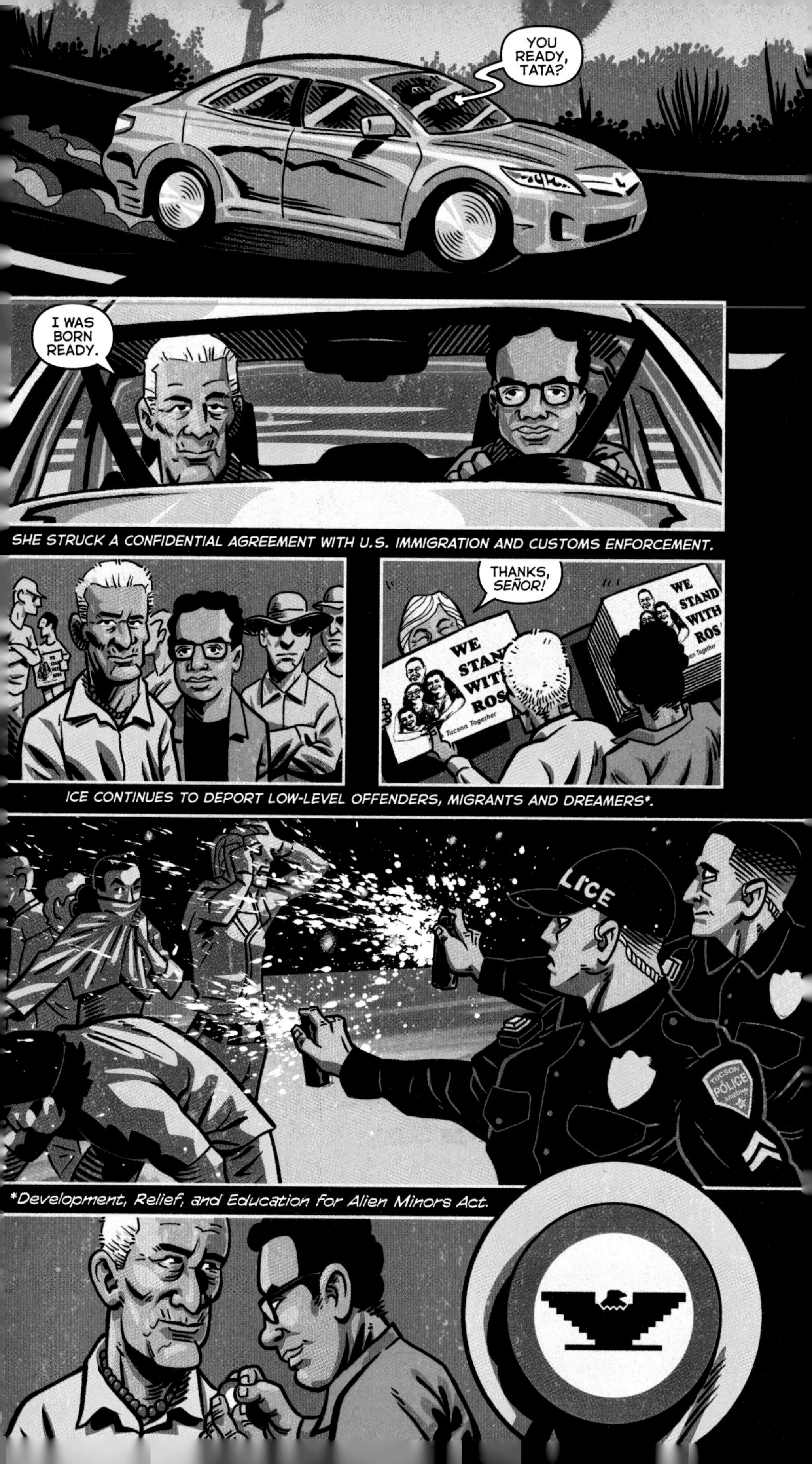
YOU READY, TATA?
I WAS BORN READY.
SHE STRUCK A CONFIDENTIAL AGREEMENT WITH U.S. IMMIGRATION AND CUSTOMS ENFORCEMENT.
THANKS, SEÑOR!
Tucson Together
ICE CONTINUES TO DEPORT LOW-LEVEL OFFENDERS, MIGRANTS AND DREAMERS*.
ICE
TUCSON POLICE ARIZONA
*Development, Relief, and Education for Alien Minors Act.

RAMON DIED ON OCTOBER 11, 2017.

IN THE 70S, RAMON HELPED THE PASCUA YAQUI TRIBE INSTALL SIDEWALKS, ROADS, ELECTRICITY, PLUMBING AND BRING JOBS TO THEIR COMMUNITY. HE CO-FOUNDED M.A.Y.O. AND THEY HELPED THE TRIBE KEEP THEIR LAND FROM BEING TAKEN BY THE CITY OF TUCSON TO MAKE WAY FOR INTERSTATE 10.

I SPENT A WHOLE MONTH INTERVIEWING RAMON AND SURVIVORS THAT WERE ACTUALLY THERE.

I SPENT YEARS RESEARCHING TO TELL TRUE FOLKLORE. NONE OF THIS WAS DOCUMENTED PROPERLY.

RAMON DIDN'T WANT ANY RECOGNITION FOR WHAT HE HAD DONE. RAMON DID A LOT BUT DIDN'T WANT THE SPOTLIGHT.

THIS IS A STORY ABOUT WHAT I CAN PROVE AND I THINK MIGHT HAVE HAPPENED.

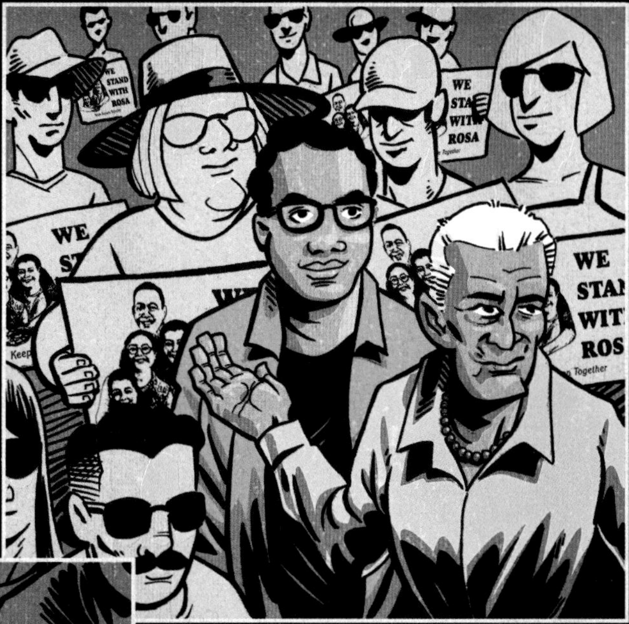
WE STAND WITH ROSA
WE STA WITH ROSA
WE STAN WIT ROS

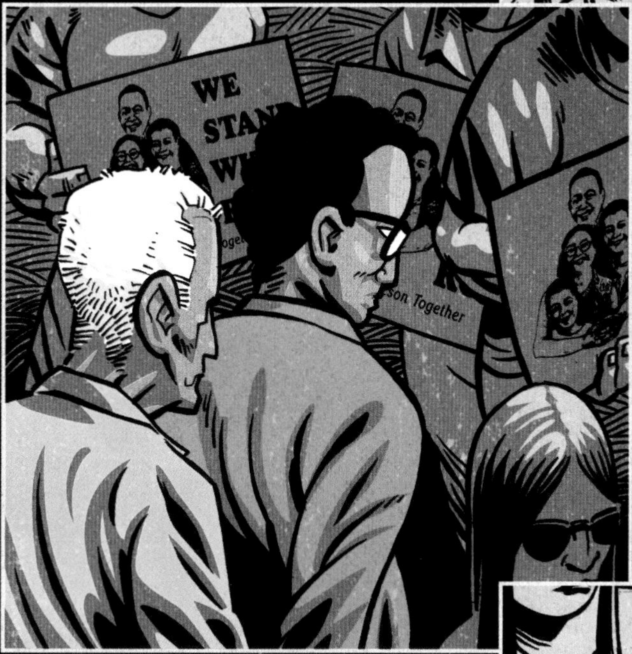
WE STAN
son Together

MY FAMILY USED TO TELL ME THAT HE WAS A GOOD MAN, AND HE HELPED A LOT OF PEOPLE-- BUT NEVER WENT INTO DETAIL ABOUT HIS ACTUAL ACCOMPLISHMENTS.

THE REPORTER IN ME COULDN'T LET THAT HAPPEN WHILE HE WAS STILL ON THIS EARTH.

SADLY, HE DIDN'T LIVE LONG ENOUGH TO READ THIS. I REALLY WANTED TO GIVE HIM A COPY SO HE COULD FINALLY SEE HIS WORK RECOGNIZED. BUT HE NEVER WANTED THAT. BUT AT THE END OF THE DAY, I HAD TO DO THIS FOR MYSELF.

I WANT TO BE ABLE TO HAND DOWN WHAT YOU'RE READING SO MY FAMILY WILL KNOW WHAT TO SAY WHEN SOMEONE IS CURIOUS ABOUT THE ORPHAN, WORLD WAR II VETERAN AND POLITICAL ACTIVIST.

MOST PEOPLE DON'T GET TO GROW UP WITH THEIR GREAT-GRANDPARENTS. I'M LUCKY TO HAVE THESE MEMORIES, INTERVIEWS, AND HIS RECORDS TO TELL THIS IMPORTANT STORY THE YAQUI TRIBE HAS EITHER CHOSEN TO OMIT OR DIDN'T HAVE THE MEANS TO DOCUMENT.

IT'S HARD TO PUBLISH THIS BECAUSE I FEEL LIKE I'M SAYING GOODBYE TO RAMON, AND I'LL NEVER BE READY FOR THAT.

THIS IS FOR THE PEOPLE OF OLD PASCUA. I HOPE THEY EMBRACE THIS AND SHARE IT WITH THEIR PEOPLE. IT'S AN IMPORTANT SLICE OF NOT ONLY THEIR HISTORY BUT FOR TUCSON AND OTHER NATIVE PEOPLE. AT THE END OF THE DAY, I HAD TO DO THIS BUT FOR MYSELF.

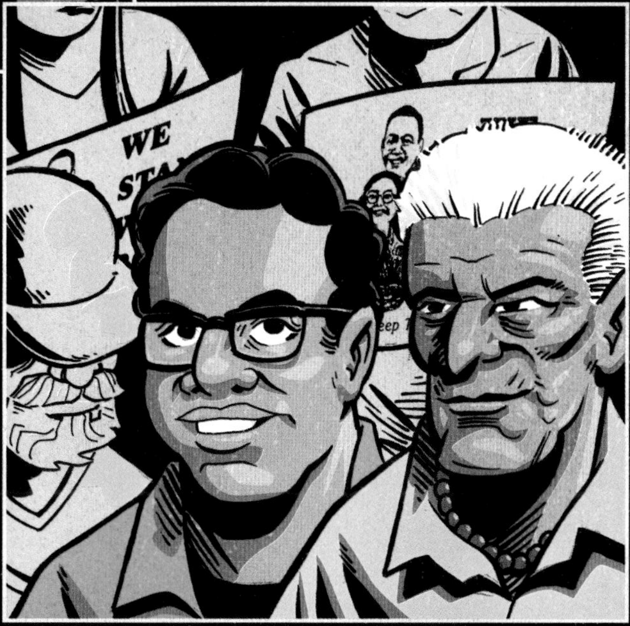
WE STA

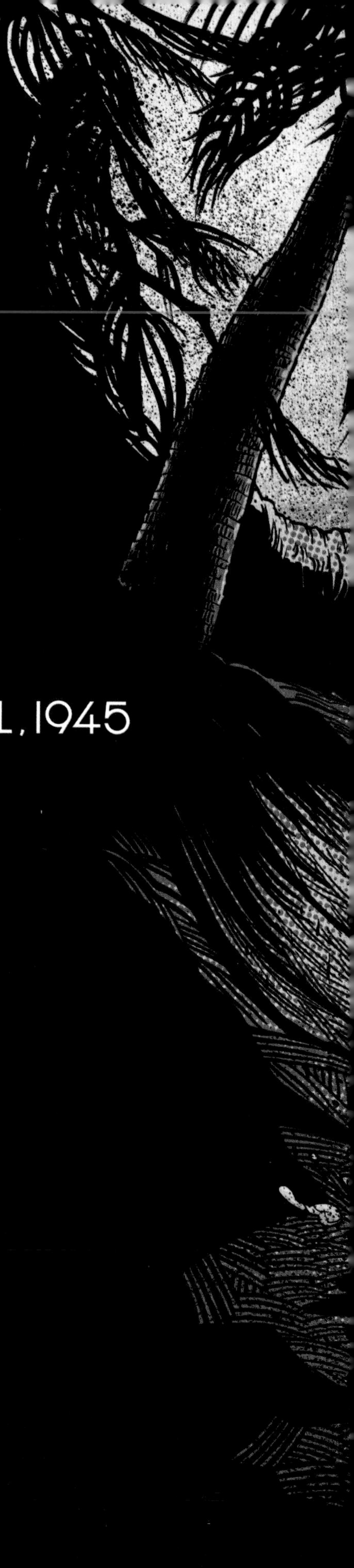

OKINAWA – APRIL, 1945

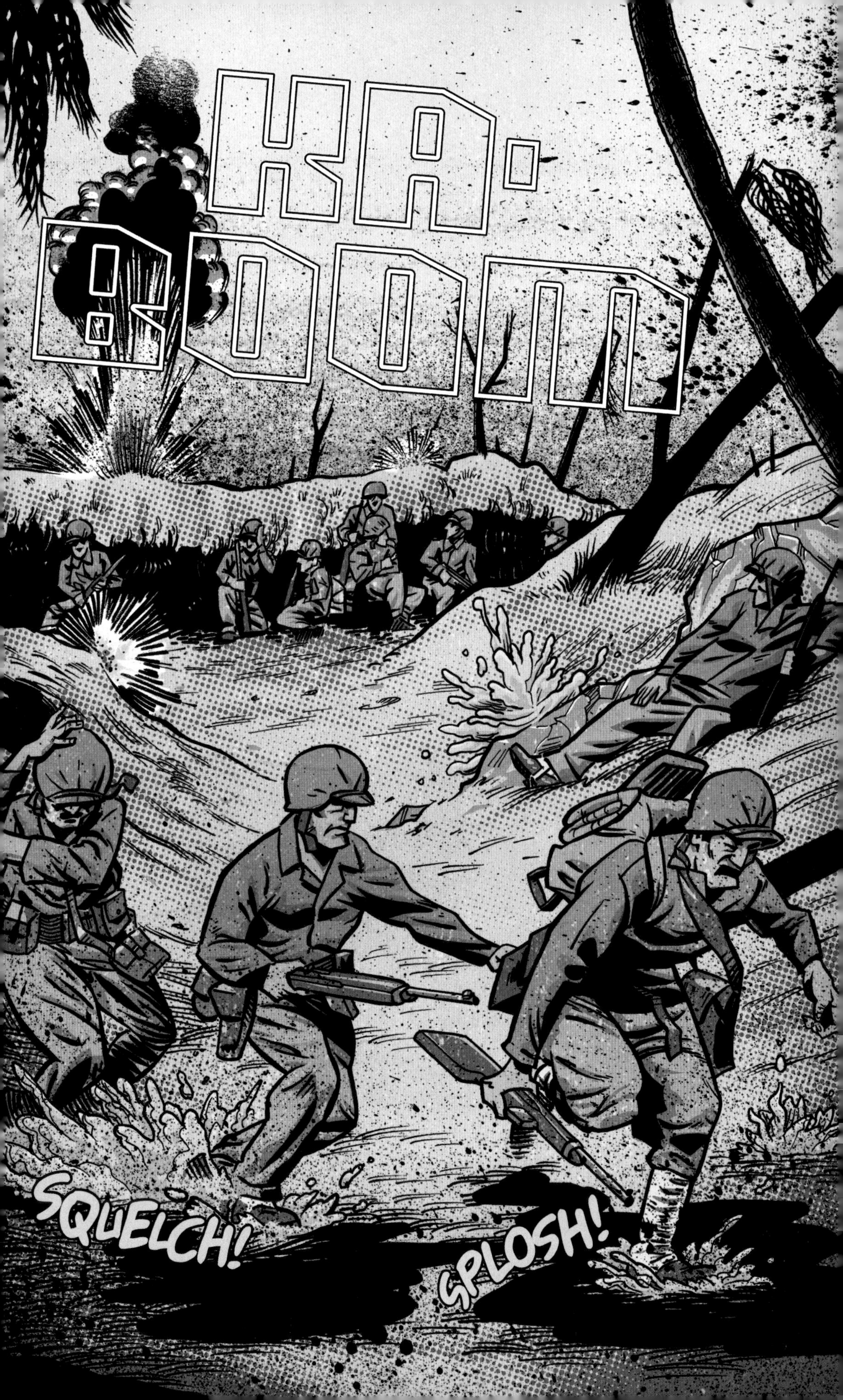
KA-BOOM
SQUELCH!
SPLOSH!

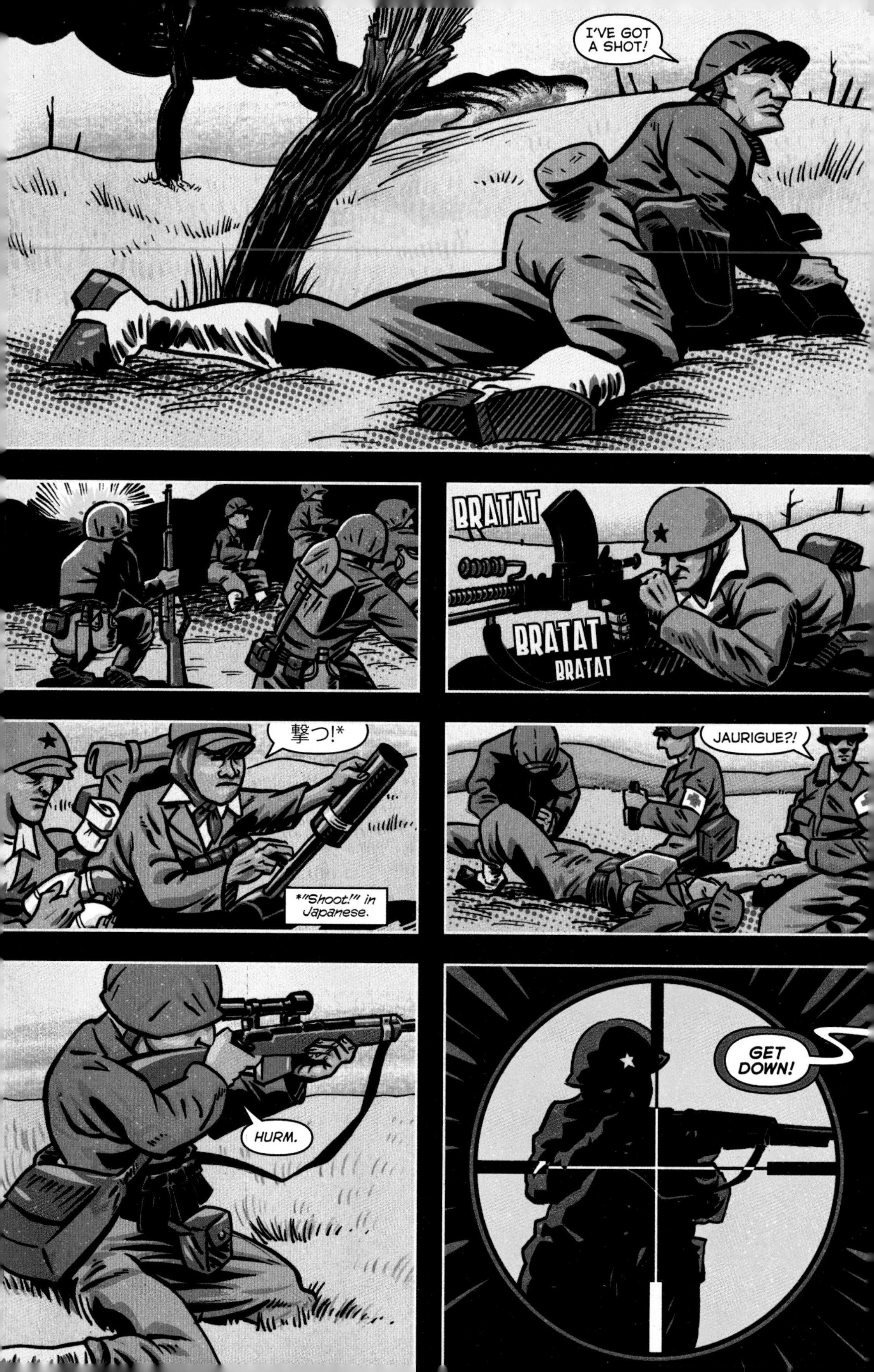
I'VE GOT A SHOT!
BRATAT
BRATAT
BRATAT
撃つ!*
*"Shoot!" in Japanese.
JAURIGUE?!
HURM.
GET DOWN!

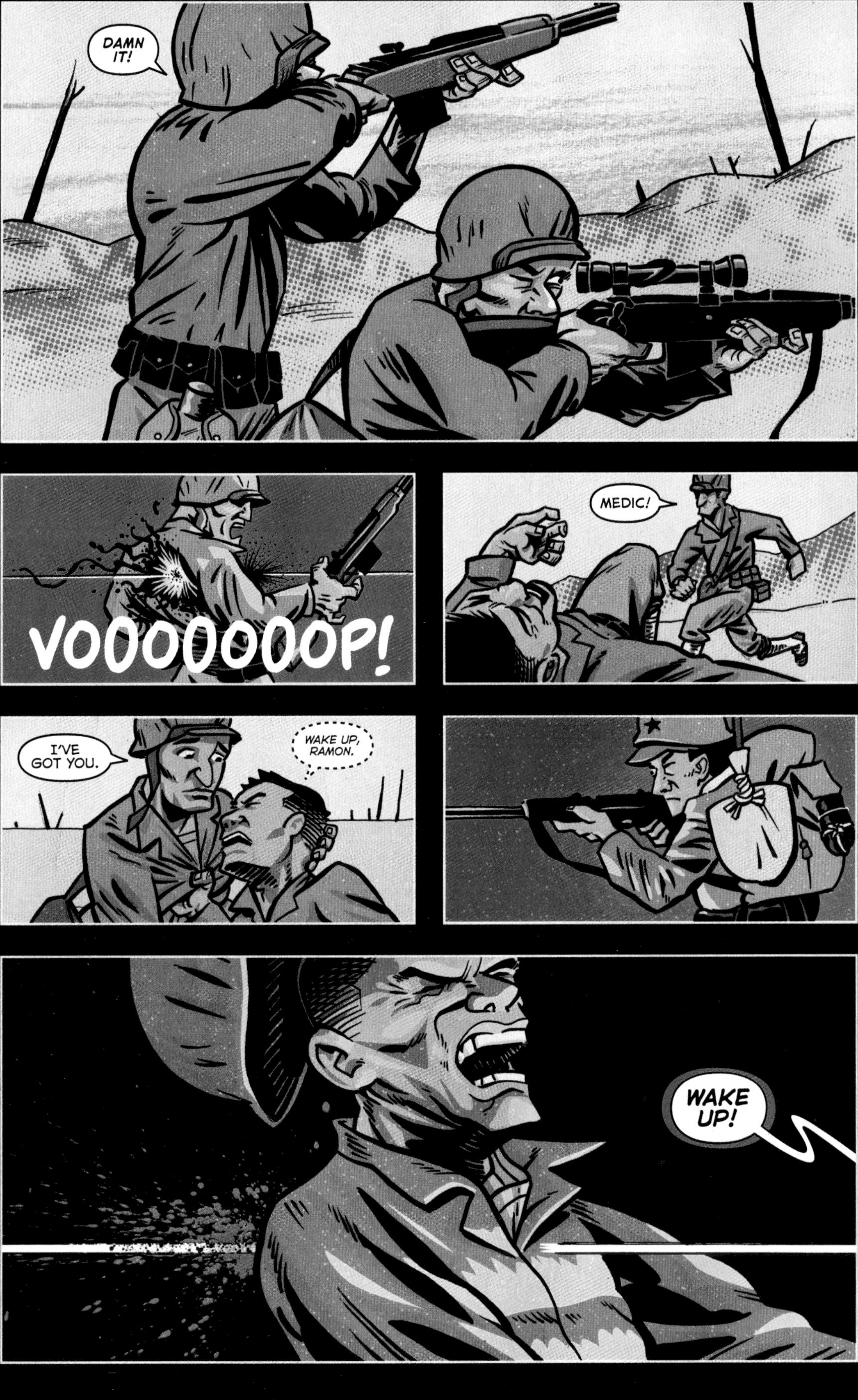
DAMN IT!
VOOOOOOOP!
MEDIC!
I'VE GOT YOU.
WAKE UP, RAMON.
WAKE UP!

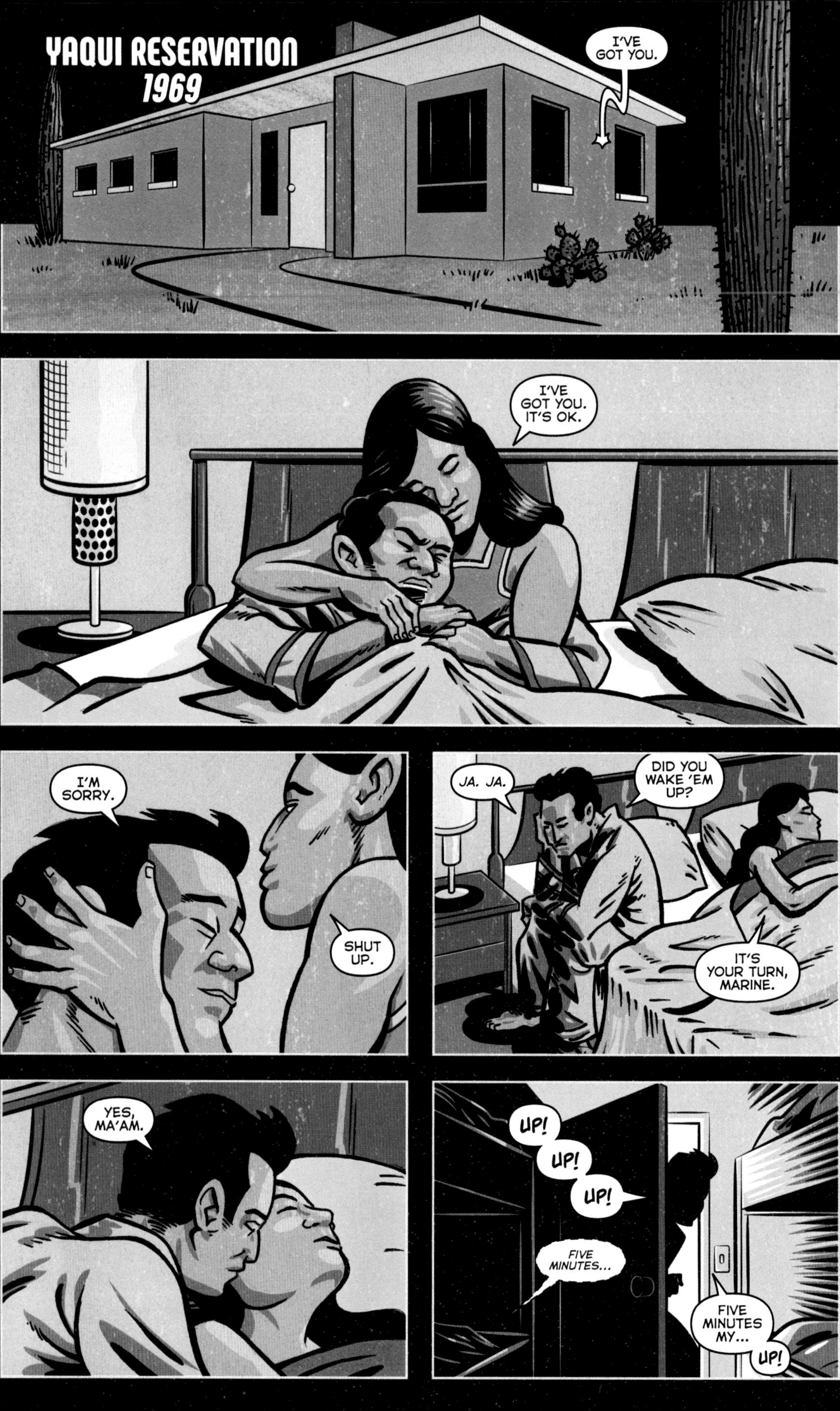
YAQUI RESERVATION
1969
I'VE GOT YOU.
I'VE GOT YOU. IT'S OK.
I'M SORRY.
SHUT UP.
JA. JA.
DID YOU WAKE 'EM UP?
IT'S YOUR TURN, MARINE.
YES, MA'AM.
UP!
UP!
UP!
FIVE MINUTES...
FIVE MINUTES MY...
UP!

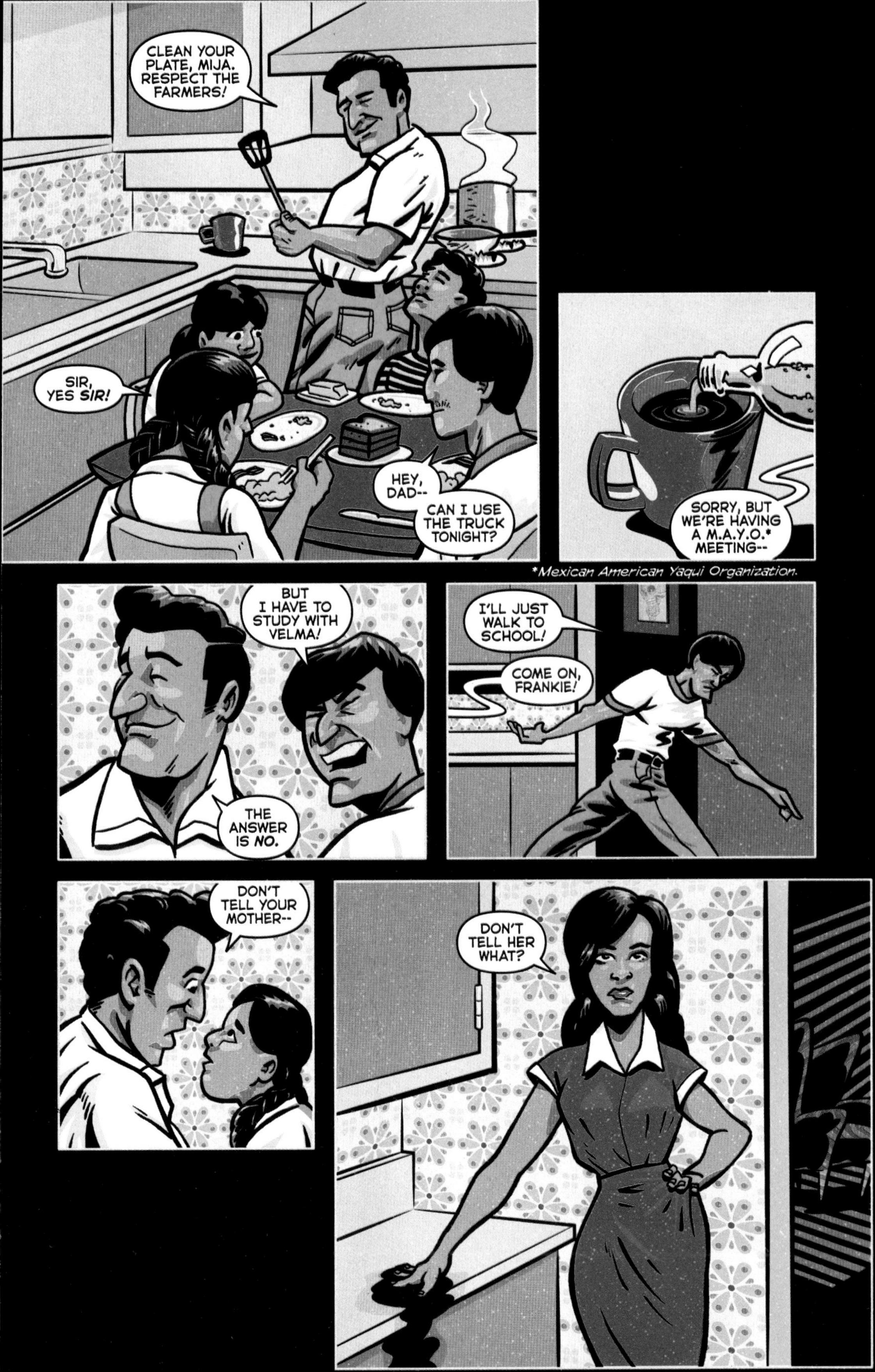
CLEAN YOUR PLATE, MIJA. RESPECT THE FARMERS!
SIR, YES SIR!
HEY, DAD--
CAN I USE THE TRUCK TONIGHT?
SORRY, BUT WE'RE HAVING A M.A.Y.O.* MEETING--
*Mexican American Yaqui Organization.
BUT I HAVE TO STUDY WITH VELMA!
THE ANSWER IS NO.
I'LL JUST WALK TO SCHOOL!
COME ON, FRANKIE!
DON'T TELL YOUR MOTHER--
DON'T TELL HER WHAT?

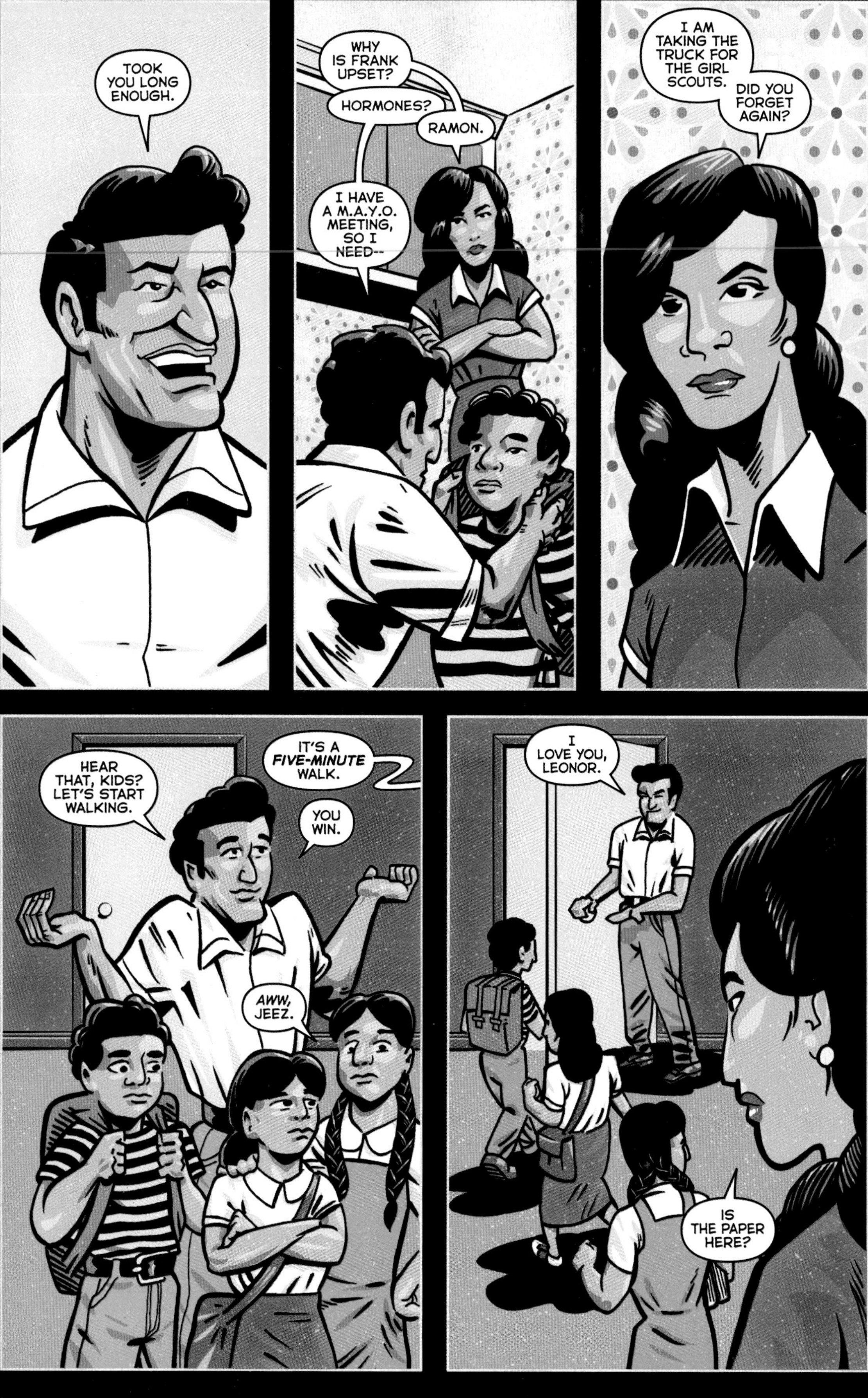

TOOK YOU LONG ENOUGH.
WHY IS FRANK UPSET?
HORMONES?
RAMON.
I HAVE A M.A.Y.O. MEETING, SO I NEED--
I AM TAKING THE TRUCK FOR THE GIRL SCOUTS.
DID YOU FORGET AGAIN?
HEAR THAT, KIDS? LET'S START WALKING.
IT'S A *FIVE-MINUTE* WALK.
YOU WIN.
AWW, JEEZ.
I LOVE YOU, LEONOR.
IS THE PAPER HERE?

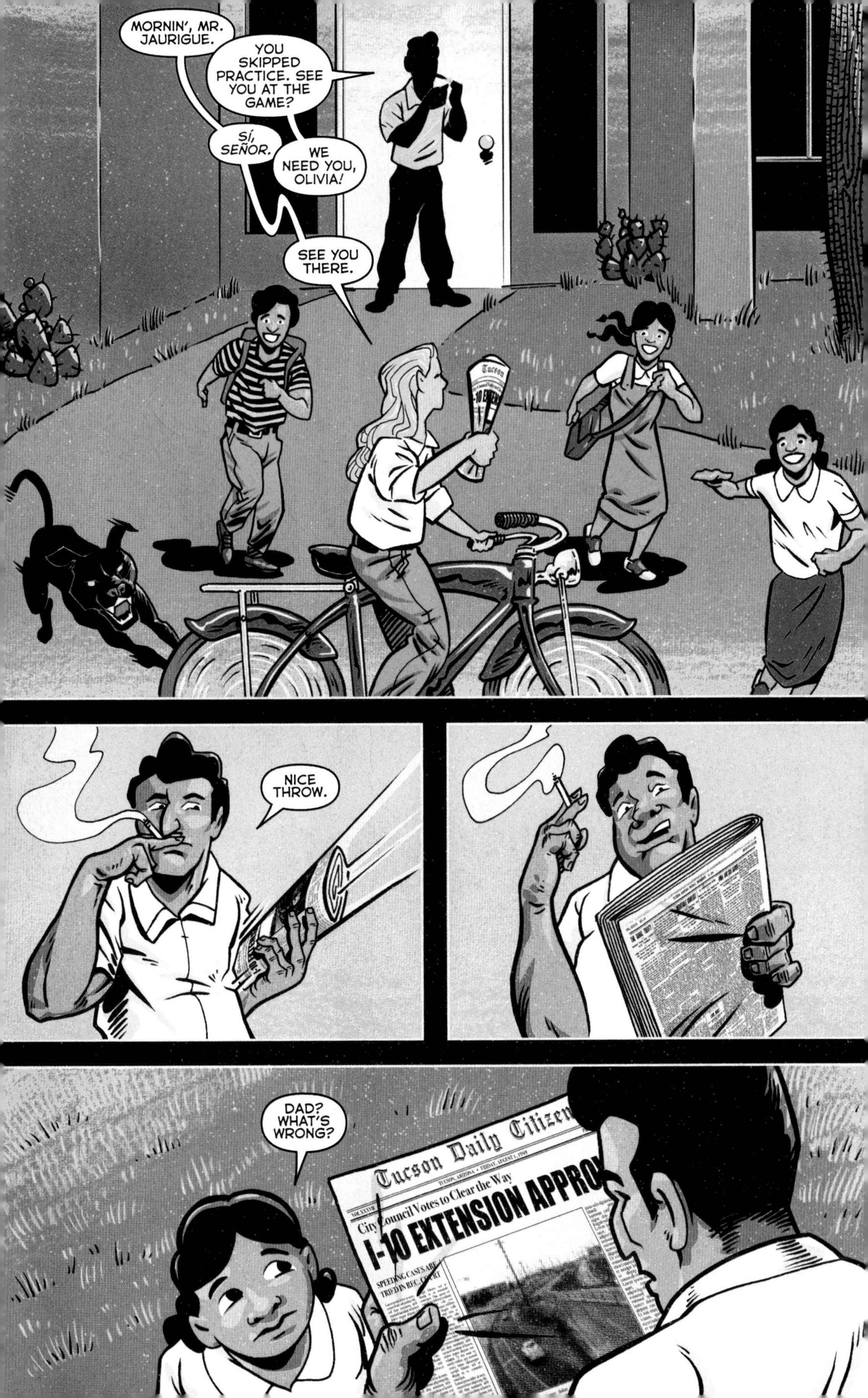
MORNIN', MR. JAURIGUE.
YOU SKIPPED PRACTICE. SEE YOU AT THE GAME?
SÍ, SEÑOR.
WE NEED YOU, OLIVIA!
SEE YOU THERE.
NICE THROW.
DAD? WHAT'S WRONG?
Tucson Daily Citizen
City Council Votes to Clear the Way
I-10 EXTENSION APPRO
SPEEDING CASES ARE TRIED IN REC. COURT

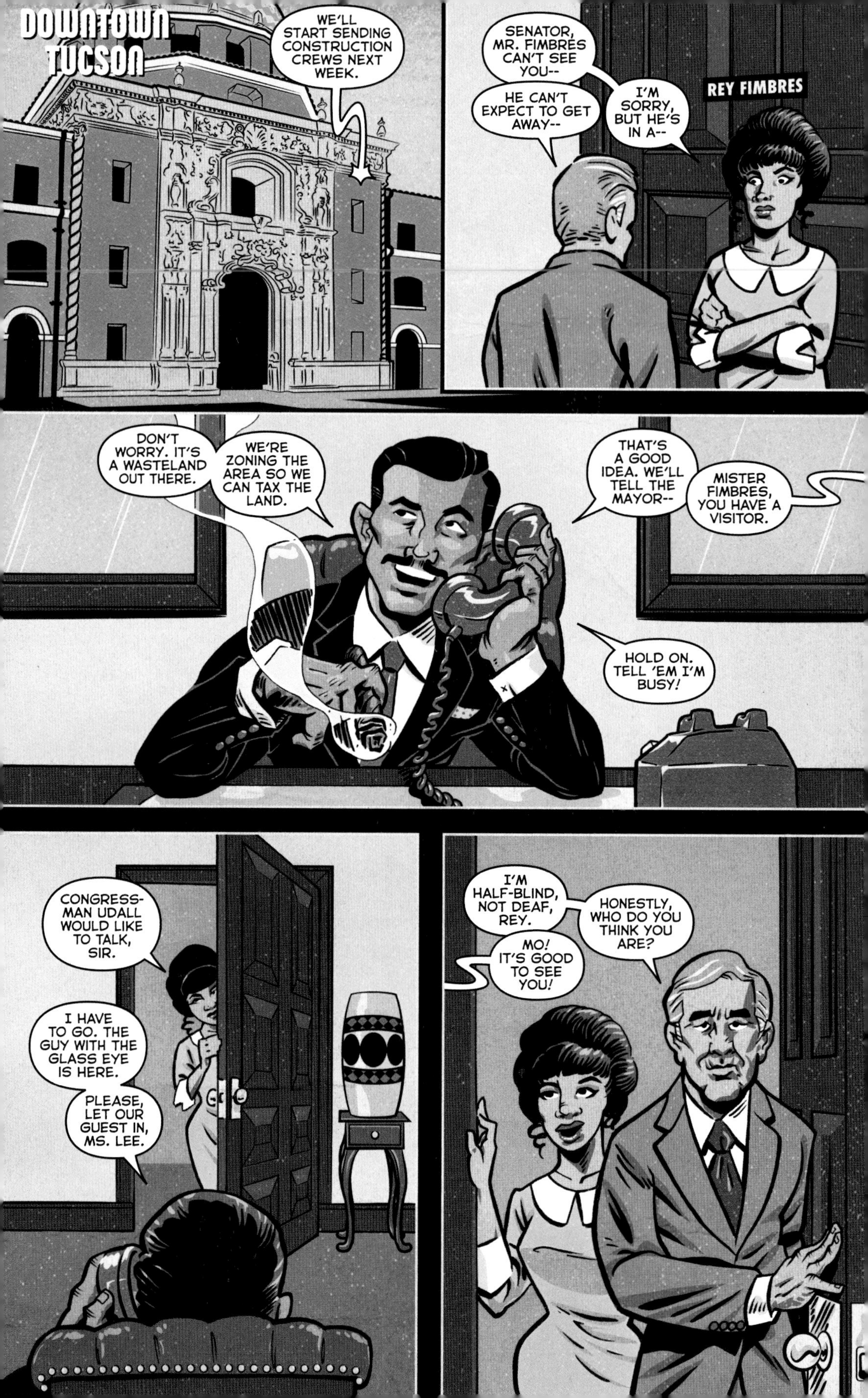
DOWNTOWN TUCSON
WE'LL START SENDING CONSTRUCTION CREWS NEXT WEEK.
SENATOR, MR. FIMBRES CAN'T SEE YOU--
HE CAN'T EXPECT TO GET AWAY--
I'M SORRY, BUT HE'S IN A--
REY FIMBRES
DON'T WORRY. IT'S A WASTELAND OUT THERE.
WE'RE ZONING THE AREA SO WE CAN TAX THE LAND.
THAT'S A GOOD IDEA. WE'LL TELL THE MAYOR--
MISTER FIMBRES, YOU HAVE A VISITOR.
HOLD ON. TELL 'EM I'M BUSY!
CONGRESS-MAN UDALL WOULD LIKE TO TALK, SIR.
I HAVE TO GO. THE GUY WITH THE GLASS EYE IS HERE.
PLEASE, LET OUR GUEST IN, MS. LEE.
I'M HALF-BLIND, NOT DEAF, REY.
HONESTLY, WHO DO YOU THINK YOU ARE?
MO! IT'S GOOD TO SEE YOU!

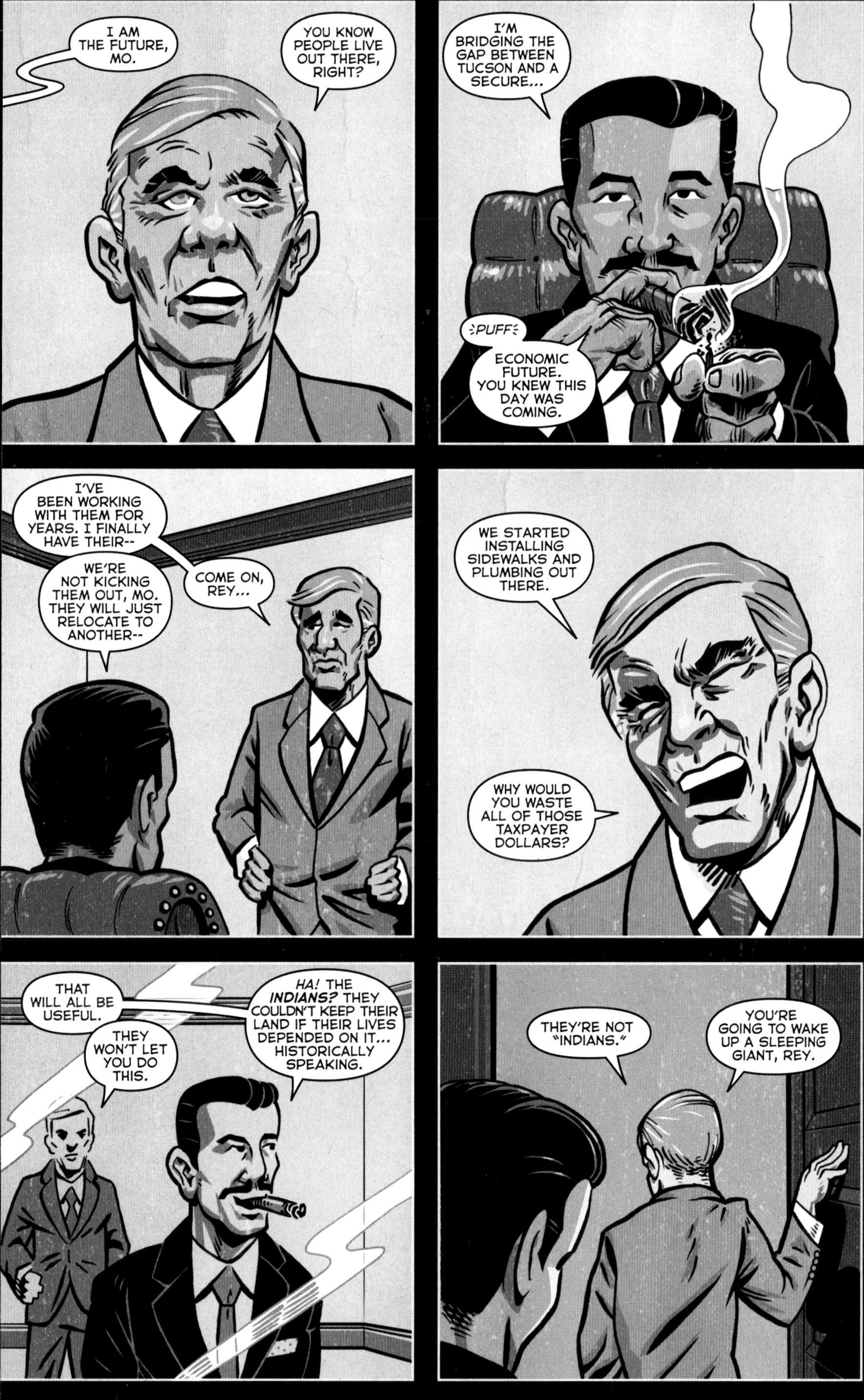
I AM THE FUTURE, MO.
YOU KNOW PEOPLE LIVE OUT THERE, RIGHT?
I'M BRIDGING THE GAP BETWEEN TUCSON AND A SECURE...
PUFF
ECONOMIC FUTURE. YOU KNEW THIS DAY WAS COMING.
I'VE BEEN WORKING WITH THEM FOR YEARS. I FINALLY HAVE THEIR--
COME ON, REY...
WE'RE NOT KICKING THEM OUT, MO. THEY WILL JUST RELOCATE TO ANOTHER--
WE STARTED INSTALLING SIDEWALKS AND PLUMBING OUT THERE.
WHY WOULD YOU WASTE ALL OF THOSE TAXPAYER DOLLARS?
THAT WILL ALL BE USEFUL.
THEY WON'T LET YOU DO THIS.
HA! THE INDIANS? THEY COULDN'T KEEP THEIR LAND IF THEIR LIVES DEPENDED ON IT... HISTORICALLY SPEAKING.
THEY'RE NOT "INDIANS."
YOU'RE GOING TO WAKE UP A SLEEPING GIANT, REY.

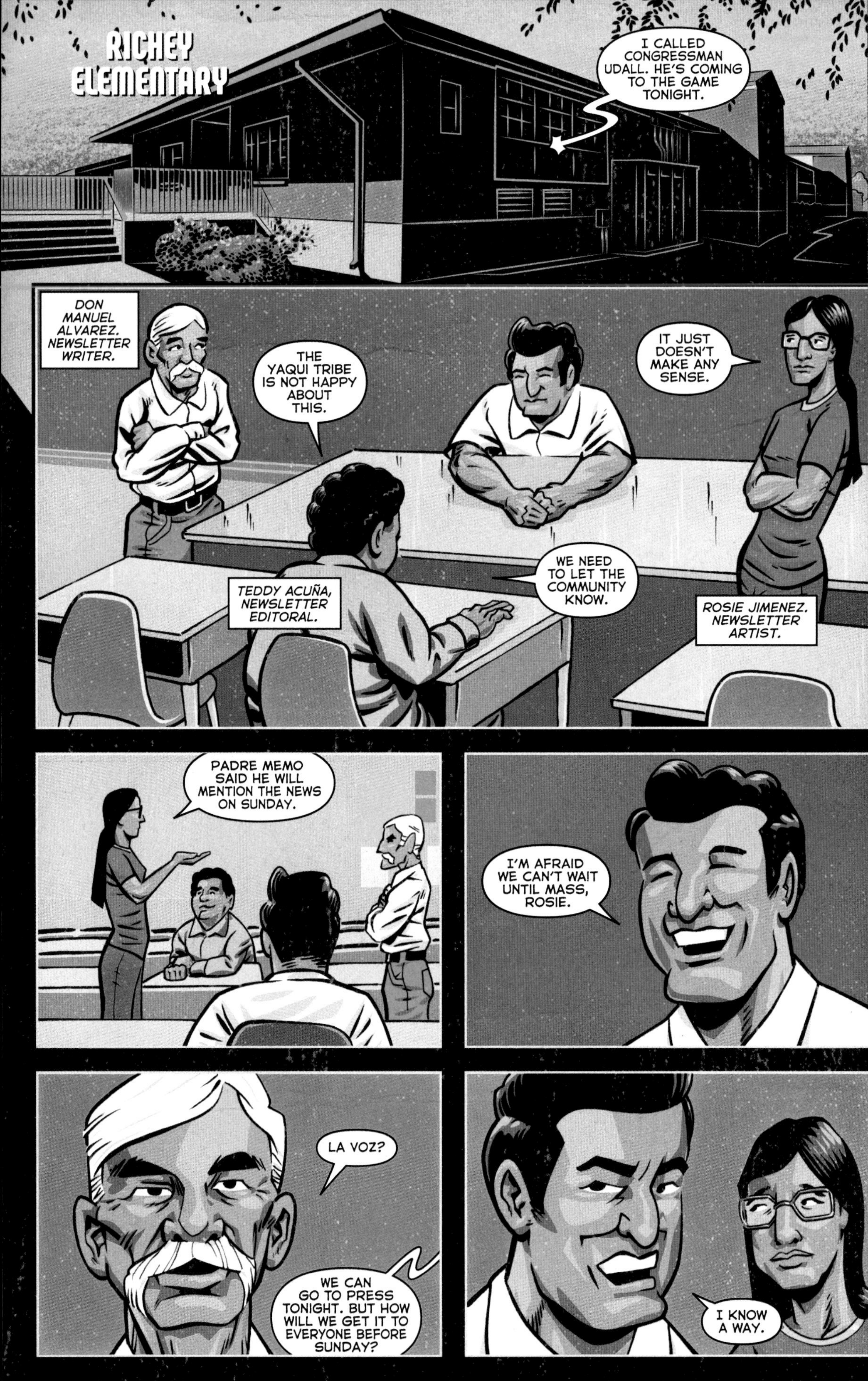
RICHEY ELEMENTARY
I CALLED CONGRESSMAN UDALL. HE'S COMING TO THE GAME TONIGHT.
DON MANUEL ALVAREZ. NEWSLETTER WRITER.
THE YAQUI TRIBE IS NOT HAPPY ABOUT THIS.
IT JUST DOESN'T MAKE ANY SENSE.
WE NEED TO LET THE COMMUNITY KNOW.
TEDDY ACUÑA, NEWSLETTER EDITORAL.
ROSIE JIMENEZ. NEWSLETTER ARTIST.
PADRE MEMO SAID HE WILL MENTION THE NEWS ON SUNDAY.
I'M AFRAID WE CAN'T WAIT UNTIL MASS, ROSIE.
LA VOZ?
WE CAN GO TO PRESS TONIGHT. BUT HOW WILL WE GET IT TO EVERYONE BEFORE SUNDAY?
I KNOW A WAY.

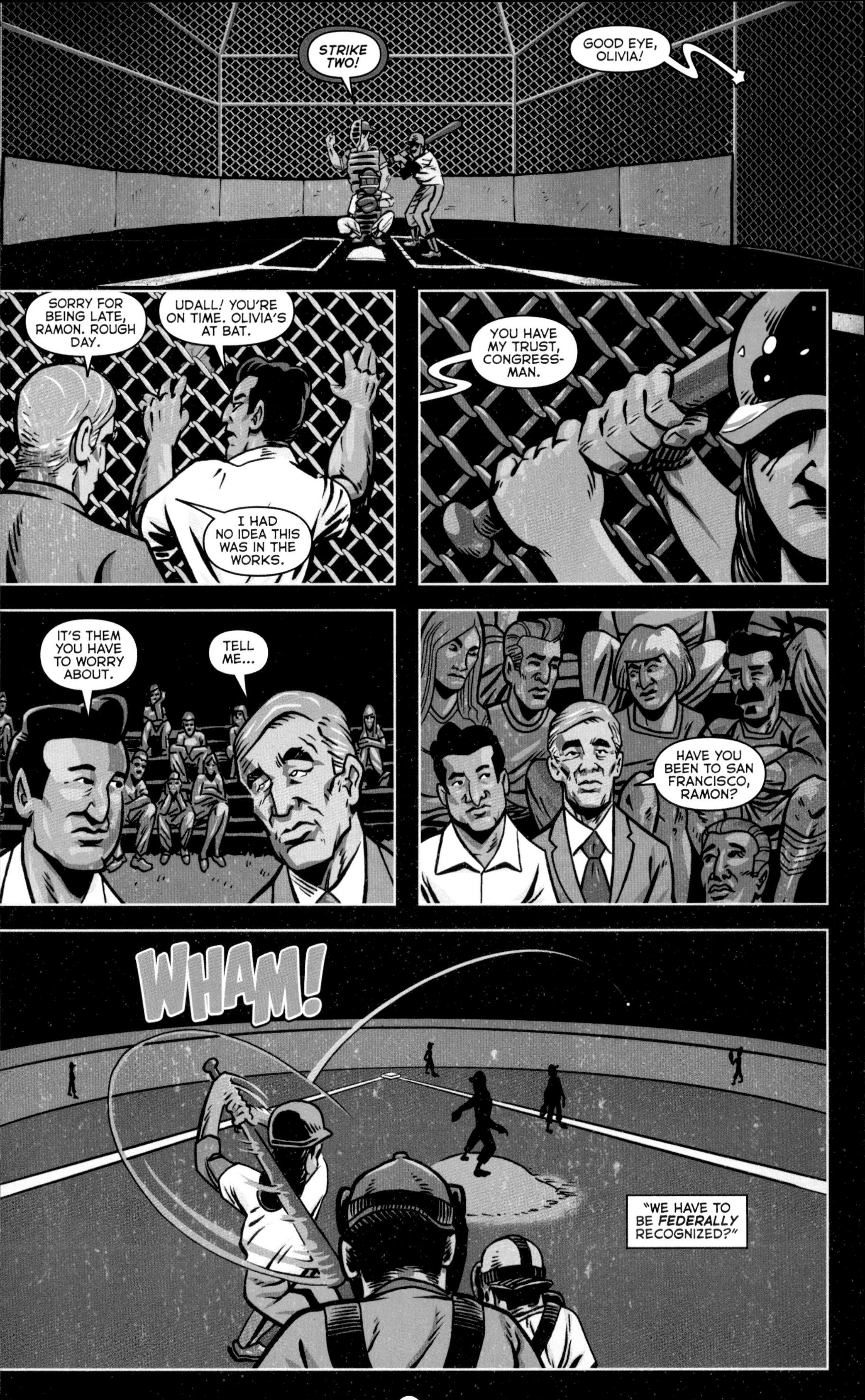
STRIKE TWO!
GOOD EYE, OLIVIA!
SORRY FOR BEING LATE, RAMON. ROUGH DAY.
UDALL! YOU'RE ON TIME. OLIVIA'S AT BAT.
I HAD NO IDEA THIS WAS IN THE WORKS.
YOU HAVE MY TRUST, CONGRESS-MAN.
IT'S THEM YOU HAVE TO WORRY ABOUT.
TELL ME...
HAVE YOU BEEN TO SAN FRANCISCO, RAMON?
WHAM!
"WE HAVE TO BE *FEDERALLY* RECOGNIZED?"

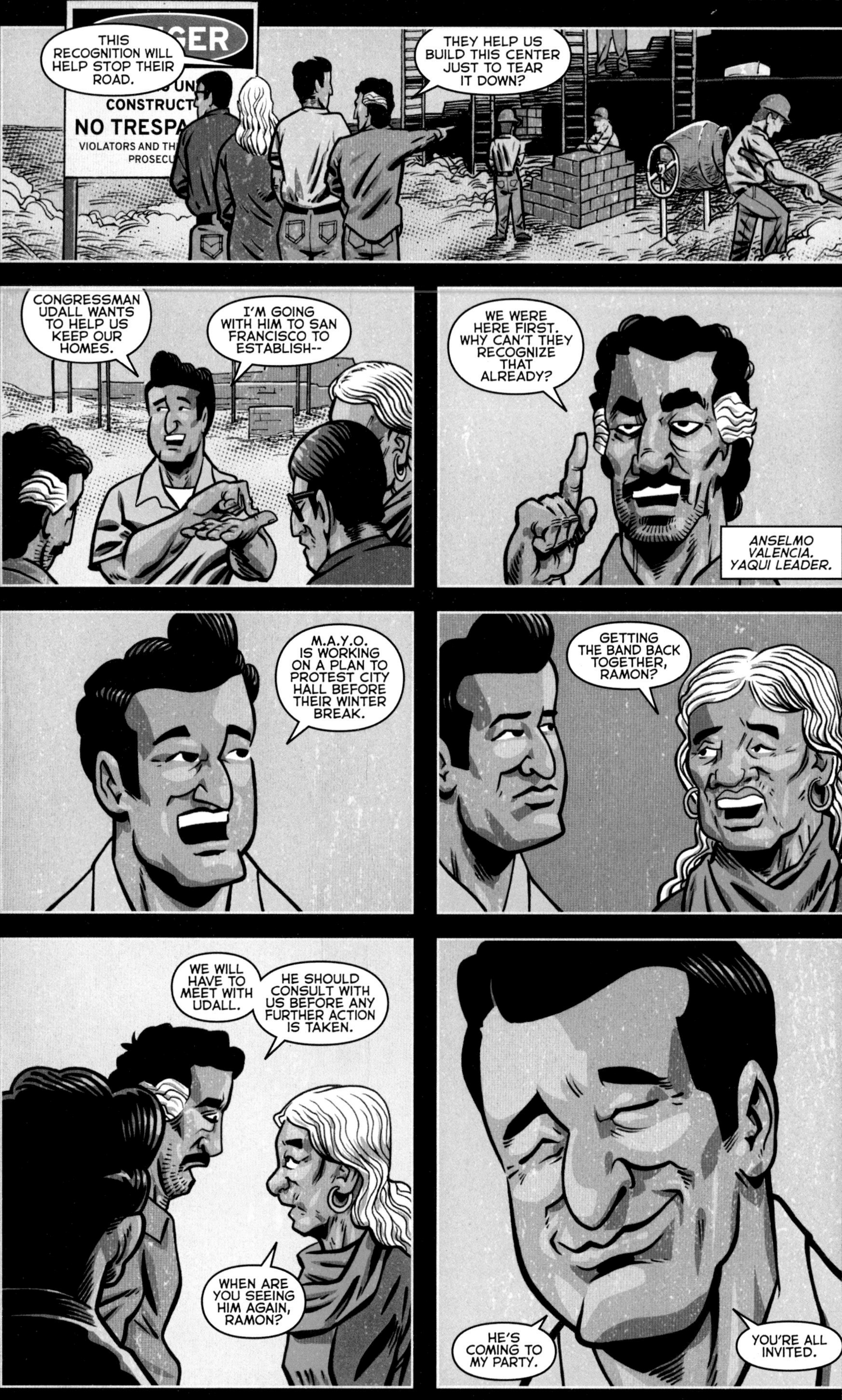

THIS RECOGNITION WILL HELP STOP THEIR ROAD.
...GER
...S UN...
CONSTRUCT...
NO TRESPA...
VIOLATORS AND TH...
PROSECU...
THEY HELP US BUILD THIS CENTER JUST TO TEAR IT DOWN?
CONGRESSMAN UDALL WANTS TO HELP US KEEP OUR HOMES.
I'M GOING WITH HIM TO SAN FRANCISCO TO ESTABLISH--
WE WERE HERE FIRST. WHY CAN'T THEY RECOGNIZE THAT ALREADY?
ANSELMO VALENCIA. YAQUI LEADER.
M.A.Y.O. IS WORKING ON A PLAN TO PROTEST CITY HALL BEFORE THEIR WINTER BREAK.
GETTING THE BAND BACK TOGETHER, RAMON?
WE WILL HAVE TO MEET WITH UDALL.
HE SHOULD CONSULT WITH US BEFORE ANY FURTHER ACTION IS TAKEN.
WHEN ARE YOU SEEING HIM AGAIN, RAMON?
HE'S COMING TO MY PARTY.
YOU'RE ALL INVITED.

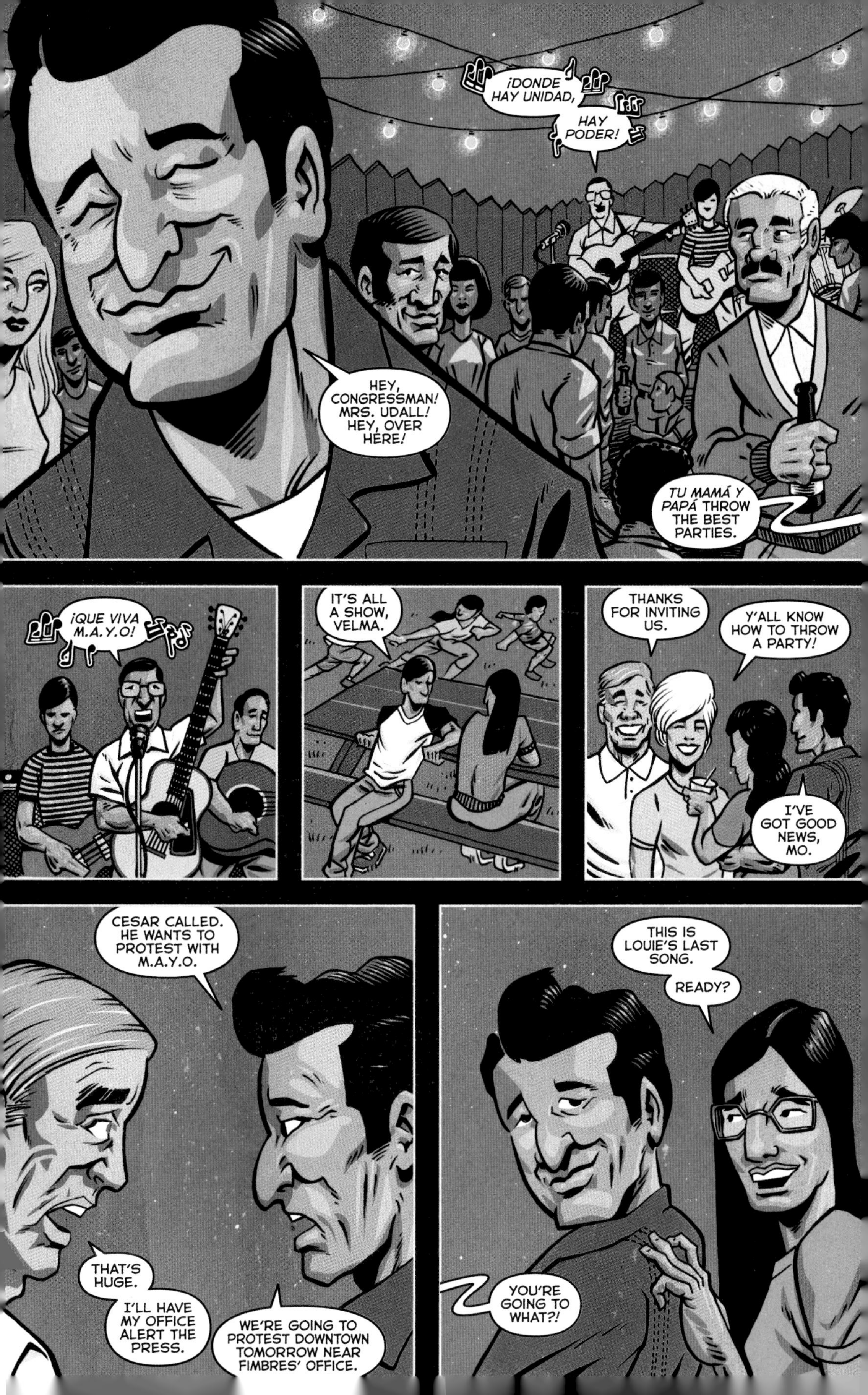
¡DONDE HAY UNIDAD,
HAY PODER!
HEY, CONGRESSMAN! MRS. UDALL! HEY, OVER HERE!
TU MAMÁ Y PAPÁ THROW THE BEST PARTIES.
¡QUE VIVA M.A.Y.O!
IT'S ALL A SHOW, VELMA.
THANKS FOR INVITING US.
Y'ALL KNOW HOW TO THROW A PARTY!
I'VE GOT GOOD NEWS, MO.
CESAR CALLED. HE WANTS TO PROTEST WITH M.A.Y.O.
THAT'S HUGE.
I'LL HAVE MY OFFICE ALERT THE PRESS.
WE'RE GOING TO PROTEST DOWNTOWN TOMORROW NEAR FIMBRES' OFFICE.
THIS IS LOUIE'S LAST SONG.
READY?
YOU'RE GOING TO WHAT?!

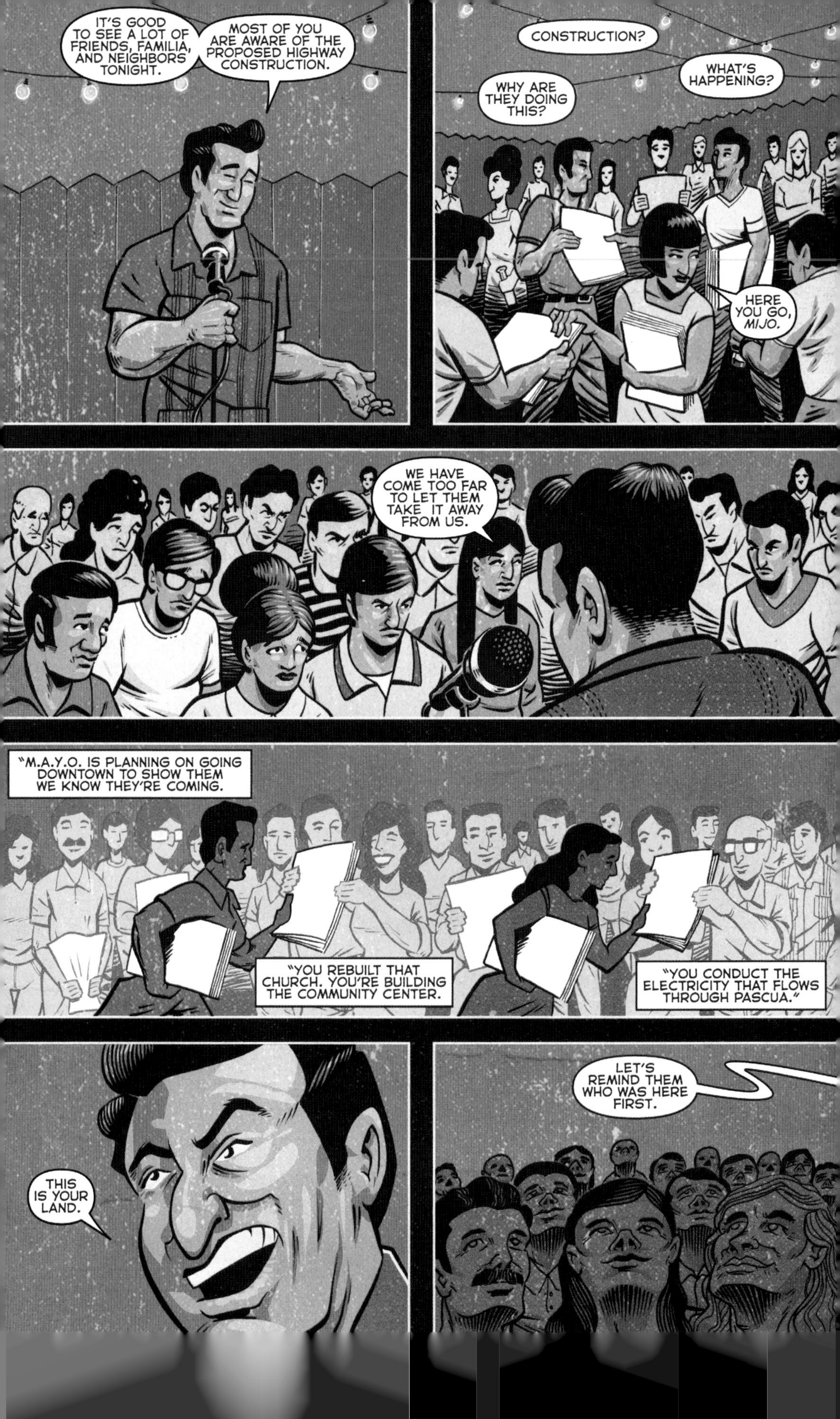
IT'S GOOD TO SEE A LOT OF FRIENDS, FAMILIA, AND NEIGHBORS' TONIGHT.
MOST OF YOU ARE AWARE OF THE PROPOSED HIGHWAY CONSTRUCTION.
CONSTRUCTION?
WHAT'S HAPPENING?
WHY ARE THEY DOING THIS?
HERE YOU GO, MIJO.
WE HAVE COME TOO FAR TO LET THEM TAKE IT AWAY FROM US.
"M.A.Y.O. IS PLANNING ON GOING DOWNTOWN TO SHOW THEM WE KNOW THEY'RE COMING.
"YOU REBUILT THAT CHURCH. YOU'RE BUILDING THE COMMUNITY CENTER.
"YOU CONDUCT THE ELECTRICITY THAT FLOWS THROUGH PASCUA."
THIS IS YOUR LAND.
LET'S REMIND THEM WHO WAS HERE FIRST.

LA VOZ DE MAYO

THE VOICE OF BARRIOS PASCUA, ADELANTO, AND ORACLE PARK (BLUE MOON) 2075 N. CALLE CENTRAL TUCSON, AZ. PHONE 622-5680
MEXICAN AMERICAN YAQUI ORGANIZATION (MAYO)   DECEMBER, 1969
VOLUME I, NUMBER 3

NUEVO ATAQUE CONTRA LOS BARRIOS

NUESTROS BARRIOS

TATPA

IN SAILAM

A new attack against the barrios has again been started through the Dept. of Community Development of the City of Tucson. They have prepared a plan called the Community Renewal Program to acquire a lot of land in the Model Cities Area which at present has many people living on it. And then they plan to change the zoning to industrial, and make an industrial park out of it.

I am speaking mainly about Old Pascua. If they succeed in doing this, we have had it!

Now they have come up with a new program which is the proposed East-West freeway (and the Butterfield freeway) which are planned to cut through the Model Cities Area. As proposed they will be very disruptive, and will destroy many homes and will destroy many schools and will erect tremendous additional barriers in the barrios. If freeway plans are passed, we have had it, even if building does not begin soon. People will be displaced in our barrios and other barrios. The total freeway plan would displace about 12000 people, 4000 homes and many schools. We must act now and protect ourselves against this unethical way of trying to get rid of our barrios!

They say that the Community Renewal Program was undertaken by the City with citizen participation and was supported by city staff and consultants, but as far as we know the citizens are the last ones to know what is being done for them, or shall we say what is being done to them. How much do we actually need freeways unless we need them to make a quick getaway from the actual problems that are present and have been for many years. Do you people think this is the way we are going to our barrios from further deterior-

that our neighbors on the East sides like to see money spent big freeways when taxes are so there are so many people who d, health care and better homes. think the citizens of Tucson rove of us losing our land and r if they are really informed.

por Manuel Alvarez

Senu o ou tuii cohaco jita junevahas-tuoo jibasu tahuic batoita anattemaine hua ajunesiyatuane. Buume o-ouwin chea jita junesiya, tequil, noopo, jiosiapo ajjoste o tui cobata jipueu, chuipia, ta inichupia ca sine agueiya, mamni taoam batoim nasuc, guepula teune amacsan, junuen vetchivo, tuisi vejee senu o ou tutulita sugua jipuetuoo. Ta itepo quia o ouwim jibba: ?Cabe iton mastac jitasa te a awene? Catem jainea sime inime, yorim, mericano, necrom, iton aniane itepo jun aneta-neco. Ta ini ama ayuc naue te tequi-yanuane, ca oviachi itomac anne ca nochaec ca nocne quia guame itomac culp-ti, ioa te jjocaine (hacer bola, huitti eme ke a jjocaja) Catem majas o ousi em ane iton asoam simeta ji-pune: empo ou caita ajoa enchi anastane, teguil, oficio, entureu caita vejetuane.

Nechem jiocole, ochalim, malam, ussi hiohuim ini ne netane: sanouate te lleutobay imi iton joarapo, Adelanto, Blue Moon, iton emania. Enou ne Lios boania utteasi.

Un nuevo ataque contra los barrios se ha empezado por el Departamento del Desarollo de la Comunidad de Tucson. Ellos han preparado un plan que se llama Community Renewal Program para conseguir mucho terreno en el area de Ciudad Modelo que ahora tiene muchos habitantes. Y quieren cambiar el zonamiento para hacer un parque industrial.

Estoy hablando principalmente de Old Pascua. Si ellos tienen éxito, ya se ha acabado todo para nosotros!

Ahora tienen un programa nuevo que es el propuesto freeway este-oeste (y Butterfield) que correrían por el area Ciudad Modelo. Van a destruir muchas casas y muchas escuelas, y levantarán nuevas y tremendas barricadas en los barrios. Si pasan los planes, todo se ha acabado, aunque la construcción no empiece muy pronto. Se sera "desemplazado" ... plan ... barrios y otros ... total desempla... mente 12,000 p... casas, y muchas escu... actuar inmediatamente ... contra este modo in... de nuestros barrios ...

Se dice que el Communi... gram fué empezado por ... participación de los c... apoyado por staff y c... ciudad, pero a nosotr... los ciudadanos son lo... oir que se es'a hacie... o diremos contra ello... sitamos los freeways ... usaran para escaparse ... actuales? ¿Creen ust... manera vamos a salv... de mas deterioración...

Dudo que nues'ros ... este de Tucson qu... tado en grandes fr... impuestos estan t... gente en necesidad ... medica, y casas. ... dadanos de Tucson ... perdiendo nuestro ... casas, si ellos e...

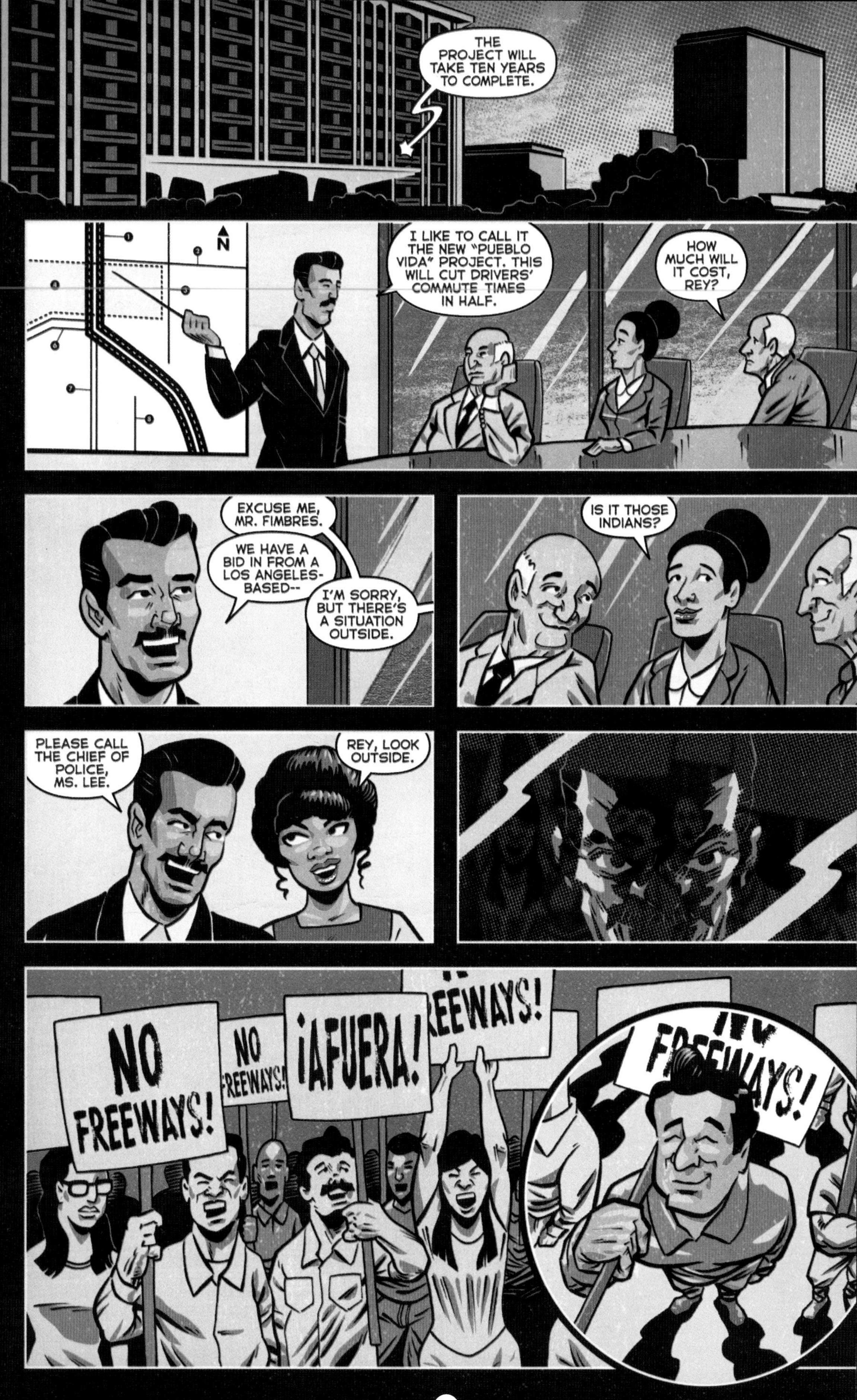
THE PROJECT WILL TAKE TEN YEARS TO COMPLETE.
I LIKE TO CALL IT THE NEW "PUEBLO VIDA" PROJECT. THIS WILL CUT DRIVERS' COMMUTE TIMES IN HALF.
HOW MUCH WILL IT COST, REY?
EXCUSE ME, MR. FIMBRES.
WE HAVE A BID IN FROM A LOS ANGELES-BASED--
I'M SORRY, BUT THERE'S A SITUATION OUTSIDE.
IS IT THOSE INDIANS?
PLEASE CALL THE CHIEF OF POLICE, MS. LEE.
REY, LOOK OUTSIDE.
NO FREEWAYS!
NO FREEWAYS!
¡AFUERA!
FREEWAYS!

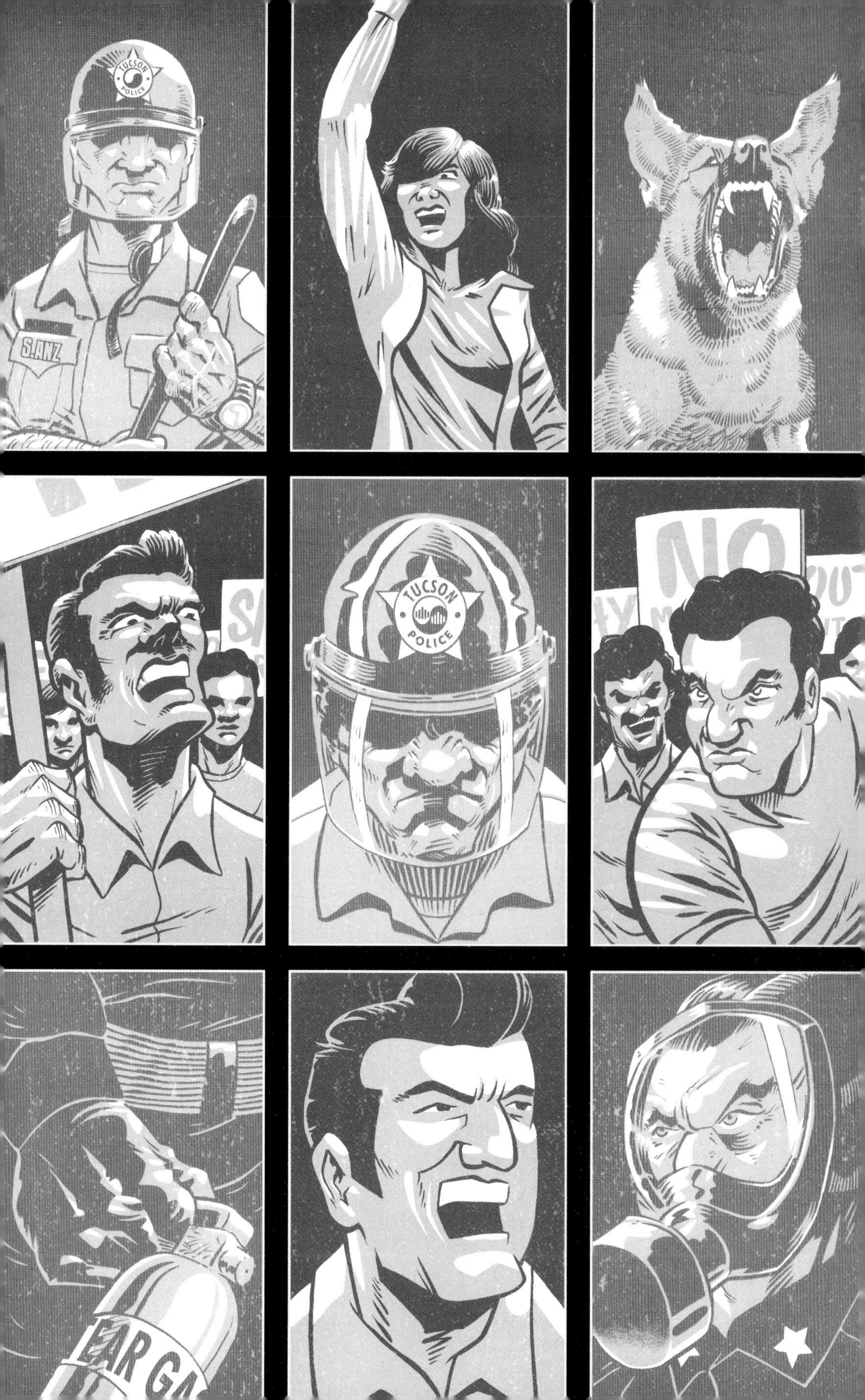
TUCSON
POLICE
S.ANZ
NO
TUCSON
POLICE

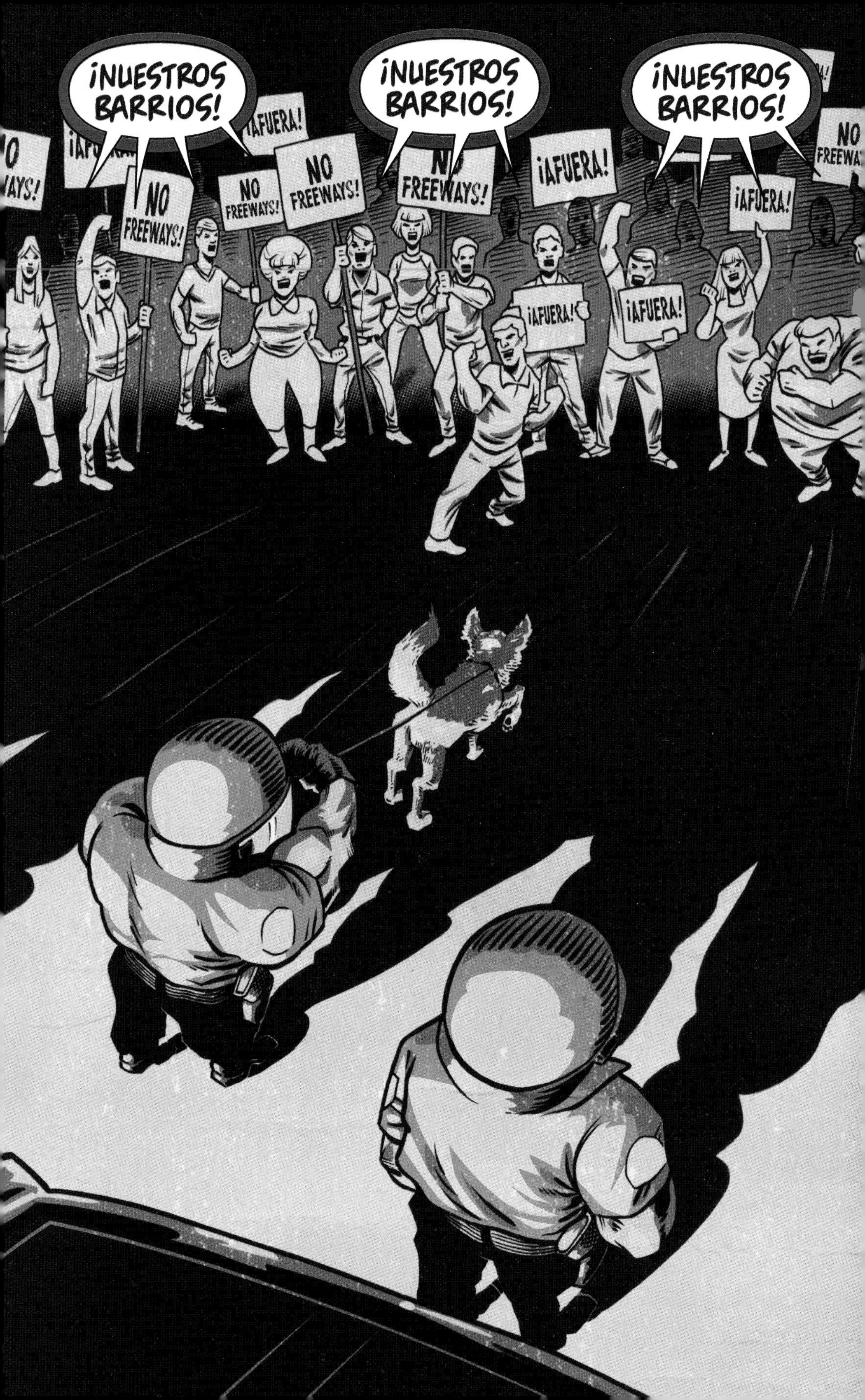

¡NUESTROS BARRIOS!
¡NUESTROS BARRIOS!
¡NUESTROS BARRIOS!
NO FREEWAYS!
NO FREEWAYS!
NO FREEWAYS!
NO FREEWAYS!
¡AFUERA!
¡AFUERA!
¡AFUERA!
¡AFUERA!

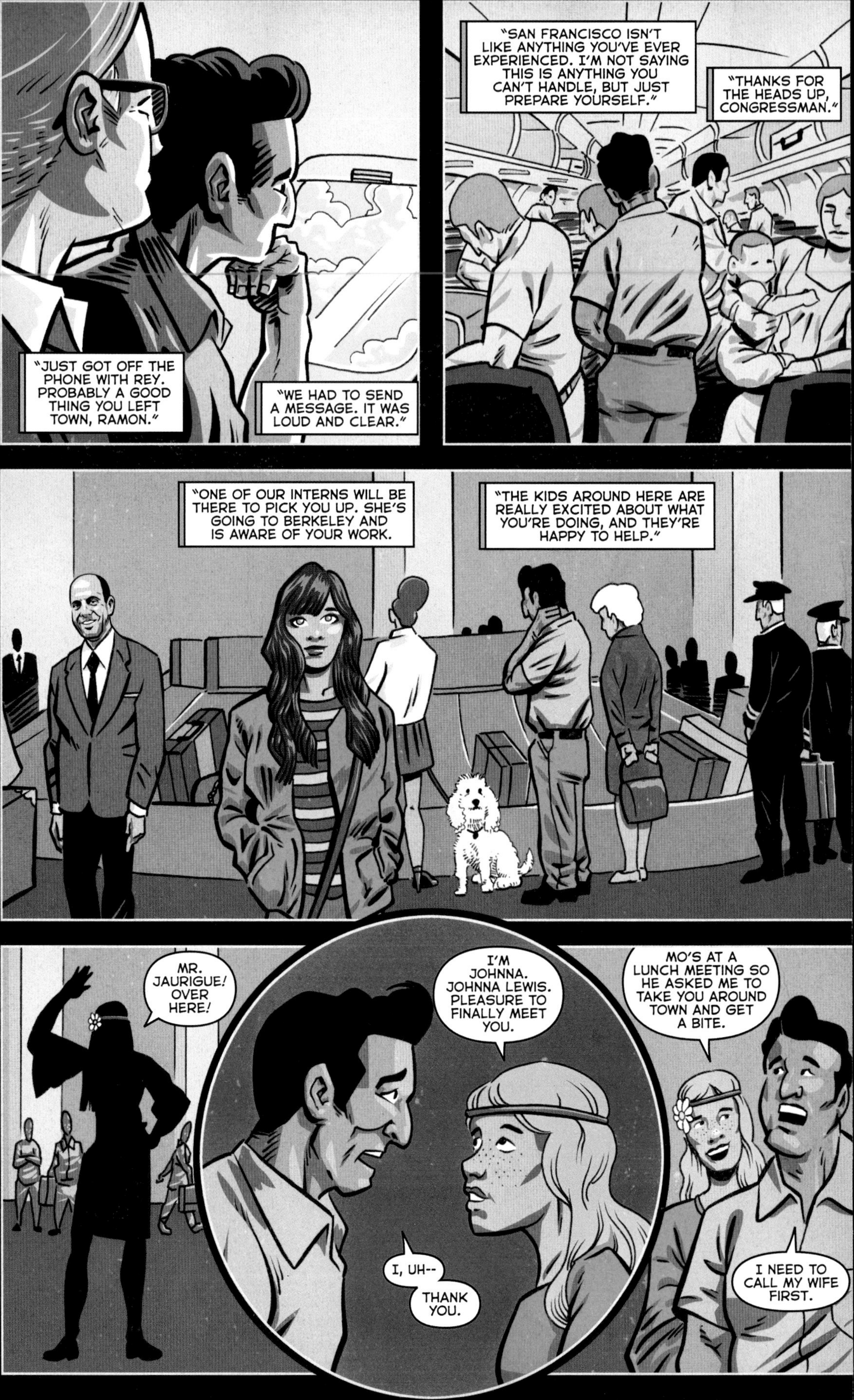
"JUST GOT OFF THE PHONE WITH REY. PROBABLY A GOOD THING YOU LEFT TOWN, RAMON."
"WE HAD TO SEND A MESSAGE. IT WAS LOUD AND CLEAR."
"SAN FRANCISCO ISN'T LIKE ANYTHING YOU'VE EVER EXPERIENCED. I'M NOT SAYING THIS IS ANYTHING YOU CAN'T HANDLE, BUT JUST PREPARE YOURSELF."
"THANKS FOR THE HEADS UP, CONGRESSMAN."
"ONE OF OUR INTERNS WILL BE THERE TO PICK YOU UP. SHE'S GOING TO BERKELEY AND IS AWARE OF YOUR WORK.
"THE KIDS AROUND HERE ARE REALLY EXCITED ABOUT WHAT YOU'RE DOING, AND THEY'RE HAPPY TO HELP."
MR. JAURIGUE! OVER HERE!
I'M JOHNNA. JOHNNA LEWIS. PLEASURE TO FINALLY MEET YOU.
I, UH--
THANK YOU.
MO'S AT A LUNCH MEETING SO HE ASKED ME TO TAKE YOU AROUND TOWN AND GET A BITE.
I NEED TO CALL MY WIFE FIRST.

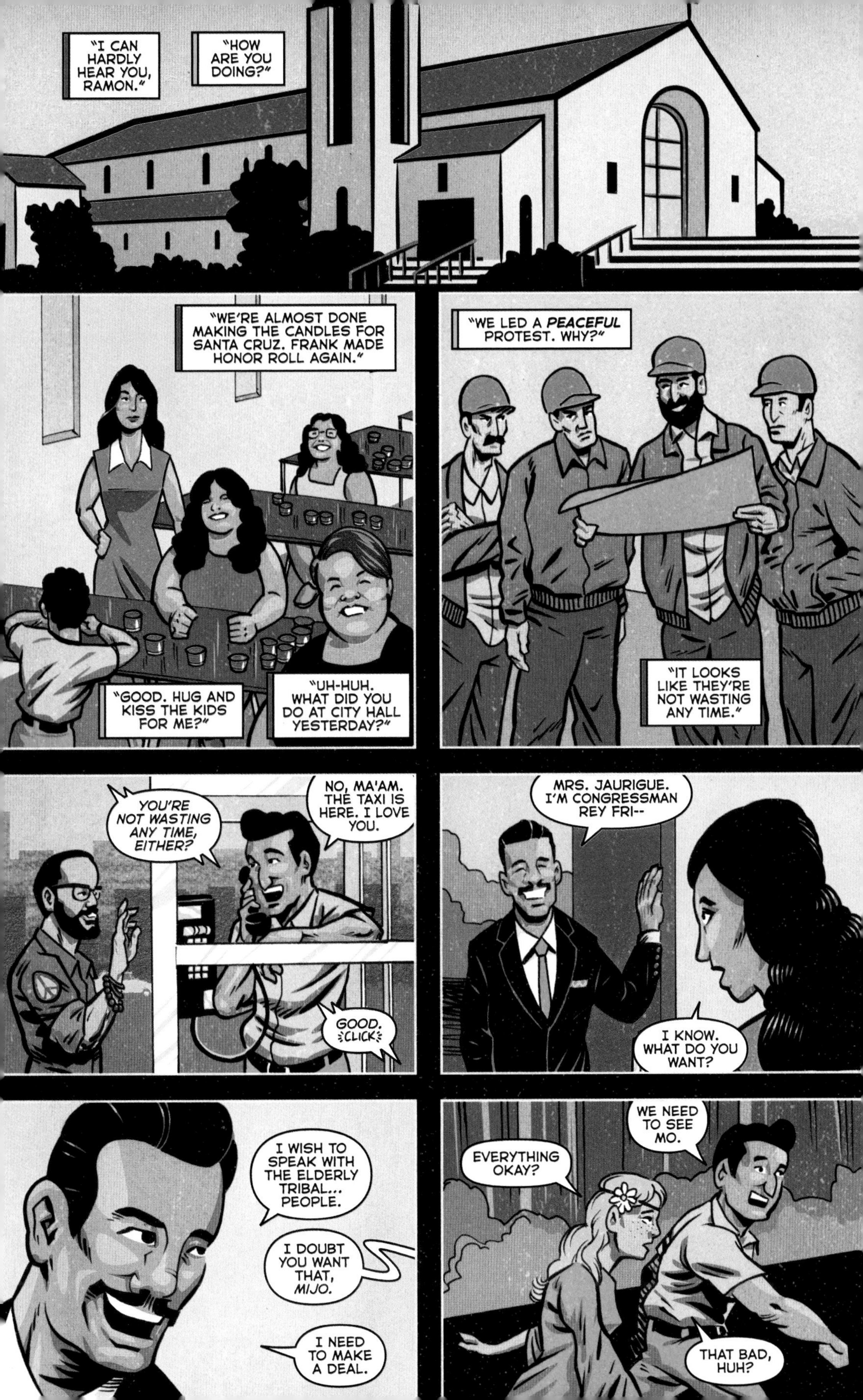
"I CAN HARDLY HEAR YOU, RAMON."
"HOW ARE YOU DOING?"
"WE'RE ALMOST DONE MAKING THE CANDLES FOR SANTA CRUZ. FRANK MADE HONOR ROLL AGAIN."
"GOOD. HUG AND KISS THE KIDS FOR ME?"
"UH-HUH. WHAT DID YOU DO AT CITY HALL YESTERDAY?"
"WE LED A *PEACEFUL* PROTEST. WHY?"
"IT LOOKS LIKE THEY'RE NOT WASTING ANY TIME."
YOU'RE NOT WASTING ANY TIME, EITHER?
NO, MA'AM. THE TAXI IS HERE. I LOVE YOU.
GOOD. *CLICK*
MRS. JAURIGUE. I'M CONGRESSMAN REY FRI--
I KNOW. WHAT DO YOU WANT?
I WISH TO SPEAK WITH THE ELDERLY TRIBAL... PEOPLE.
I DOUBT YOU WANT THAT, *MIJO.*
I NEED TO MAKE A DEAL.
WE NEED TO SEE MO.
EVERYTHING OKAY?
THAT BAD, HUH?

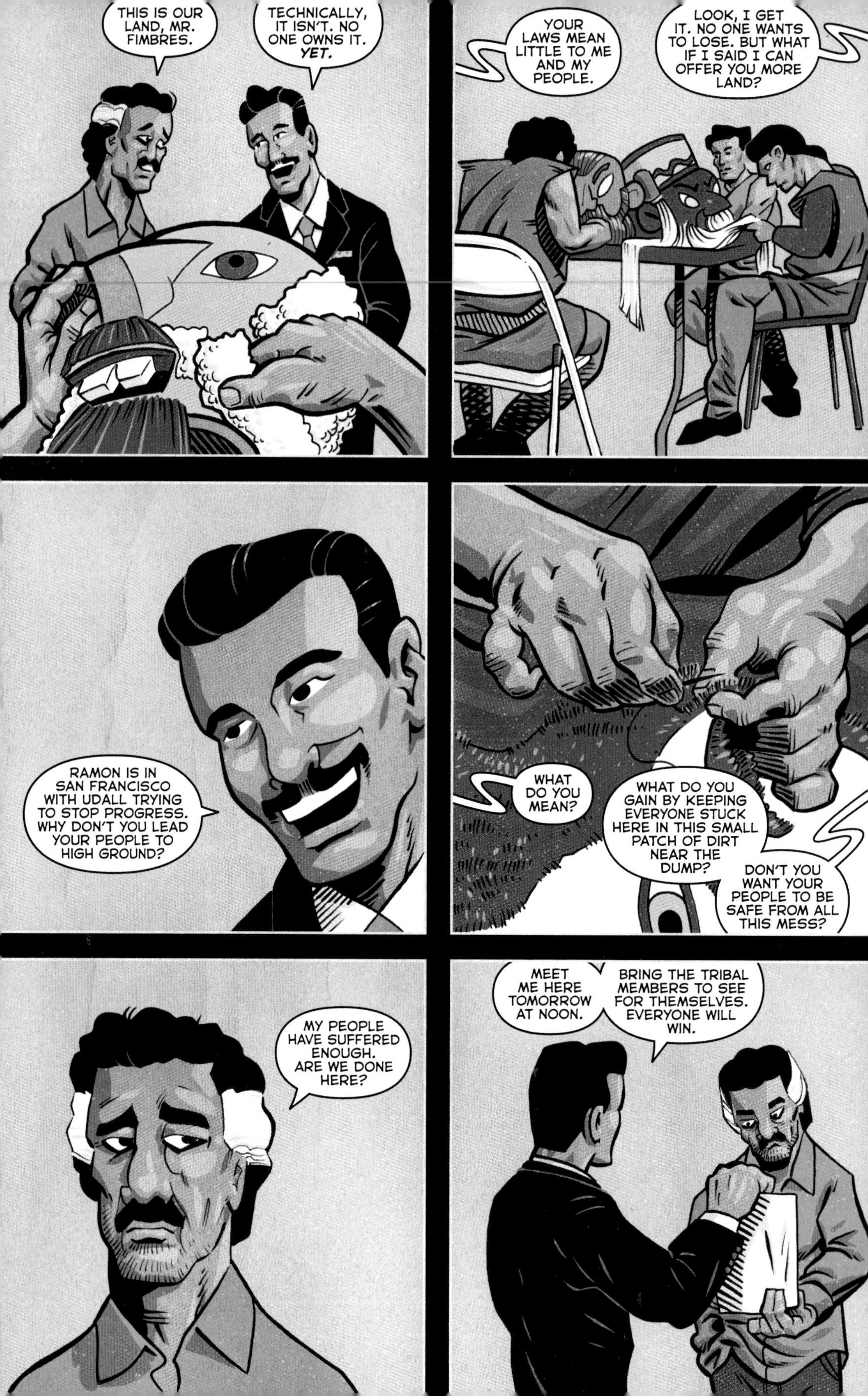

THIS IS OUR LAND, MR. FIMBRES.
TECHNICALLY, IT ISN'T. NO ONE OWNS IT. *YET.*
YOUR LAWS MEAN LITTLE TO ME AND MY PEOPLE.
LOOK, I GET IT. NO ONE WANTS TO LOSE. BUT WHAT IF I SAID I CAN OFFER YOU MORE LAND?
RAMON IS IN SAN FRANCISCO WITH UDALL TRYING TO STOP PROGRESS. WHY DON'T YOU LEAD YOUR PEOPLE TO HIGH GROUND?
WHAT DO YOU MEAN?
WHAT DO YOU GAIN BY KEEPING EVERYONE STUCK HERE IN THIS SMALL PATCH OF DIRT NEAR THE DUMP?
DON'T YOU WANT YOUR PEOPLE TO BE SAFE FROM ALL THIS MESS?
MY PEOPLE HAVE SUFFERED ENOUGH. ARE WE DONE HERE?
MEET ME HERE TOMORROW AT NOON.
BRING THE TRIBAL MEMBERS TO SEE FOR THEMSELVES. EVERYONE WILL WIN.

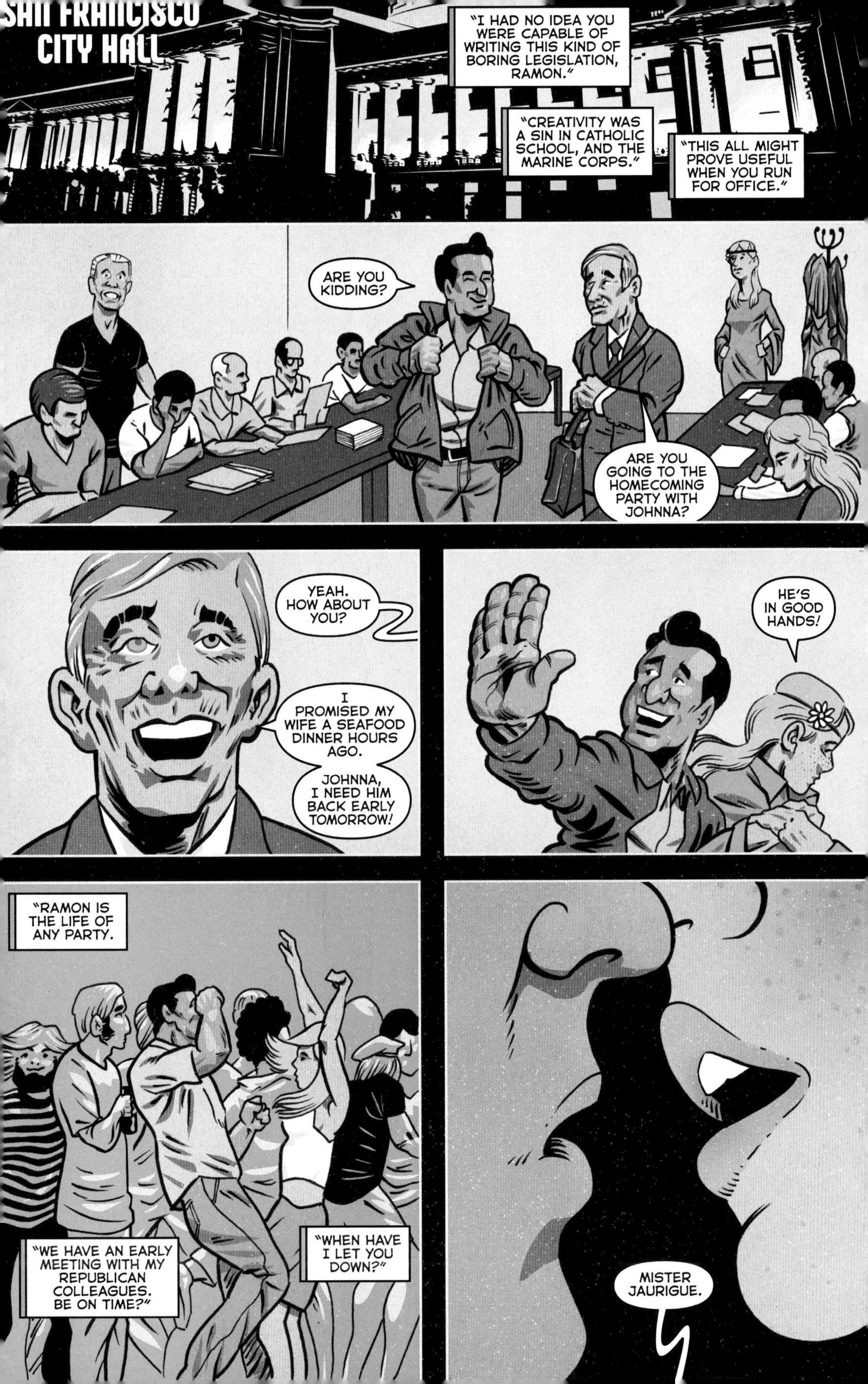
SAN FRANCISCO CITY HALL
"I HAD NO IDEA YOU WERE CAPABLE OF WRITING THIS KIND OF BORING LEGISLATION, RAMON."
"CREATIVITY WAS A SIN IN CATHOLIC SCHOOL, AND THE MARINE CORPS."
"THIS ALL MIGHT PROVE USEFUL WHEN YOU RUN FOR OFFICE."
ARE YOU KIDDING?
ARE YOU GOING TO THE HOMECOMING PARTY WITH JOHNNA?
YEAH. HOW ABOUT YOU?
I PROMISED MY WIFE A SEAFOOD DINNER HOURS AGO.
JOHNNA, I NEED HIM BACK EARLY TOMORROW!
HE'S IN GOOD HANDS!
"RAMON IS THE LIFE OF ANY PARTY.
"WE HAVE AN EARLY MEETING WITH MY REPUBLICAN COLLEAGUES. BE ON TIME?"
"WHEN HAVE I LET YOU DOWN?"
MISTER JAURIGUE.

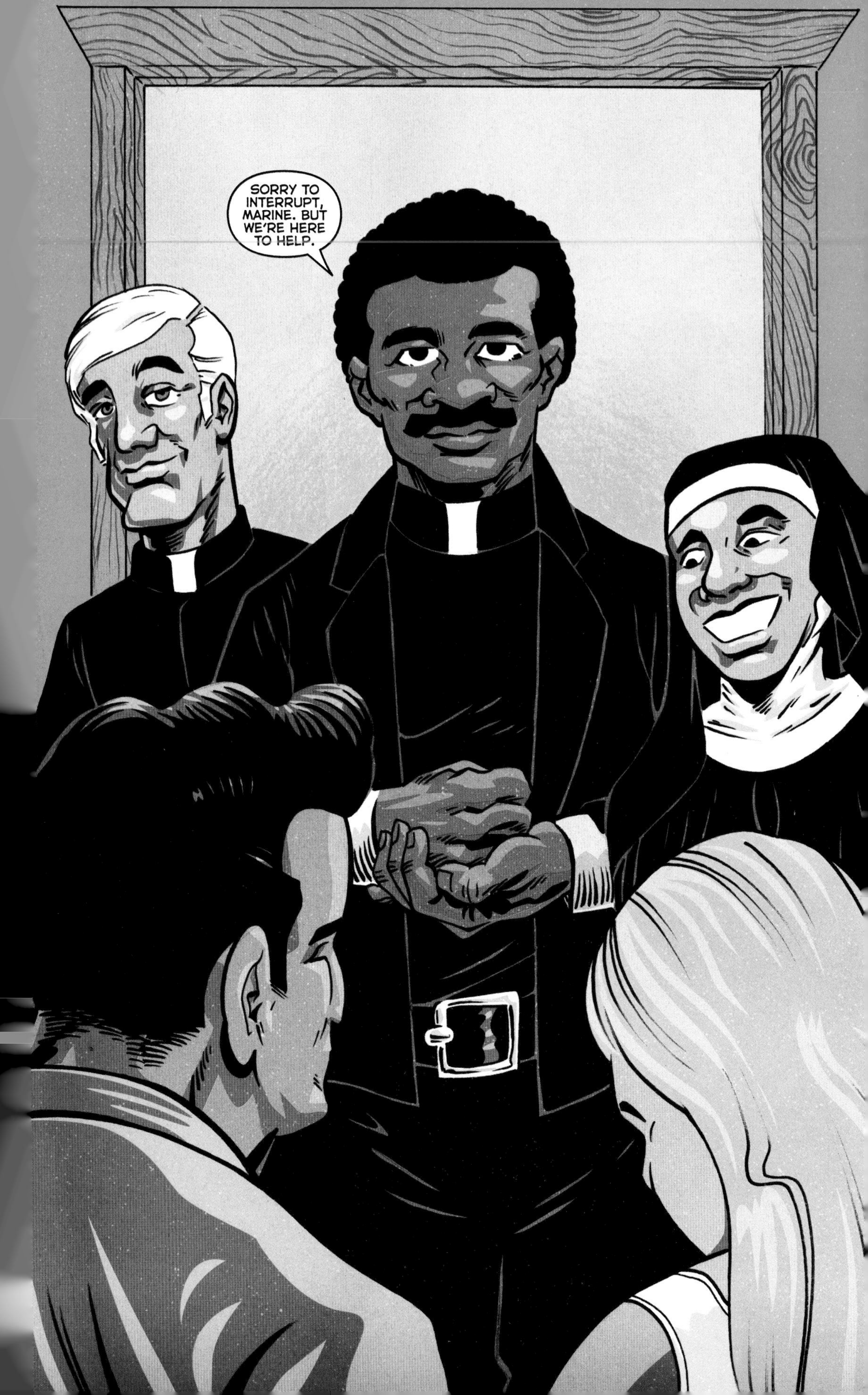
SORRY TO INTERRUPT, MARINE. BUT WE'RE HERE TO HELP.

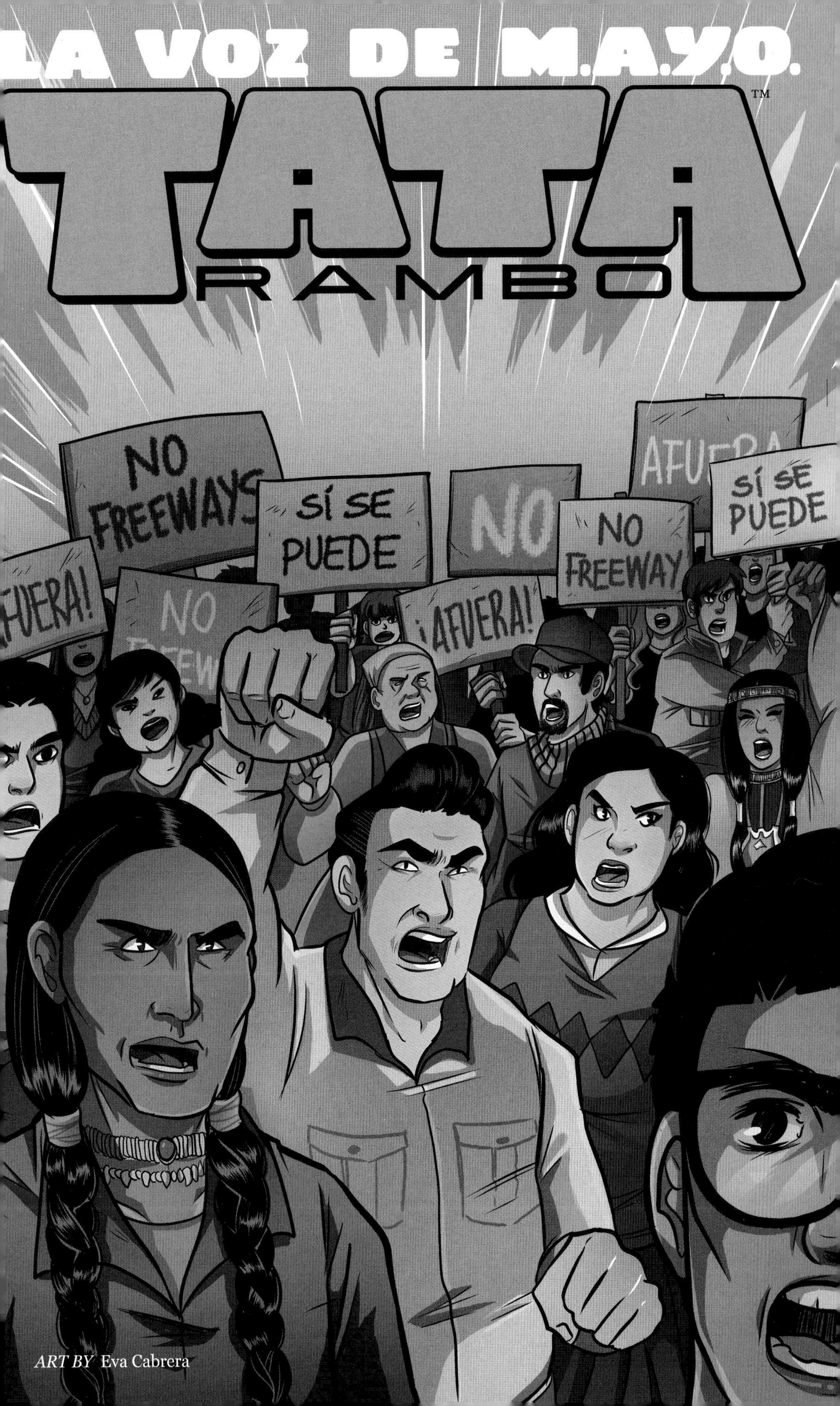
LA VOZ DE M.A.Y.O.
TATA RAMBO™
NO FREEWAYS
SÍ SE PUEDE
NO
SÍ SE PUEDE
NO FREEWAY
¡AFUERA!
NO
ART BY Eva Cabrera

CHAPTER TWO:

¡SÍ SE PUEDE!

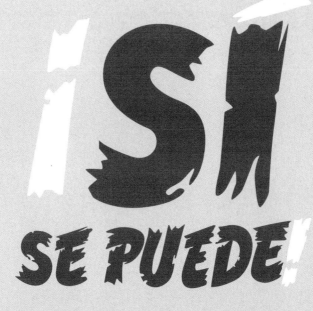

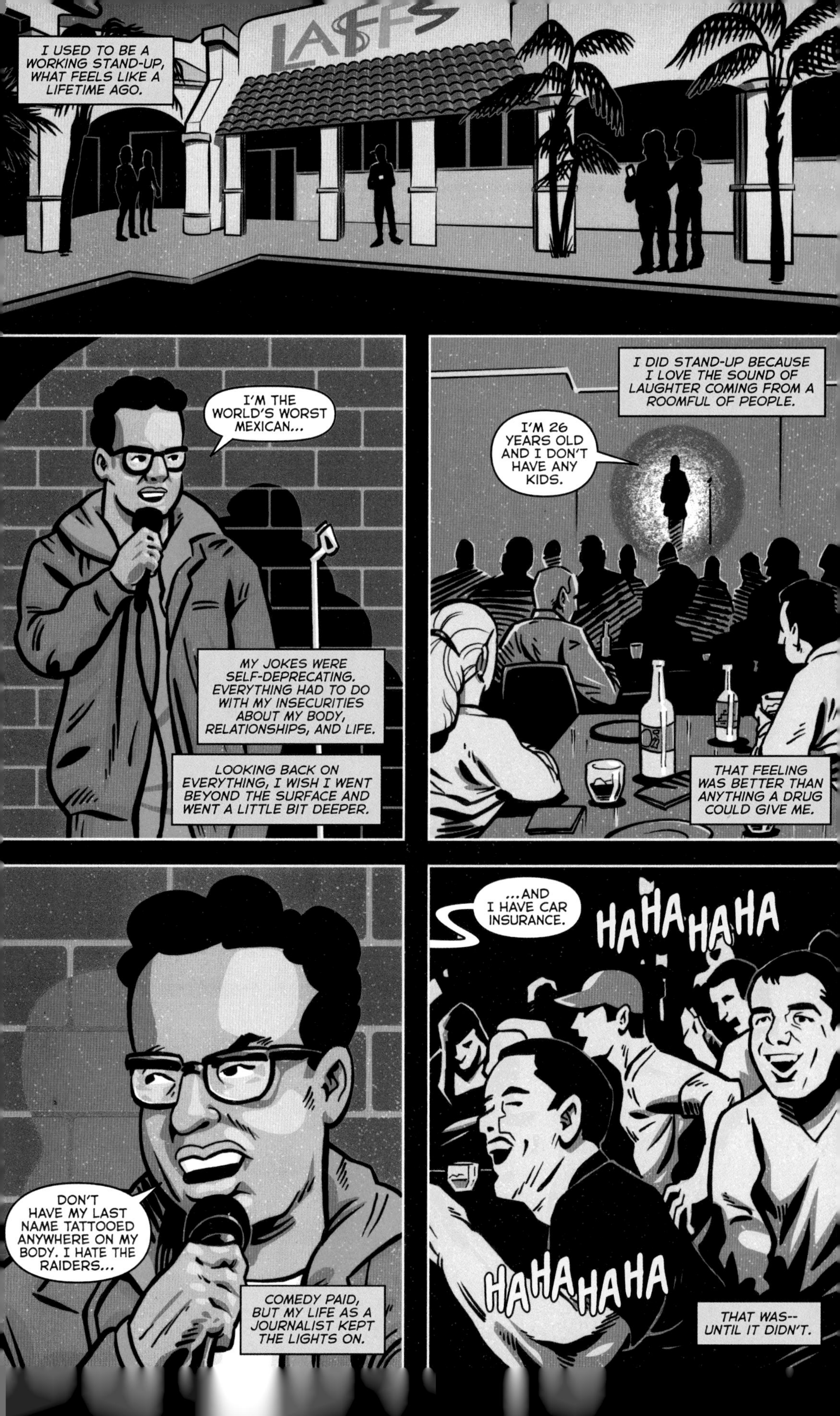
LAFFS
I USED TO BE A WORKING STAND-UP, WHAT FEELS LIKE A LIFETIME AGO.
I'M THE WORLD'S WORST MEXICAN...
MY JOKES WERE SELF-DEPRECATING. EVERYTHING HAD TO DO WITH MY INSECURITIES ABOUT MY BODY, RELATIONSHIPS, AND LIFE.
LOOKING BACK ON EVERYTHING, I WISH I WENT BEYOND THE SURFACE AND WENT A LITTLE BIT DEEPER.
I DID STAND-UP BECAUSE I LOVE THE SOUND OF LAUGHTER COMING FROM A ROOMFUL OF PEOPLE.
I'M 26 YEARS OLD AND I DON'T HAVE ANY KIDS.
THAT FEELING WAS BETTER THAN ANYTHING A DRUG COULD GIVE ME.
DON'T HAVE MY LAST NAME TATTOOED ANYWHERE ON MY BODY. I HATE THE RAIDERS...
COMEDY PAID, BUT MY LIFE AS A JOURNALIST KEPT THE LIGHTS ON.
...AND I HAVE CAR INSURANCE.
HAHAHAHAHA
HAHAHAHAHA
THAT WAS-- UNTIL IT DIDN'T.

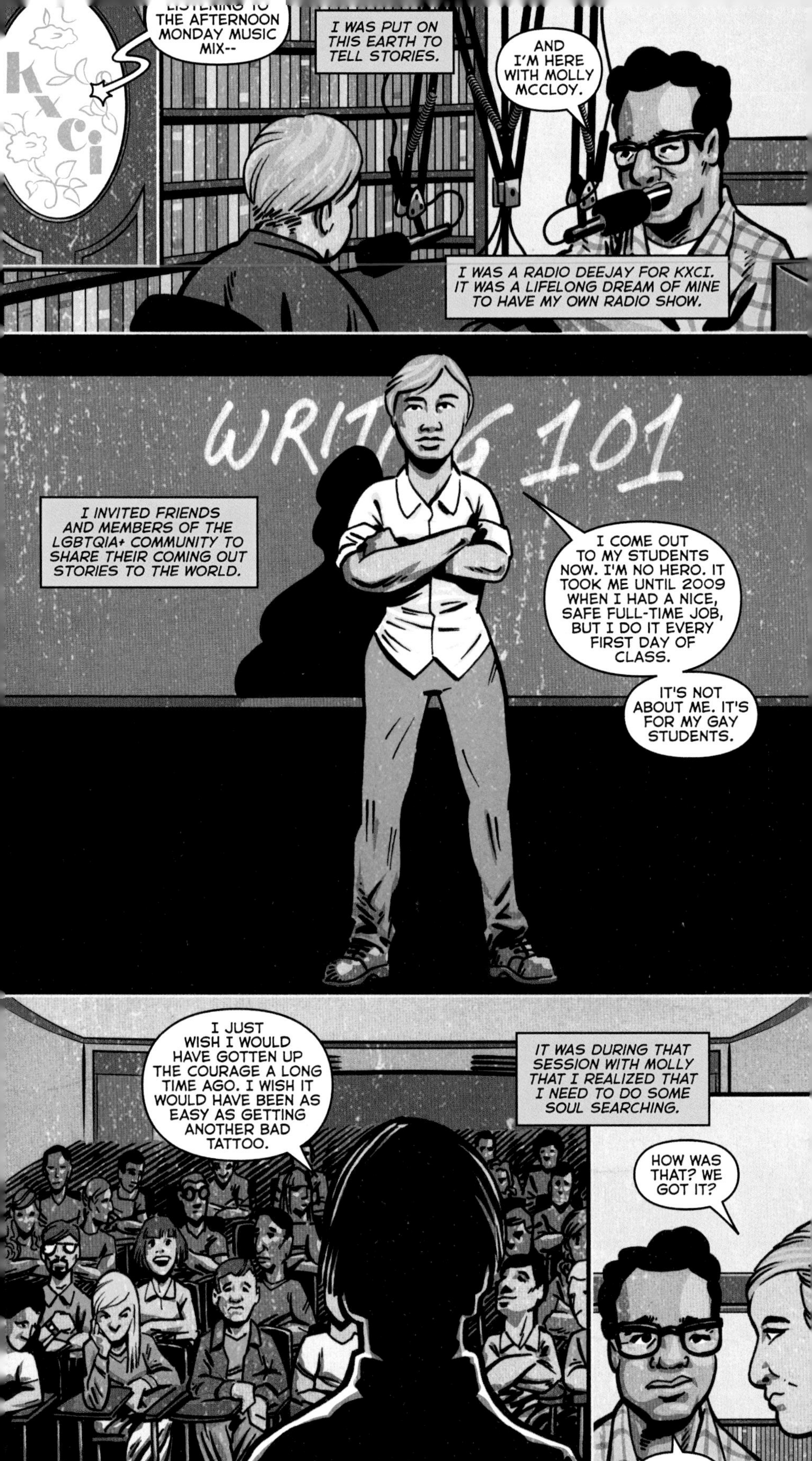
kxci
THE AFTERNOON MONDAY MUSIC MIX--
I WAS PUT ON THIS EARTH TO TELL STORIES.
AND I'M HERE WITH MOLLY MCCLOY.
I WAS A RADIO DEEJAY FOR KXCI. IT WAS A LIFELONG DREAM OF MINE TO HAVE MY OWN RADIO SHOW.
WRITING 101
I INVITED FRIENDS AND MEMBERS OF THE LGBTQIA+ COMMUNITY TO SHARE THEIR COMING OUT STORIES TO THE WORLD.
I COME OUT TO MY STUDENTS NOW. I'M NO HERO. IT TOOK ME UNTIL 2009 WHEN I HAD A NICE, SAFE FULL-TIME JOB, BUT I DO IT EVERY FIRST DAY OF CLASS.
IT'S NOT ABOUT ME. IT'S FOR MY GAY STUDENTS.
I JUST WISH I WOULD HAVE GOTTEN UP THE COURAGE A LONG TIME AGO. I WISH IT WOULD HAVE BEEN AS EASY AS GETTING ANOTHER BAD TATTOO.
IT WAS DURING THAT SESSION WITH MOLLY THAT I REALIZED THAT I NEED TO DO SOME SOUL SEARCHING.
HOW WAS THAT? WE GOT IT?
I THINK I'VE GOT

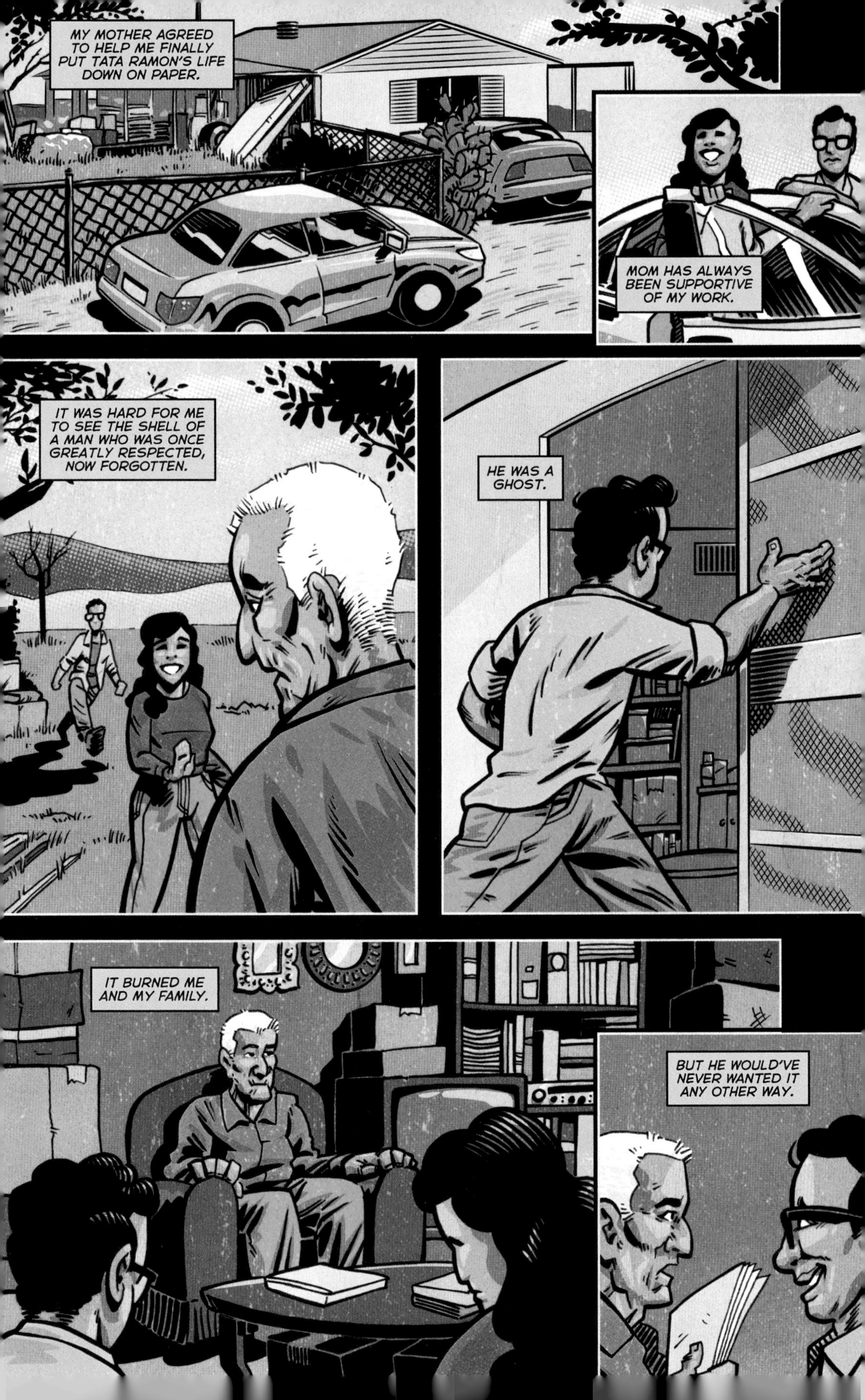
MY MOTHER AGREED TO HELP ME FINALLY PUT TATA RAMON'S LIFE DOWN ON PAPER.
MOM HAS ALWAYS BEEN SUPPORTIVE OF MY WORK.
IT WAS HARD FOR ME TO SEE THE SHELL OF A MAN WHO WAS ONCE GREATLY RESPECTED, NOW FORGOTTEN.
HE WAS A GHOST.
IT BURNED ME AND MY FAMILY.
BUT HE WOULD'VE NEVER WANTED IT ANY OTHER WAY.

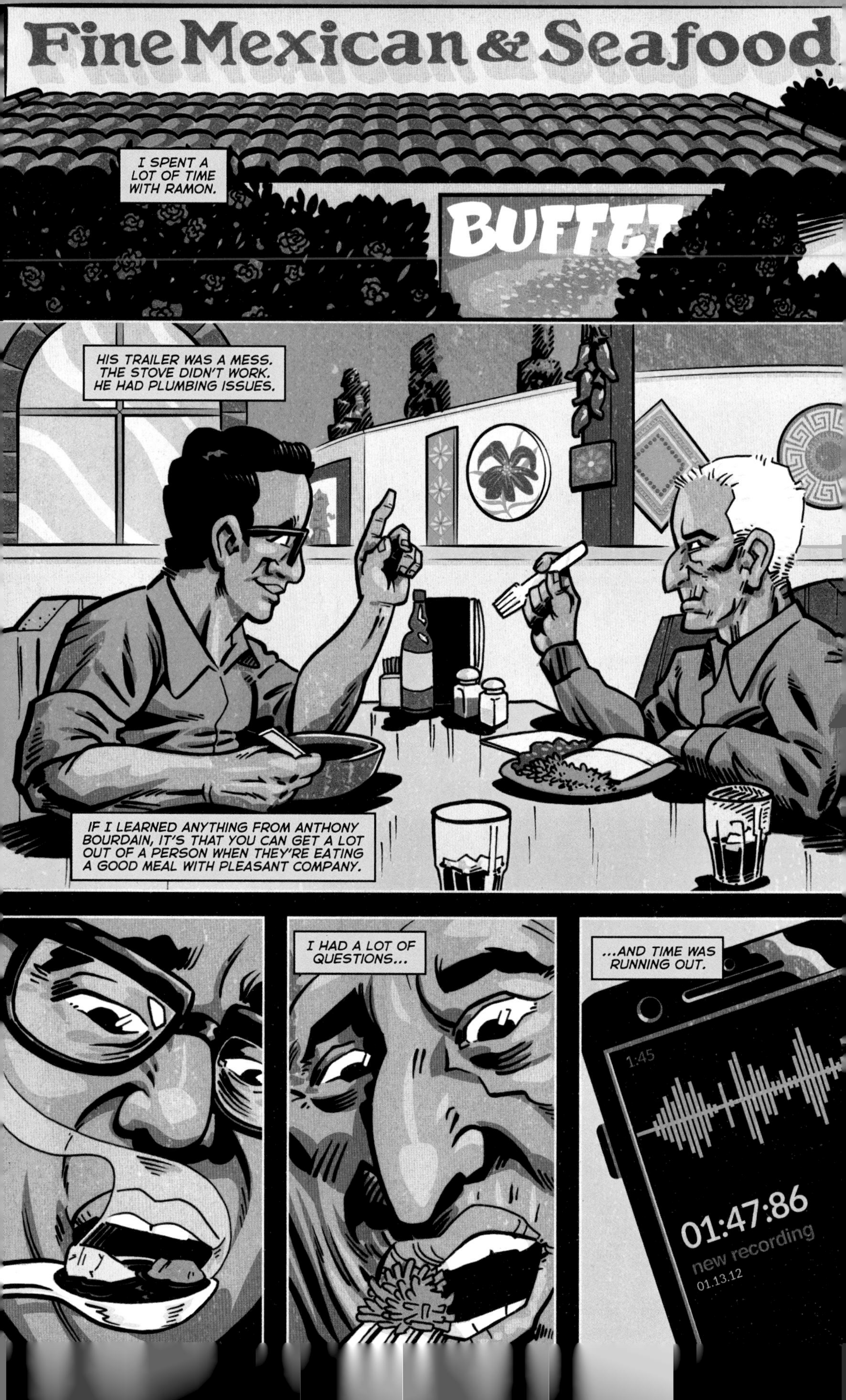
Fine Mexican & Seafood
I SPENT A LOT OF TIME WITH RAMON.
BUFFET
HIS TRAILER WAS A MESS. THE STOVE DIDN'T WORK. HE HAD PLUMBING ISSUES.
IF I LEARNED ANYTHING FROM ANTHONY BOURDAIN, IT'S THAT YOU CAN GET A LOT OUT OF A PERSON WHEN THEY'RE EATING A GOOD MEAL WITH PLEASANT COMPANY.
I HAD A LOT OF QUESTIONS...
...AND TIME WAS RUNNING OUT.
1:45
01:47:86
new recording
01.13.12

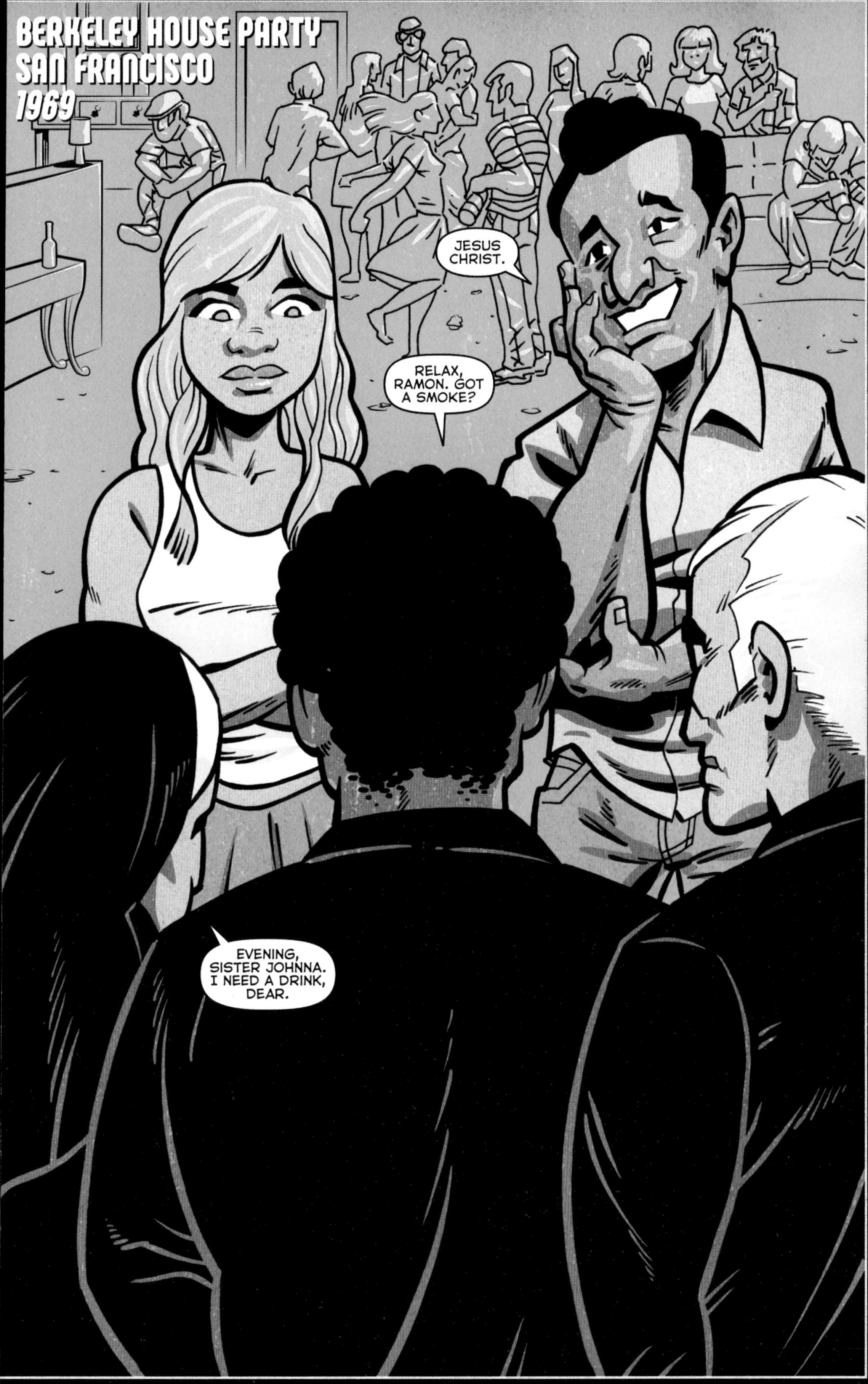
BERKELEY HOUSE PARTY
SAN FRANCISCO
1969
JESUS CHRIST.
RELAX, RAMON. GOT A SMOKE?
EVENING, SISTER JOHNNA. I NEED A DRINK, DEAR.

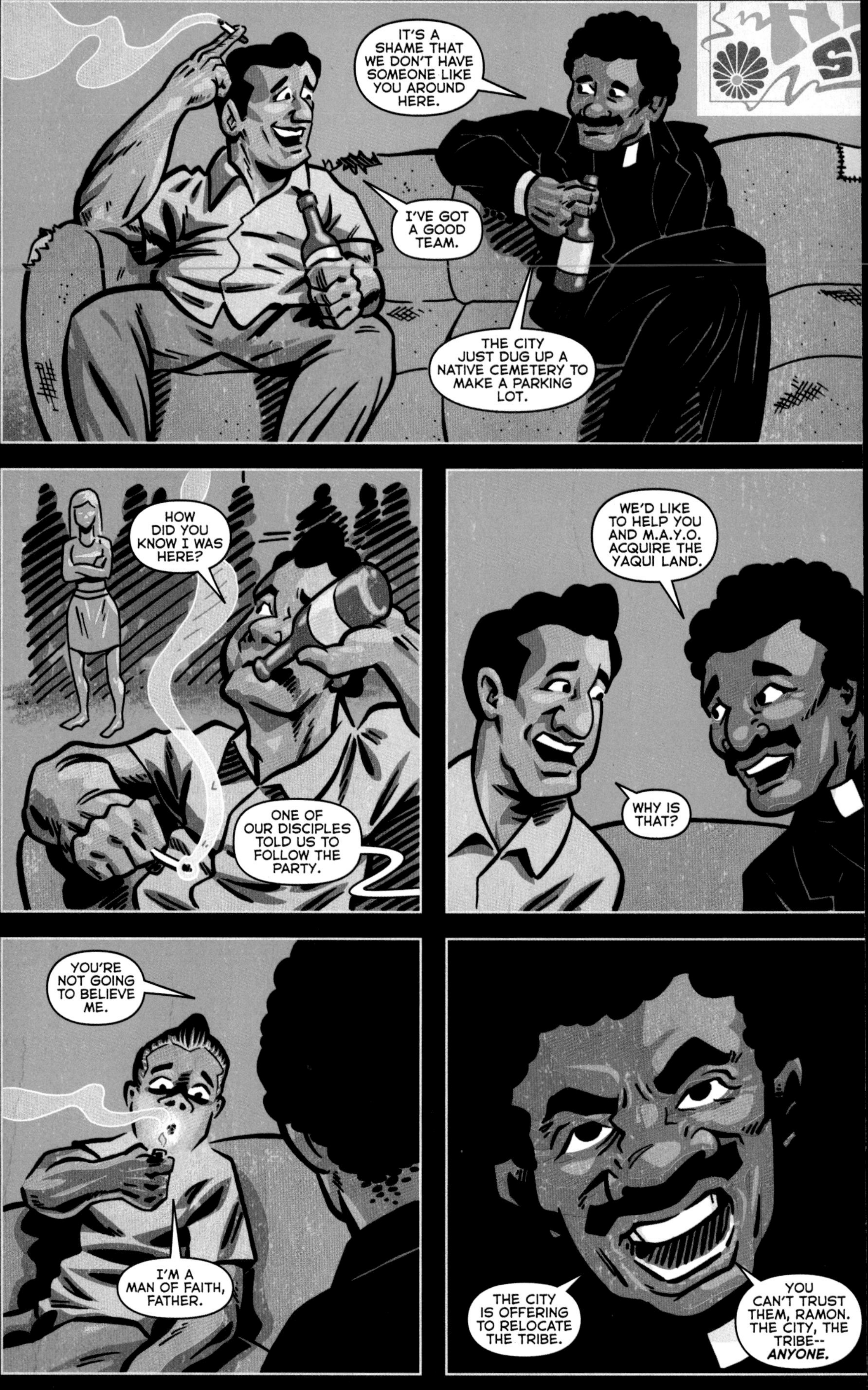
IT'S A SHAME THAT WE DON'T HAVE SOMEONE LIKE YOU AROUND HERE.
I'VE GOT A GOOD TEAM.
THE CITY JUST DUG UP A NATIVE CEMETERY TO MAKE A PARKING LOT.
HOW DID YOU KNOW I WAS HERE?
ONE OF OUR DISCIPLES TOLD US TO FOLLOW THE PARTY.
WE'D LIKE TO HELP YOU AND M.A.Y.O. ACQUIRE THE YAQUI LAND.
WHY IS THAT?
YOU'RE NOT GOING TO BELIEVE ME.
I'M A MAN OF FAITH, FATHER.
THE CITY IS OFFERING TO RELOCATE THE TRIBE.
YOU CAN'T TRUST THEM, RAMON. THE CITY, THE TRIBE-- *ANYONE.*

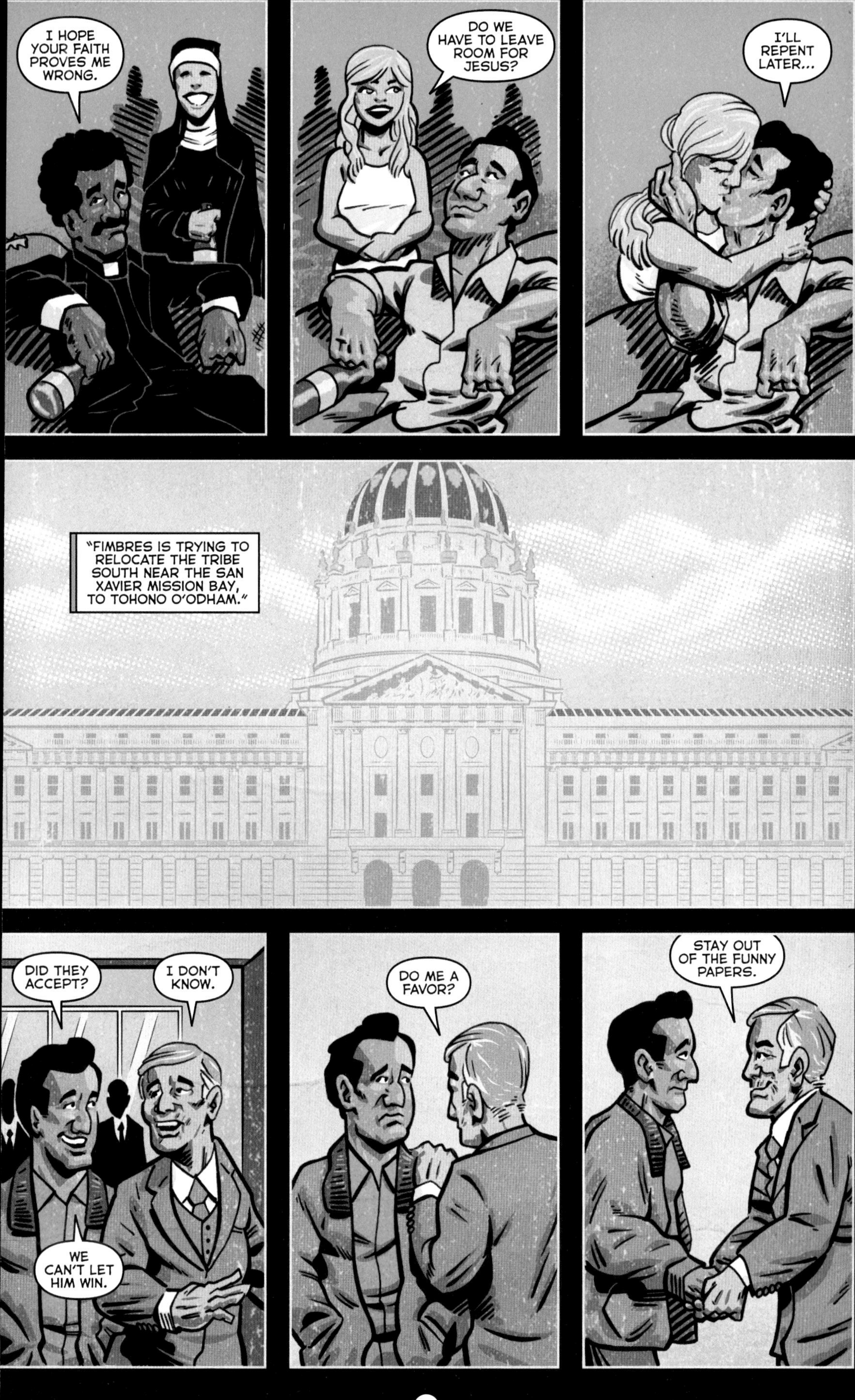
I HOPE YOUR FAITH PROVES ME WRONG.
DO WE HAVE TO LEAVE ROOM FOR JESUS?
I'LL REPENT LATER...
"FIMBRES IS TRYING TO RELOCATE THE TRIBE SOUTH NEAR THE SAN XAVIER MISSION BAY, TO TOHONO O'ODHAM."
DID THEY ACCEPT?
I DON'T KNOW.
WE CAN'T LET HIM WIN.
DO ME A FAVOR?
STAY OUT OF THE FUNNY PAPERS.

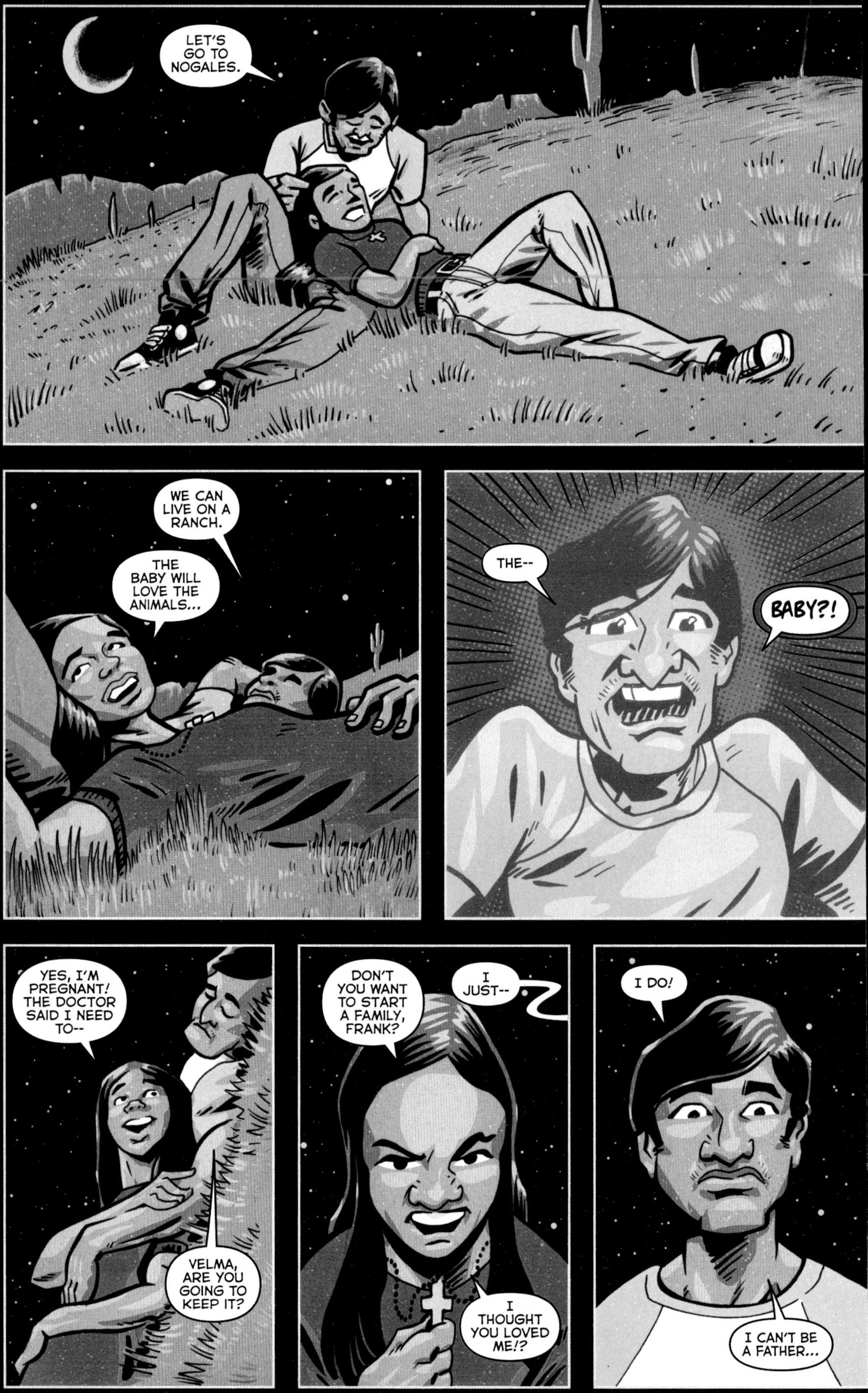
LET'S GO TO NOGALES.
WE CAN LIVE ON A RANCH.
THE BABY WILL LOVE THE ANIMALS...
THE--
BABY?!
YES, I'M PREGNANT! THE DOCTOR SAID I NEED TO--
VELMA, ARE YOU GOING TO KEEP IT?
DON'T YOU WANT TO START A FAMILY, FRANK?
I JUST--
I THOUGHT YOU LOVED ME!?
I DO!
I CAN'T BE A FATHER...

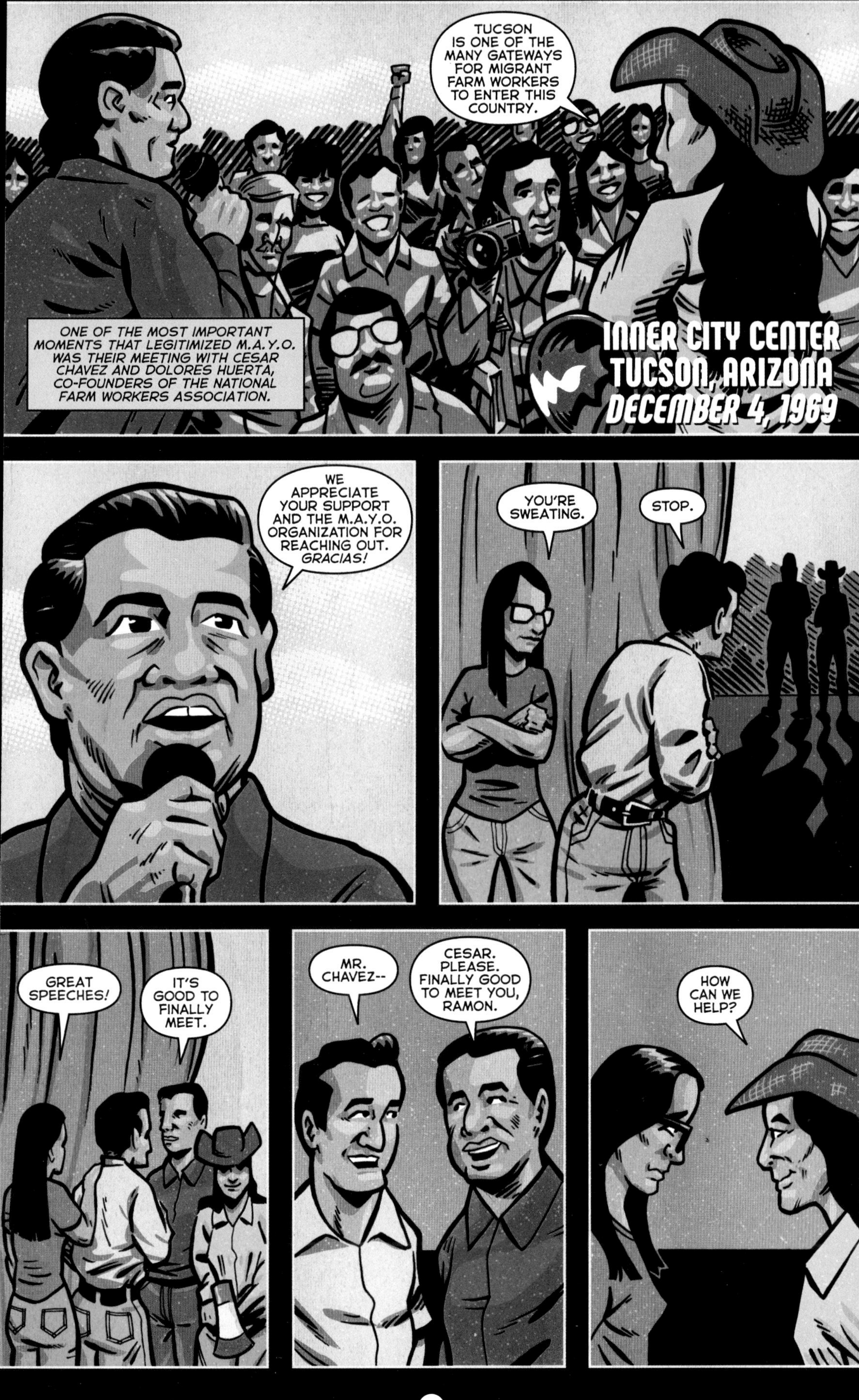
TUCSON IS ONE OF THE MANY GATEWAYS FOR MIGRANT FARM WORKERS TO ENTER THIS COUNTRY.
ONE OF THE MOST IMPORTANT MOMENTS THAT LEGITIMIZED M.A.Y.O. WAS THEIR MEETING WITH CESAR CHAVEZ AND DOLORES HUERTA, CO-FOUNDERS OF THE NATIONAL FARM WORKERS ASSOCIATION.
INNER CITY CENTER
TUCSON, ARIZONA
DECEMBER 4, 1969
WE APPRECIATE YOUR SUPPORT AND THE M.A.Y.O. ORGANIZATION FOR REACHING OUT. *GRACIAS!*
YOU'RE SWEATING.
STOP.
GREAT SPEECHES!
IT'S GOOD TO FINALLY MEET.
MR. CHAVEZ--
CESAR. PLEASE. FINALLY GOOD TO MEET YOU, RAMON.
HOW CAN WE HELP?

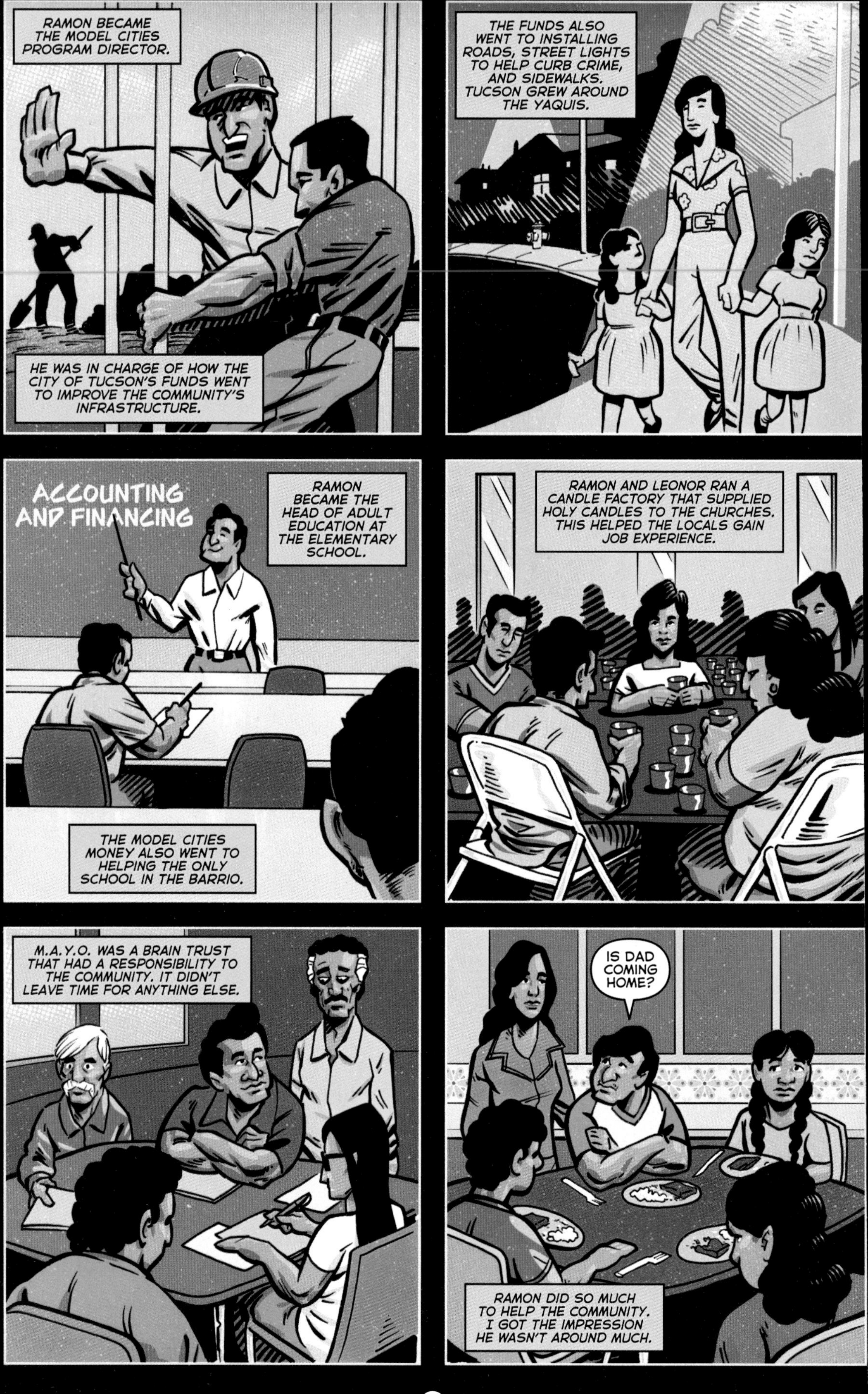
RAMON BECAME THE MODEL CITIES PROGRAM DIRECTOR.
HE WAS IN CHARGE OF HOW THE CITY OF TUCSON'S FUNDS WENT TO IMPROVE THE COMMUNITY'S INFRASTRUCTURE.
THE FUNDS ALSO WENT TO INSTALLING ROADS, STREET LIGHTS TO HELP CURB CRIME, AND SIDEWALKS. TUCSON GREW AROUND THE YAQUIS.
ACCOUNTING AND FINANCING
RAMON BECAME THE HEAD OF ADULT EDUCATION AT THE ELEMENTARY SCHOOL.
THE MODEL CITIES MONEY ALSO WENT TO HELPING THE ONLY SCHOOL IN THE BARRIO.
RAMON AND LEONOR RAN A CANDLE FACTORY THAT SUPPLIED HOLY CANDLES TO THE CHURCHES. THIS HELPED THE LOCALS GAIN JOB EXPERIENCE.
M.A.Y.O. WAS A BRAIN TRUST THAT HAD A RESPONSIBILITY TO THE COMMUNITY. IT DIDN'T LEAVE TIME FOR ANYTHING ELSE.
IS DAD COMING HOME?
RAMON DID SO MUCH TO HELP THE COMMUNITY. I GOT THE IMPRESSION HE WASN'T AROUND MUCH.

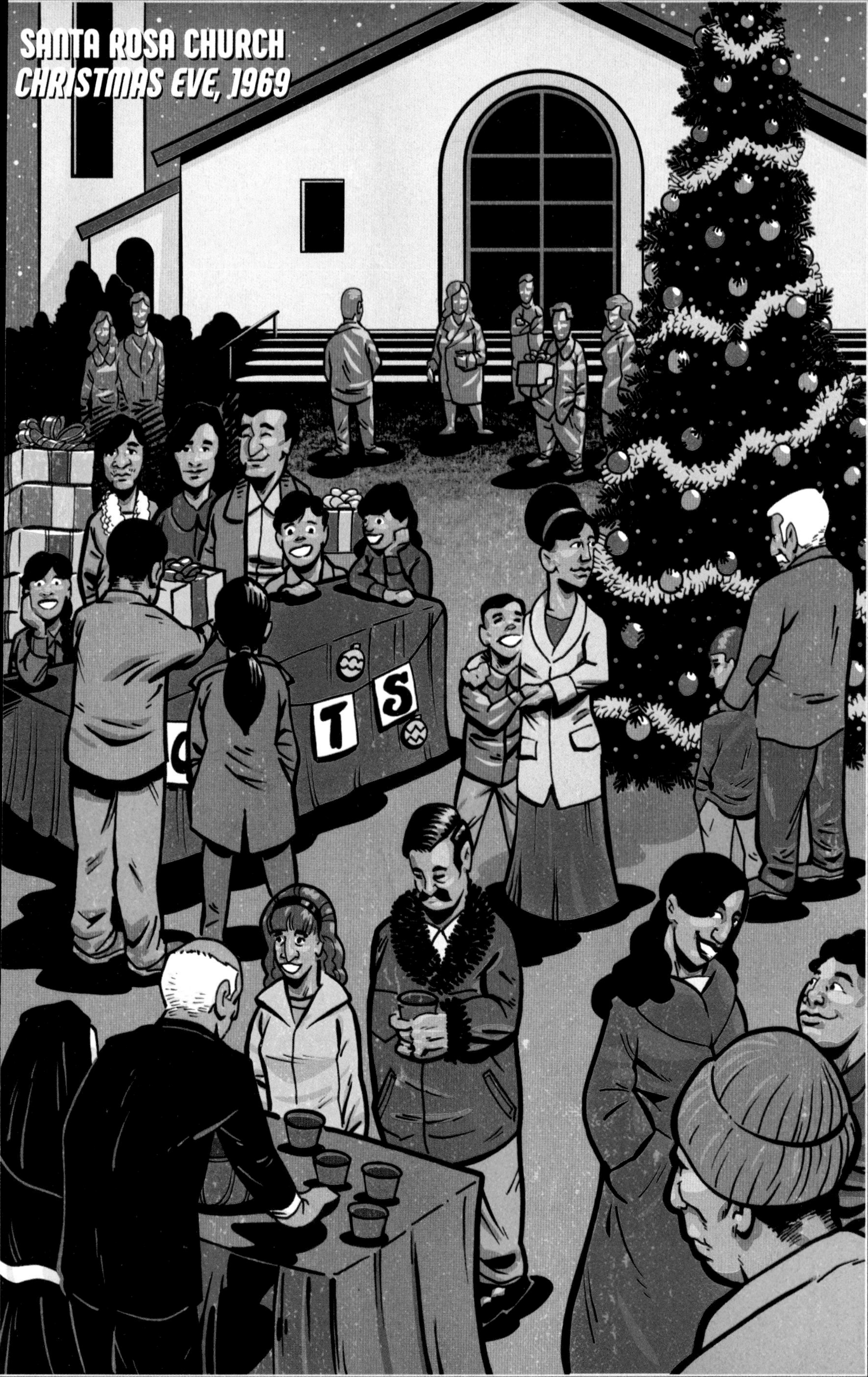
SANTA ROSA CHURCH
CHRISTMAS EVE, 1969
TS

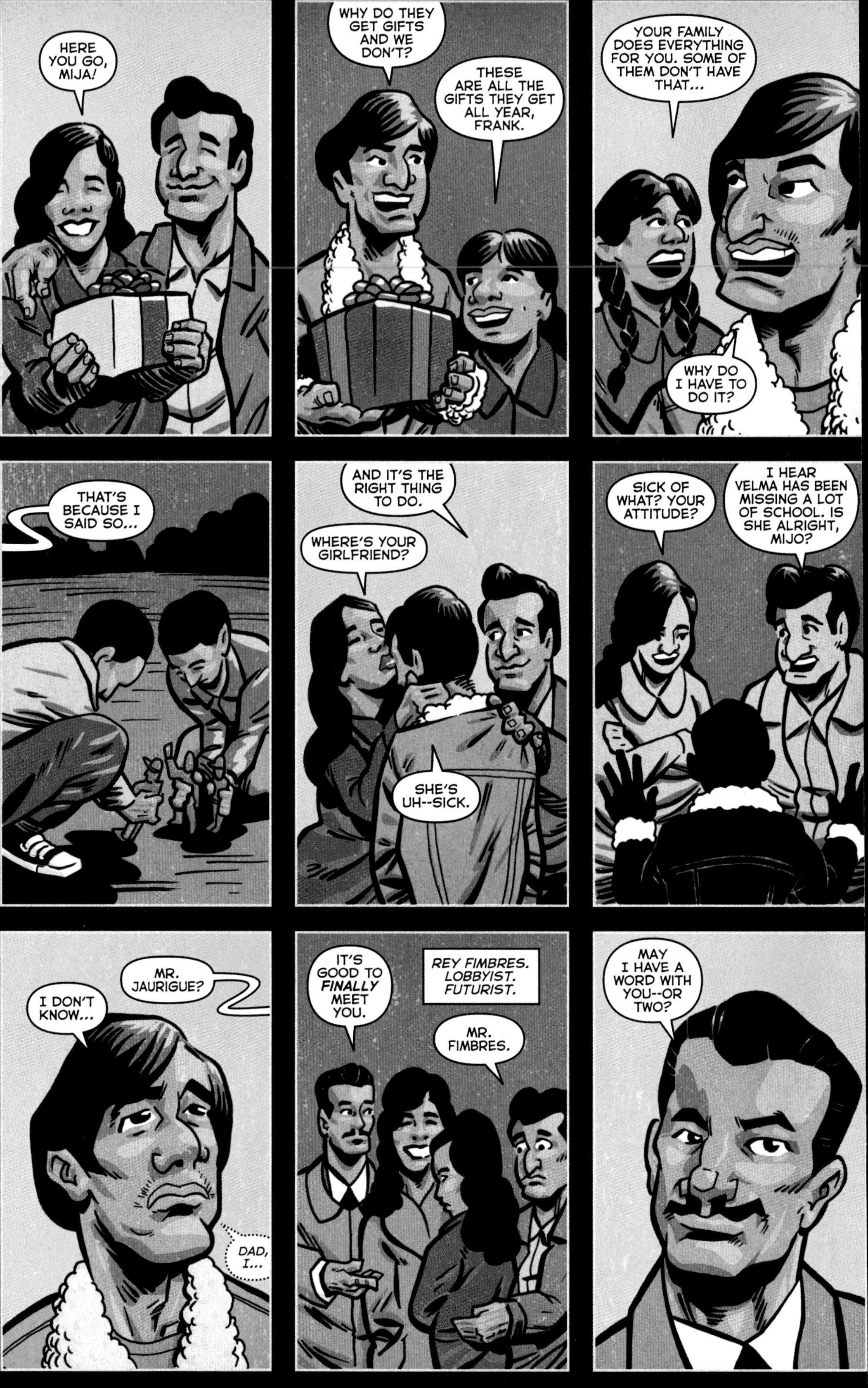
HERE YOU GO, MIJA!
WHY DO THEY GET GIFTS AND WE DON'T?
THESE ARE ALL THE GIFTS THEY GET ALL YEAR, FRANK.
YOUR FAMILY DOES EVERYTHING FOR YOU. SOME OF THEM DON'T HAVE THAT...
WHY DO I HAVE TO DO IT?
THAT'S BECAUSE I SAID SO...
AND IT'S THE RIGHT THING TO DO.
WHERE'S YOUR GIRLFRIEND?
SHE'S UH--SICK.
SICK OF WHAT? YOUR ATTITUDE?
I HEAR VELMA HAS BEEN MISSING A LOT OF SCHOOL. IS SHE ALRIGHT, MIJO?
MR. JAURIGUE?
I DON'T KNOW...
DAD, I...
IT'S GOOD TO FINALLY MEET YOU.
REY FIMBRES. LOBBYIST. FUTURIST.
MR. FIMBRES.
MAY I HAVE A WORD WITH YOU--OR TWO?

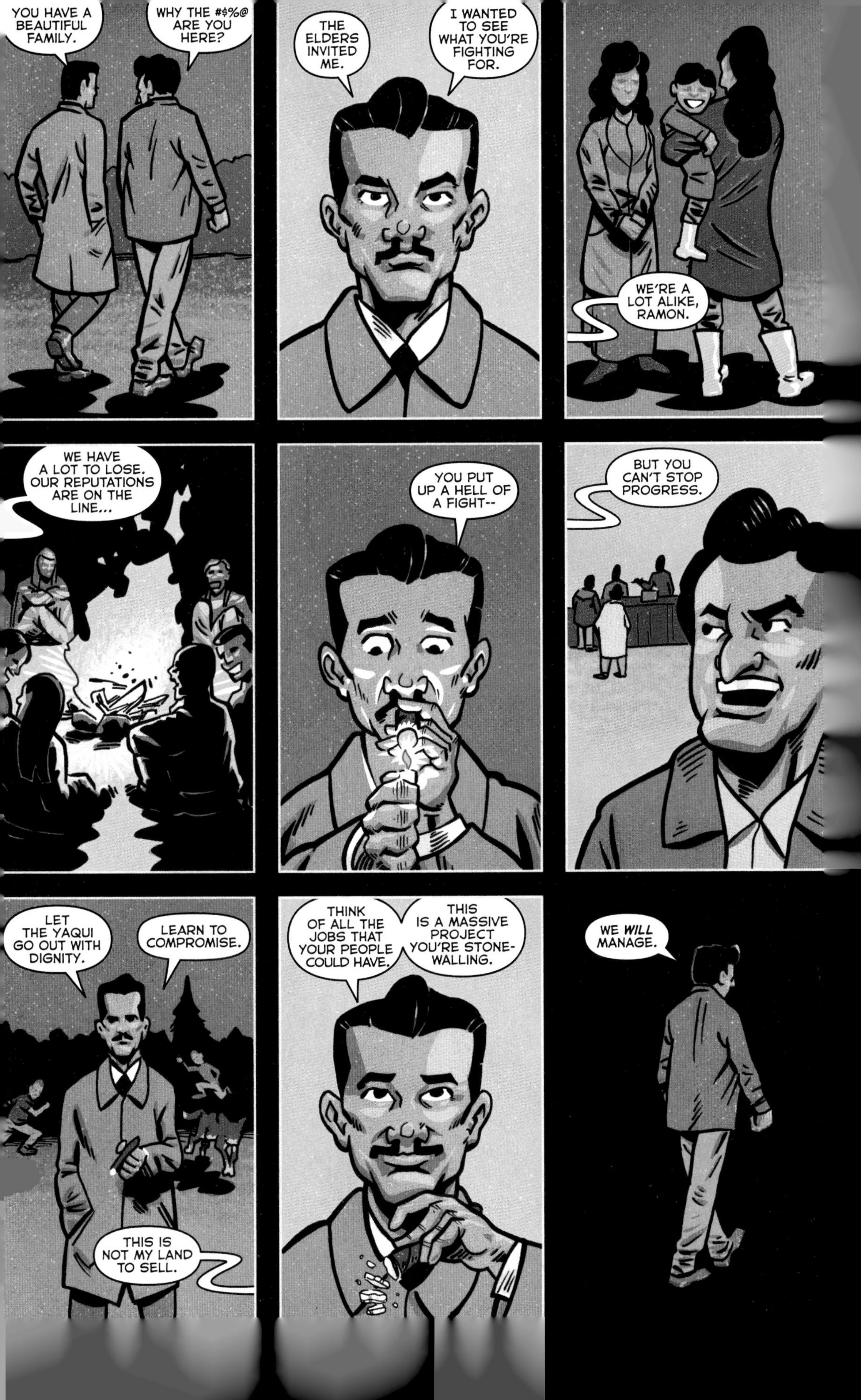
YOU HAVE A BEAUTIFUL FAMILY.
WHY THE #$%@ ARE YOU HERE?
THE ELDERS INVITED ME.
I WANTED TO SEE WHAT YOU'RE FIGHTING FOR.
WE'RE A LOT ALIKE, RAMON.
WE HAVE A LOT TO LOSE. OUR REPUTATIONS ARE ON THE LINE...
YOU PUT UP A HELL OF A FIGHT--
BUT YOU CAN'T STOP PROGRESS.
LET THE YAQUI GO OUT WITH DIGNITY.
LEARN TO COMPROMISE.
THIS IS NOT MY LAND TO SELL.
THINK OF ALL THE JOBS THAT YOUR PEOPLE COULD HAVE.
THIS IS A MASSIVE PROJECT YOU'RE STONE-WALLING.
WE *WILL* MANAGE.

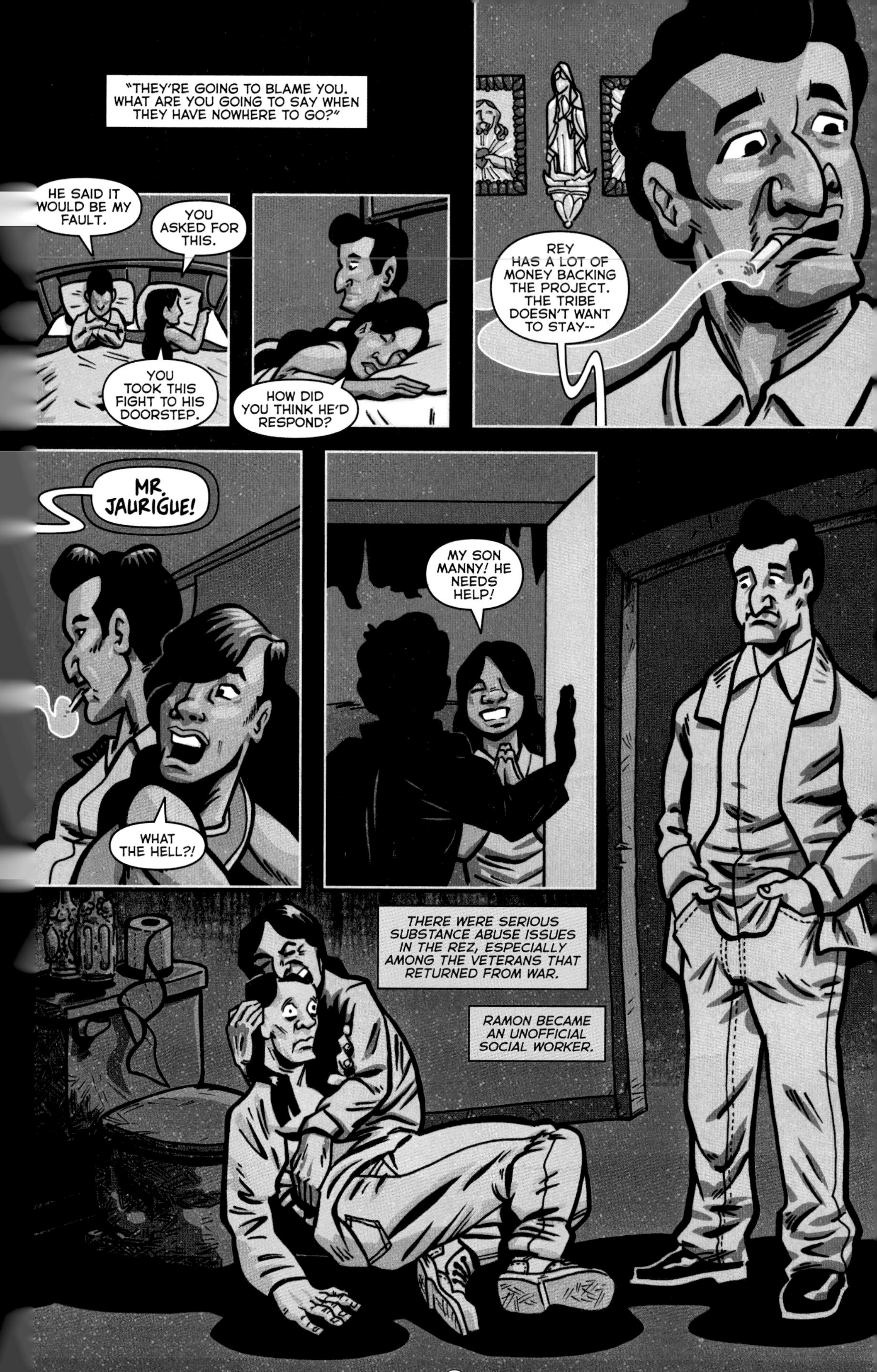
"THEY'RE GOING TO BLAME YOU. WHAT ARE YOU GOING TO SAY WHEN THEY HAVE NOWHERE TO GO?"
HE SAID IT WOULD BE MY FAULT.
YOU ASKED FOR THIS.
YOU TOOK THIS FIGHT TO HIS DOORSTEP.
HOW DID YOU THINK HE'D RESPOND?
REY HAS A LOT OF MONEY BACKING THE PROJECT. THE TRIBE DOESN'T WANT TO STAY--
MR. JAURIGUE!
WHAT THE HELL?!
MY SON MANNY! HE NEEDS HELP!
THERE WERE SERIOUS SUBSTANCE ABUSE ISSUES IN THE REZ, ESPECIALLY AMONG THE VETERANS THAT RETURNED FROM WAR.
RAMON BECAME AN UNOFFICIAL SOCIAL WORKER.

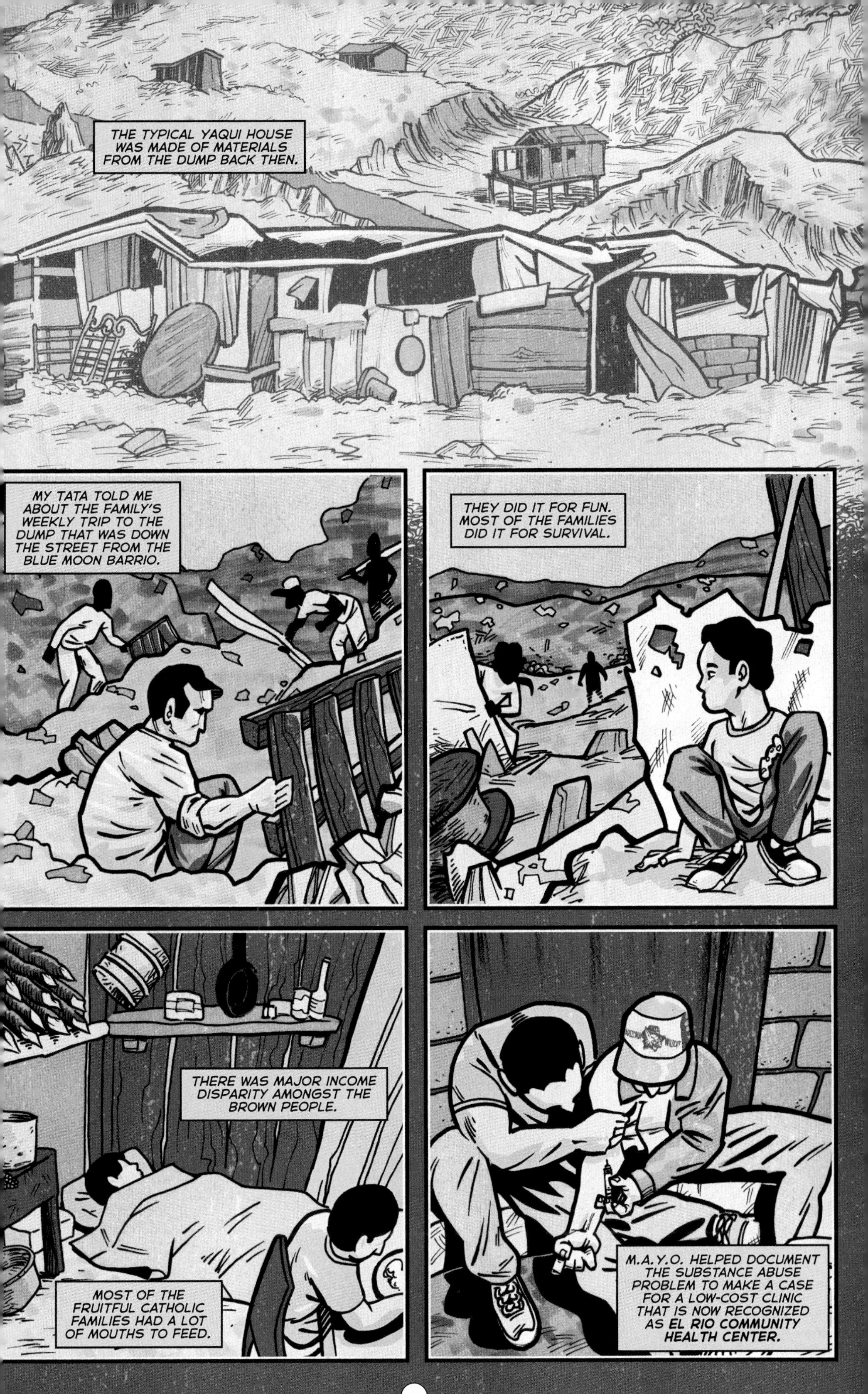
THE TYPICAL YAQUI HOUSE WAS MADE OF MATERIALS FROM THE DUMP BACK THEN.
MY TATA TOLD ME ABOUT THE FAMILY'S WEEKLY TRIP TO THE DUMP THAT WAS DOWN THE STREET FROM THE BLUE MOON BARRIO.
THEY DID IT FOR FUN. MOST OF THE FAMILIES DID IT FOR SURVIVAL.
THERE WAS MAJOR INCOME DISPARITY AMONGST THE BROWN PEOPLE.
MOST OF THE FRUITFUL CATHOLIC FAMILIES HAD A LOT OF MOUTHS TO FEED.
M.A.Y.O. HELPED DOCUMENT THE SUBSTANCE ABUSE PROBLEM TO MAKE A CASE FOR A LOW-COST CLINIC THAT IS NOW RECOGNIZED AS EL RIO COMMUNITY HEALTH CENTER.

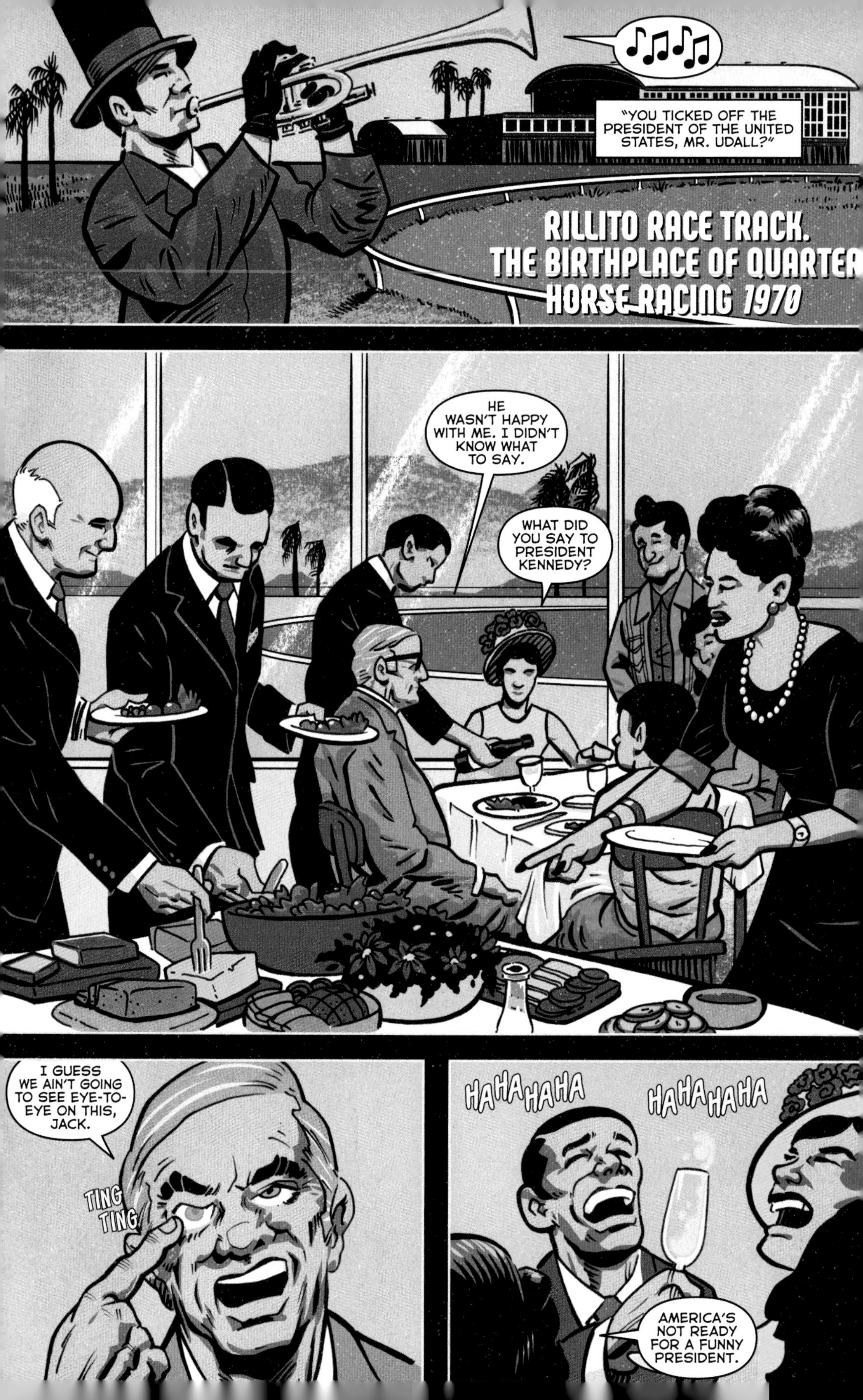
♫♫♫♫
"YOU TICKED OFF THE PRESIDENT OF THE UNITED STATES, MR. UDALL?"
RILLITO RACE TRACK. THE BIRTHPLACE OF QUARTER HORSE RACING 1970
HE WASN'T HAPPY WITH ME. I DIDN'T KNOW WHAT TO SAY.
WHAT DID YOU SAY TO PRESIDENT KENNEDY?
I GUESS WE AIN'T GOING TO SEE EYE-TO-EYE ON THIS, JACK.
TING TING
HAHAHAHA
HAHAHAHA
AMERICA'S NOT READY FOR A FUNNY PRESIDENT.

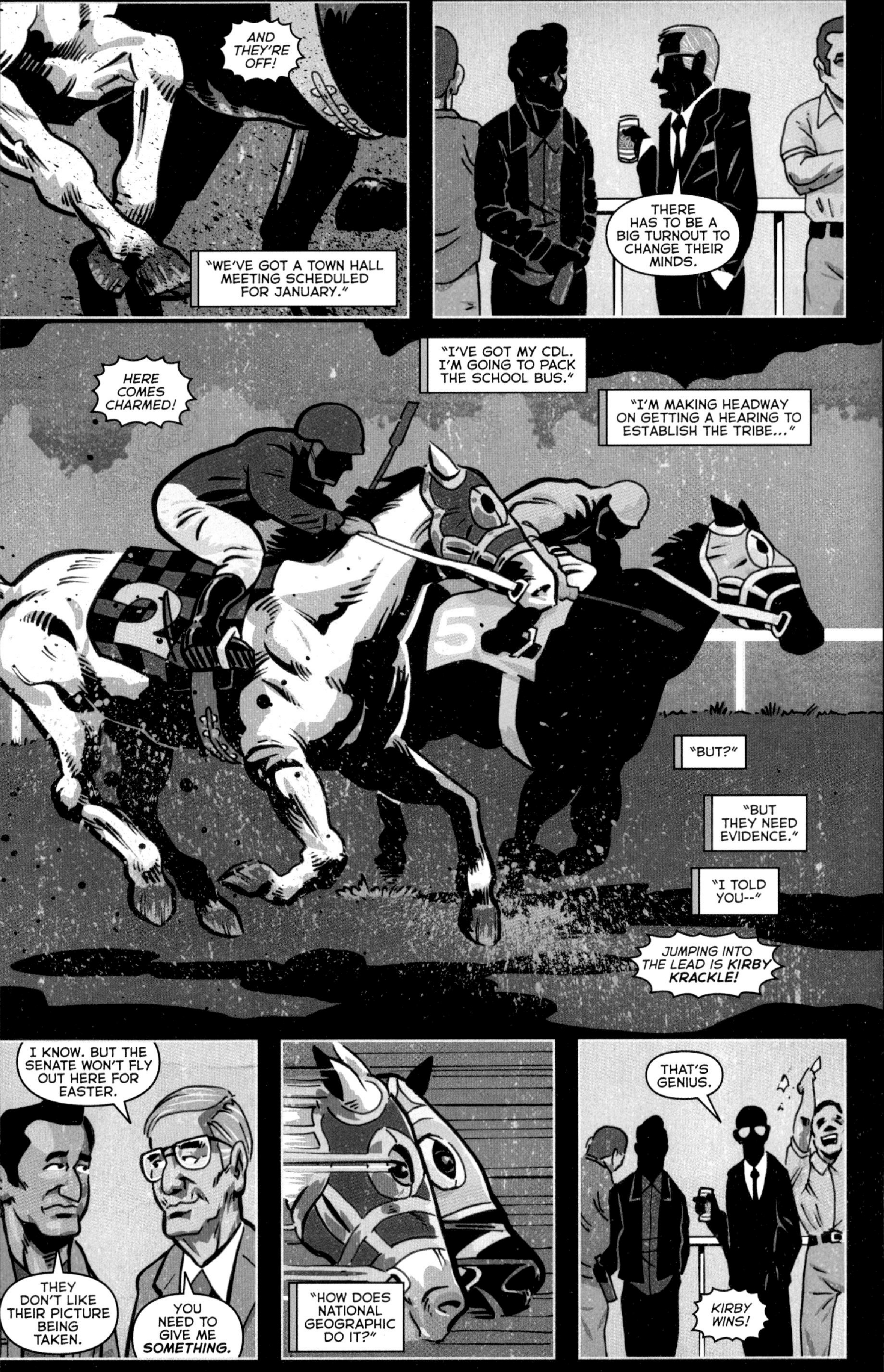
AND THEY'RE OFF!
"WE'VE GOT A TOWN HALL MEETING SCHEDULED FOR JANUARY."
THERE HAS TO BE A BIG TURNOUT TO CHANGE THEIR MINDS.
"I'VE GOT MY CDL. I'M GOING TO PACK THE SCHOOL BUS."
HERE COMES CHARMED!
"I'M MAKING HEADWAY ON GETTING A HEARING TO ESTABLISH THE TRIBE..."
"BUT?"
"BUT THEY NEED EVIDENCE."
"I TOLD YOU--"
JUMPING INTO THE LEAD IS KIRBY KRACKLE!
I KNOW. BUT THE SENATE WON'T FLY OUT HERE FOR EASTER.
THEY DON'T LIKE THEIR PICTURE BEING TAKEN.
YOU NEED TO GIVE ME SOMETHING.
"HOW DOES NATIONAL GEOGRAPHIC DO IT?"
THAT'S GENIUS.
KIRBY WINS!

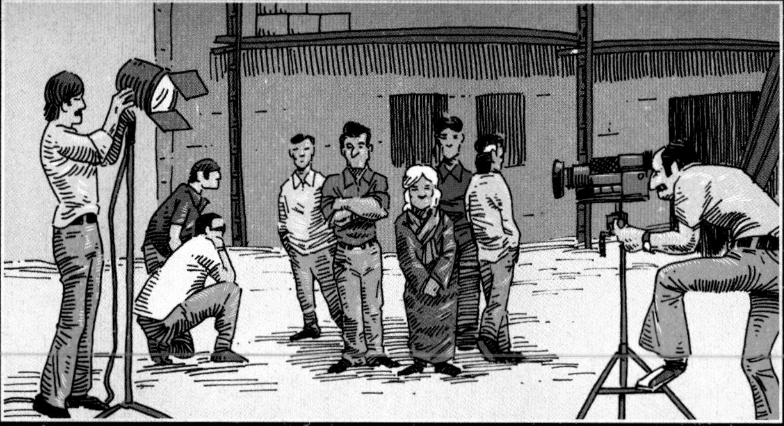

TATA RAMBO AND VALENCIA HAD CLOSE TIES WITH THE UNIVERSITY OF ARIZONA. THEY WERE ESSENTIAL IN CRAFTING THE ARGUMENT THAT THE YAQUIS LIVED IN THE SONORAN DESERT FIRST.

TRADITIONALLY, NATIVES DON'T LIKE THEIR PICTURE TAKEN. THERE ARE A COUPLE OF REASONS: THE OLDER GENERATIONS BELIEVED THAT PHOTOGRAPHS STOLE THEIR SOULS. IT'S TRUE.

SOME OF THE ELDERS DIDN'T WANT THEIR PICTURES TAKEN IN FEAR THAT THE MEXICAN GOVERNMENT WOULD FIND THEM. EVENTUALLY, THEY BROKE DOWN AND ALLOWED THE UA TO FILM AND RECORD THE ANNUAL EASTER-TIME CEREMONIES, HUNDREDS OF YEARS OLD; CHRISTIAN TEACHINGS AND ANCIENT YAQUI TRADITIONS.

LIKE ALL NATIVE PEOPLE, YAQUI HAVE A BLOODY, WAR-FILLED PAST.

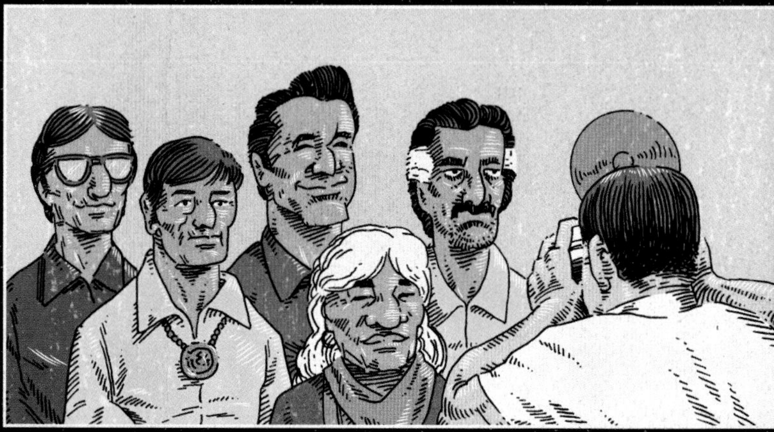

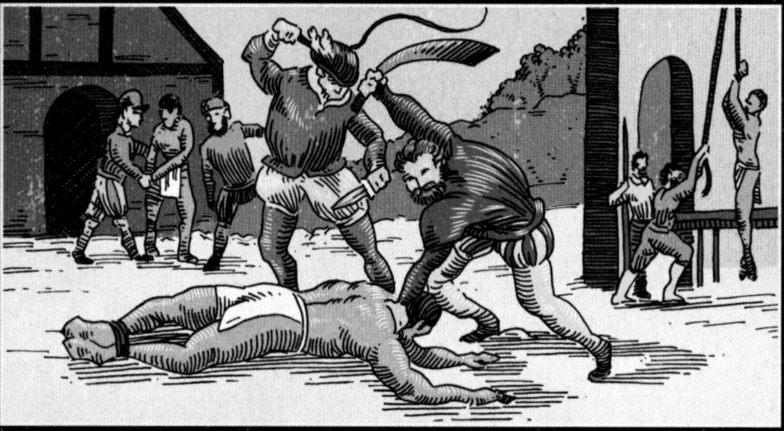

THE YAQUI PEOPLE-- ORIGINALLY KNOWN AS YOEME-- HAVE BEEN FIGHTING FOR LAND DATING BACK TO 1533. SPANISH COLONISTS SLAUGHTERED, RAPED AND PILLAGED THE INDIGENOUS TRIBES, FORCING THEM INTO FIGHT OR FLIGHT.

EVENTUALLY, THE YOEME BANDED WITH THE M.A.Y.O., OPATA AND PIMA TRIBES TO DRIVE THE COLONISTS OUT OF THE SONORAN DESERT.

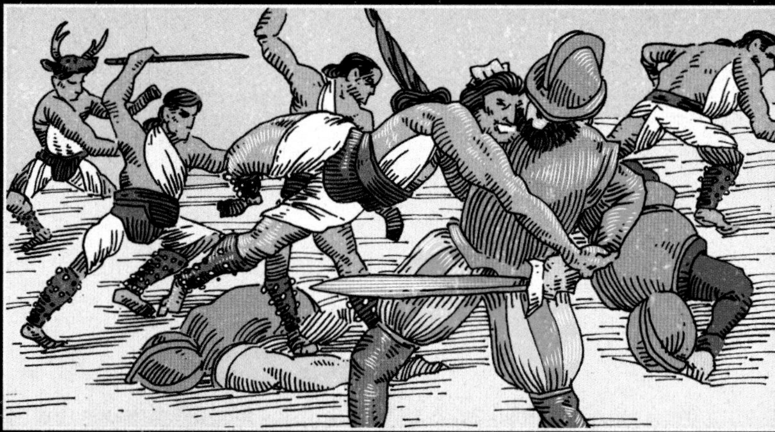

THE YAQUI ALLIED WITH THE FRENCH TO FIGHT THE MEXICAN GOVERNMENT. THEY WON SOME BATTLES...

...BUT LOST THE WAR.

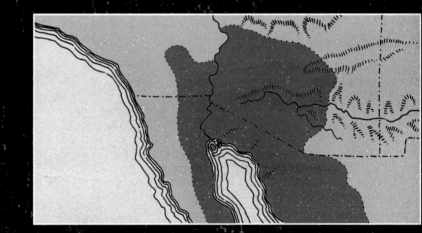

THE YAQUI FLED NORTH OF THE SONORAN DESERT. TO SURVIVE, THEY HAD TO VENTURE BEYOND THE BORDER THAT CROSSED THEM.

IT HAS BEEN DOCUMENTED THAT THE TRIBE'S LEADER--ANSELMO VALENCIA--ENVISIONED A LAND NEAR THE SAN XAVIER. HE WANTED TO TAKE THE PEOPLE TO THE PROMISED LAND SO THEY WOULDN'T HAVE TO DEAL WITH THE CRIME, DRUGS AND ALCOHOLISM THAT PLAGUED THEM. THE HISTORY BOOKS TEND TO FORGET M.A.Y.O. AND NEARLY NINE YEARS OF WORK BY THE COMMUNITY AT LARGE.

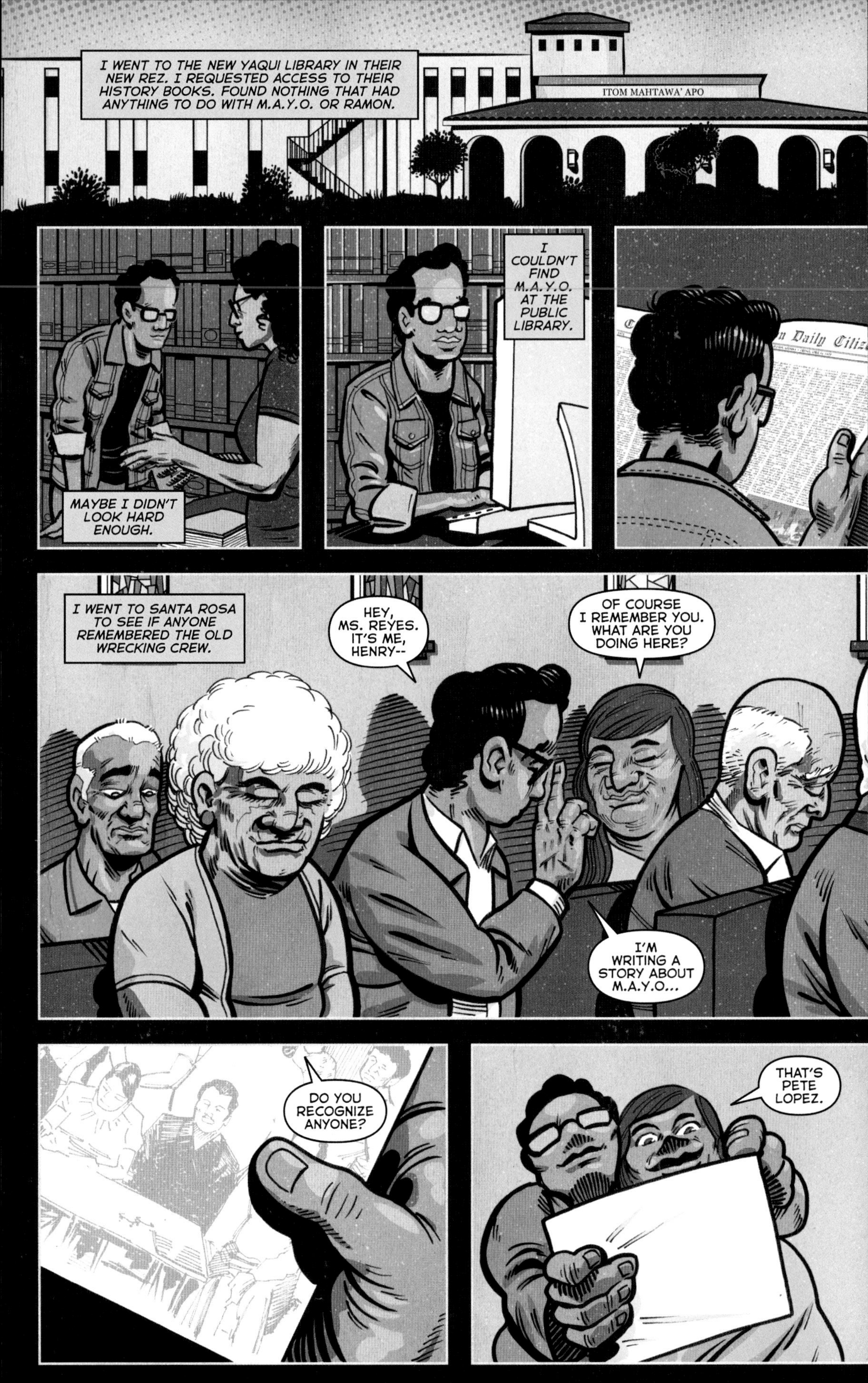
I WENT TO THE NEW YAQUI LIBRARY IN THEIR NEW REZ. I REQUESTED ACCESS TO THEIR HISTORY BOOKS. FOUND NOTHING THAT HAD ANYTHING TO DO WITH M.A.Y.O. OR RAMON.
ITOM MAHTAWA' APO
MAYBE I DIDN'T LOOK HARD ENOUGH.
I COULDN'T FIND M.A.Y.O. AT THE PUBLIC LIBRARY.
I WENT TO SANTA ROSA TO SEE IF ANYONE REMEMBERED THE OLD WRECKING CREW.
HEY, MS. REYES. IT'S ME, HENRY--
OF COURSE I REMEMBER YOU. WHAT ARE YOU DOING HERE?
I'M WRITING A STORY ABOUT M.A.Y.O...
DO YOU RECOGNIZE ANYONE?
THAT'S PETE LOPEZ.

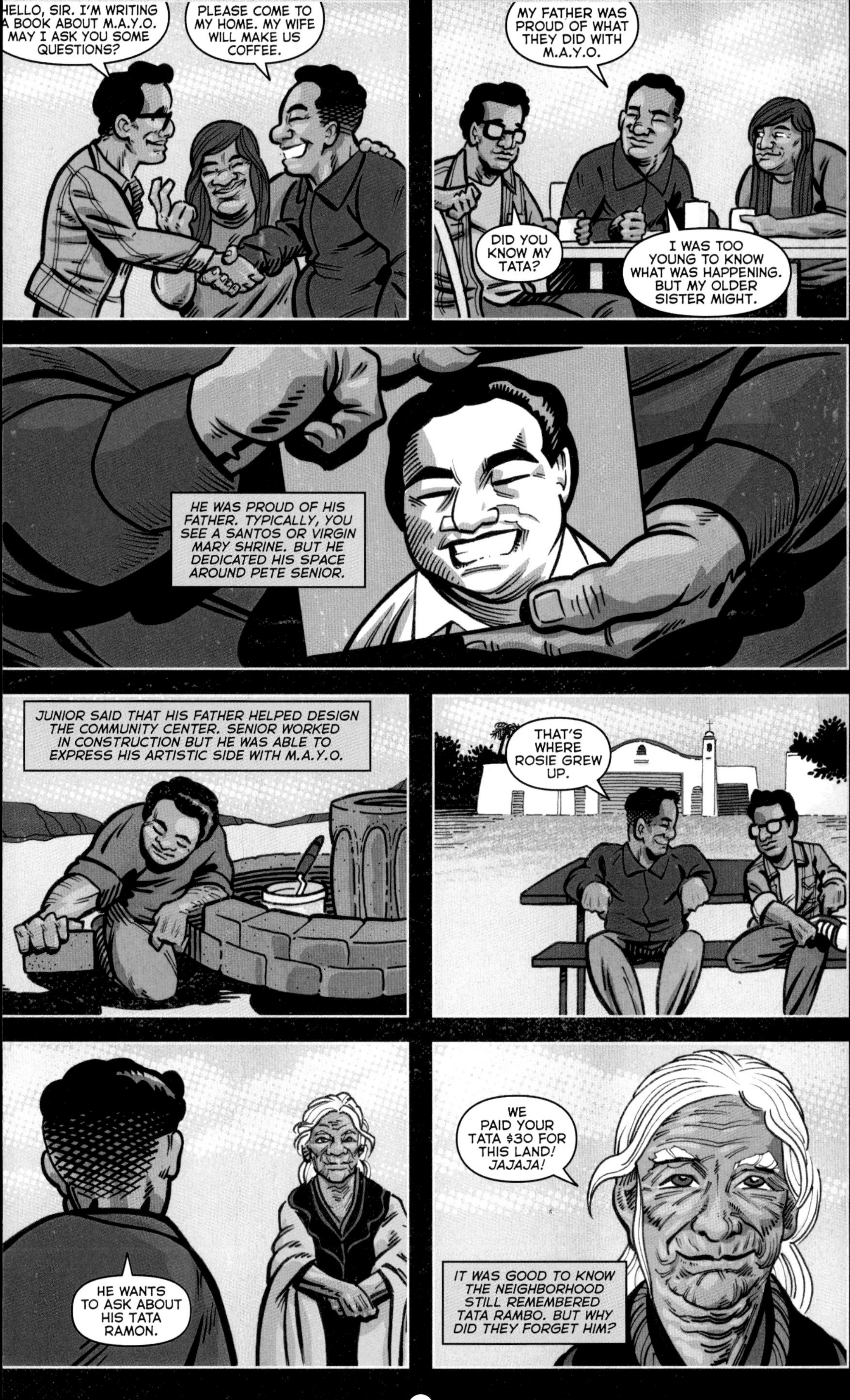
HELLO, SIR. I'M WRITING A BOOK ABOUT M.A.Y.O. MAY I ASK YOU SOME QUESTIONS?
PLEASE COME TO MY HOME. MY WIFE WILL MAKE US COFFEE.
MY FATHER WAS PROUD OF WHAT THEY DID WITH M.A.Y.O.
DID YOU KNOW MY TATA?
I WAS TOO YOUNG TO KNOW WHAT WAS HAPPENING. BUT MY OLDER SISTER MIGHT.
HE WAS PROUD OF HIS FATHER. TYPICALLY, YOU SEE A SANTOS OR VIRGIN MARY SHRINE. BUT HE DEDICATED HIS SPACE AROUND PETE SENIOR.
JUNIOR SAID THAT HIS FATHER HELPED DESIGN THE COMMUNITY CENTER. SENIOR WORKED IN CONSTRUCTION BUT HE WAS ABLE TO EXPRESS HIS ARTISTIC SIDE WITH M.A.Y.O.
THAT'S WHERE ROSIE GREW UP.
HE WANTS TO ASK ABOUT HIS TATA RAMON.
WE PAID YOUR TATA $30 FOR THIS LAND! JAJAJA!
IT WAS GOOD TO KNOW THE NEIGHBORHOOD STILL REMEMBERED TATA RAMBO. BUT WHY DID THEY FORGET HIM?

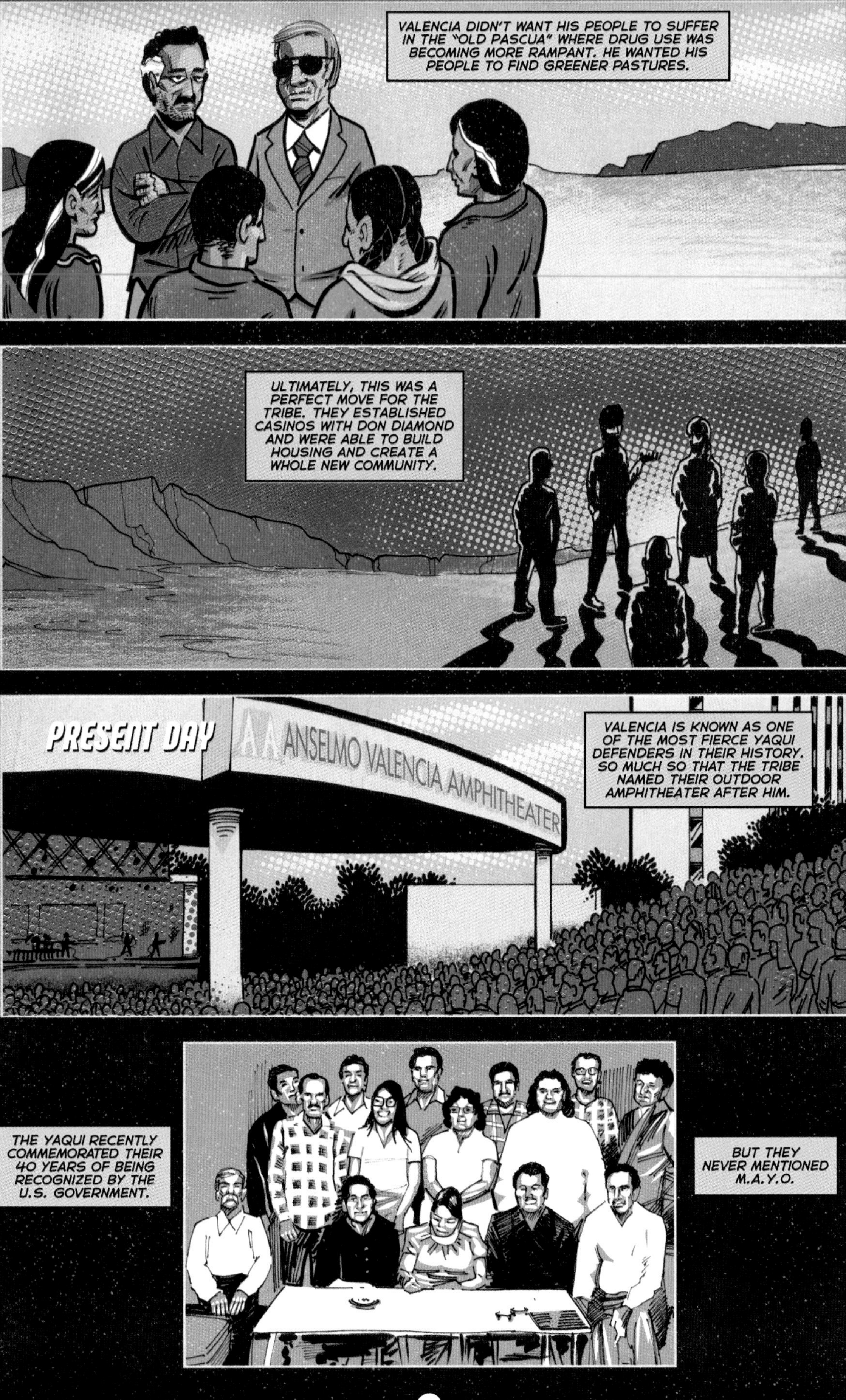
VALENCIA DIDN'T WANT HIS PEOPLE TO SUFFER IN THE "OLD PASCUA" WHERE DRUG USE WAS BECOMING MORE RAMPANT. HE WANTED HIS PEOPLE TO FIND GREENER PASTURES.
ULTIMATELY, THIS WAS A PERFECT MOVE FOR THE TRIBE. THEY ESTABLISHED CASINOS WITH DON DIAMOND AND WERE ABLE TO BUILD HOUSING AND CREATE A WHOLE NEW COMMUNITY.
PRESENT DAY
ANSELMO VALENCIA AMPHITHEATER
VALENCIA IS KNOWN AS ONE OF THE MOST FIERCE YAQUI DEFENDERS IN THEIR HISTORY. SO MUCH SO THAT THE TRIBE NAMED THEIR OUTDOOR AMPHITHEATER AFTER HIM.
THE YAQUI RECENTLY COMMEMORATED THEIR 40 YEARS OF BEING RECOGNIZED BY THE U.S. GOVERNMENT.
BUT THEY NEVER MENTIONED M.A.Y.O.

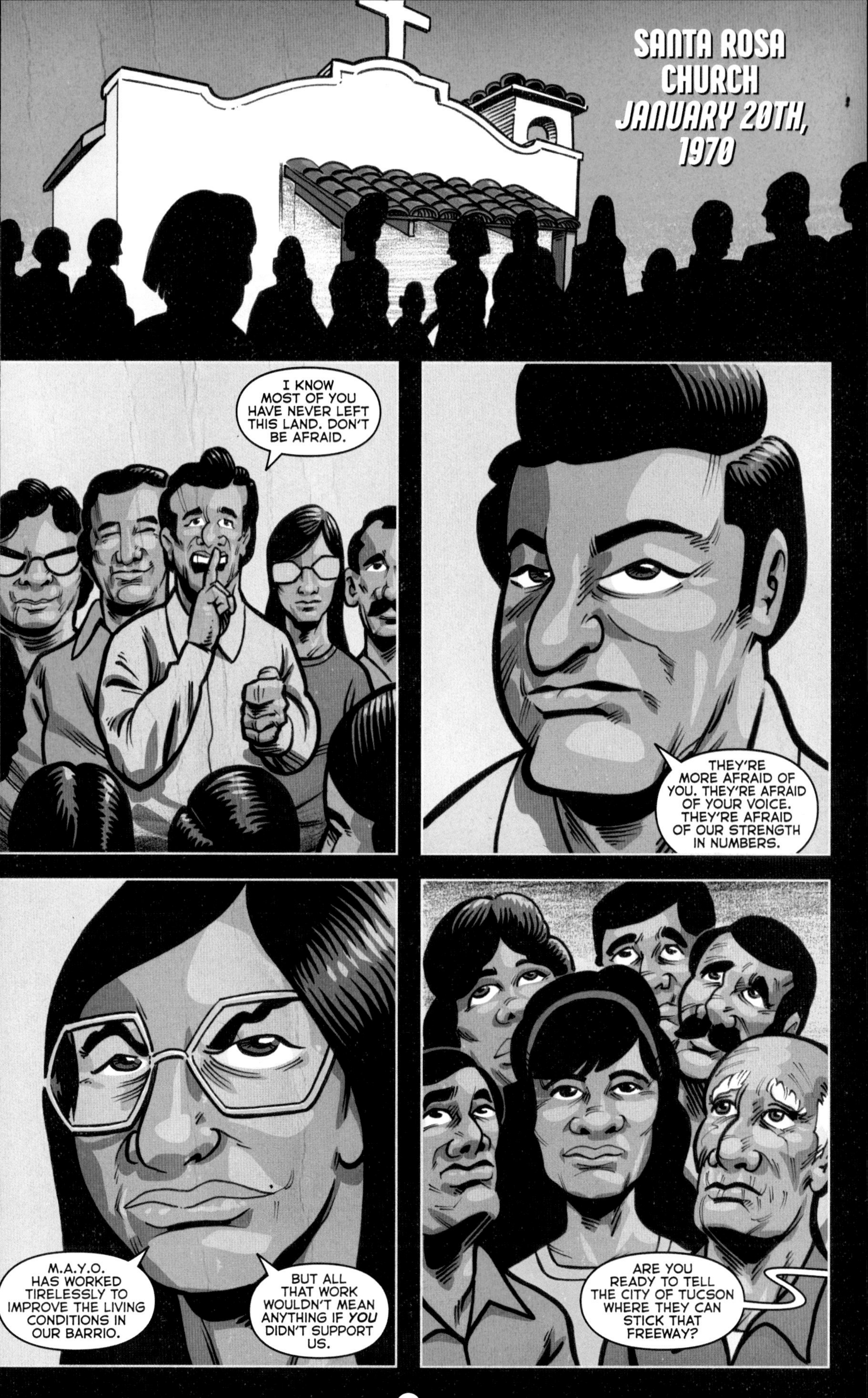
SANTA ROSA CHURCH JANUARY 20TH, 1970
I KNOW MOST OF YOU HAVE NEVER LEFT THIS LAND. DON'T BE AFRAID.
THEY'RE MORE AFRAID OF YOU. THEY'RE AFRAID OF YOUR VOICE. THEY'RE AFRAID OF OUR STRENGTH IN NUMBERS.
M.A.Y.O. HAS WORKED TIRELESSLY TO IMPROVE THE LIVING CONDITIONS IN OUR BARRIO.
BUT ALL THAT WORK WOULDN'T MEAN ANYTHING IF *YOU* DIDN'T SUPPORT US.
ARE YOU READY TO TELL THE CITY OF TUCSON WHERE THEY CAN STICK THAT FREEWAY?

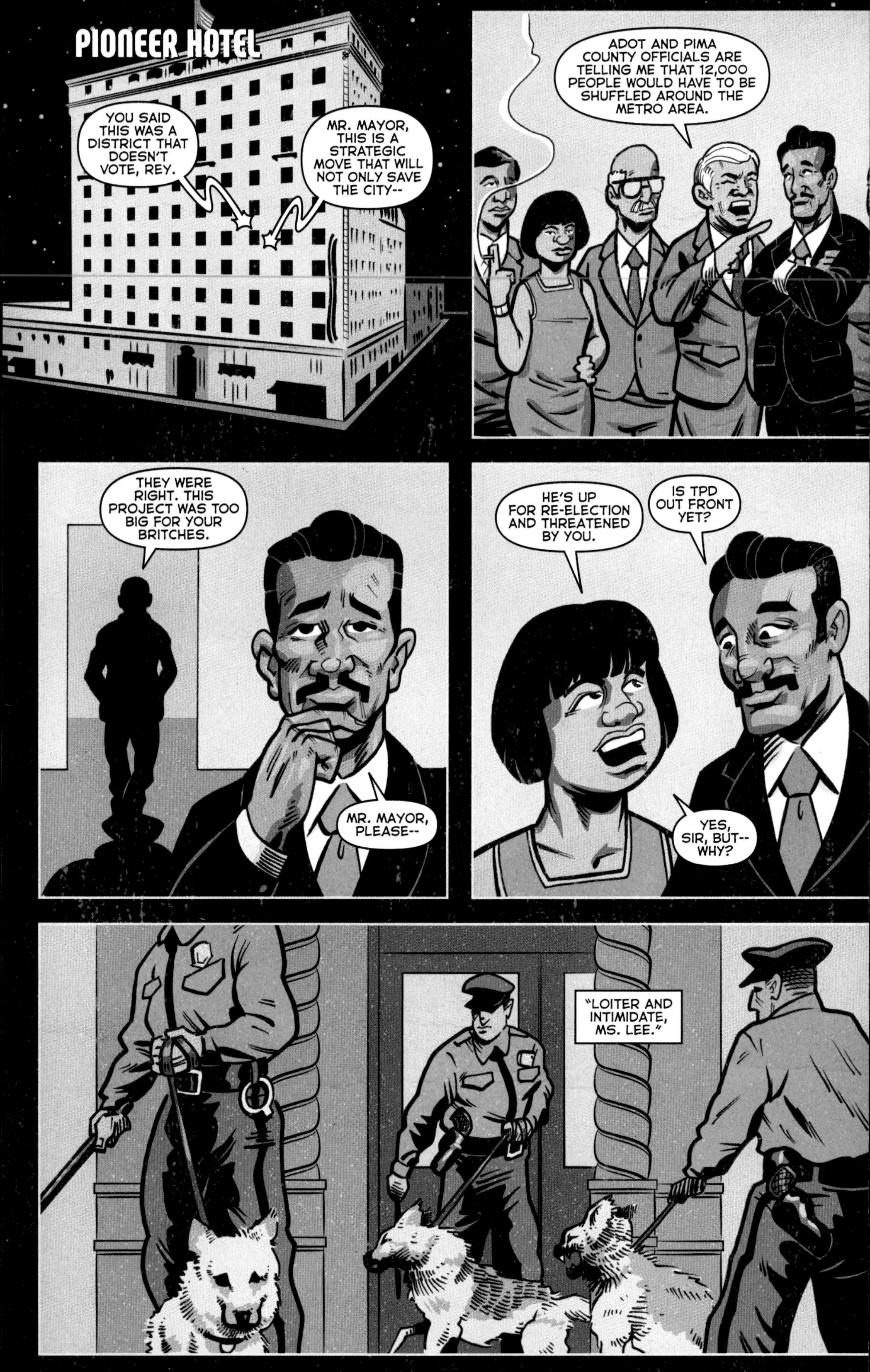
PIONEER HOTEL
YOU SAID THIS WAS A DISTRICT THAT DOESN'T VOTE, REY.
MR. MAYOR, THIS IS A STRATEGIC MOVE THAT WILL NOT ONLY SAVE THE CITY--
ADOT AND PIMA COUNTY OFFICIALS ARE TELLING ME THAT 12,000 PEOPLE WOULD HAVE TO BE SHUFFLED AROUND THE METRO AREA.
THEY WERE RIGHT. THIS PROJECT WAS TOO BIG FOR YOUR BRITCHES.
MR. MAYOR, PLEASE--
HE'S UP FOR RE-ELECTION AND THREATENED BY YOU.
IS TPD OUT FRONT YET?
YES, SIR, BUT-- WHY?
"LOITER AND INTIMIDATE, MS. LEE."

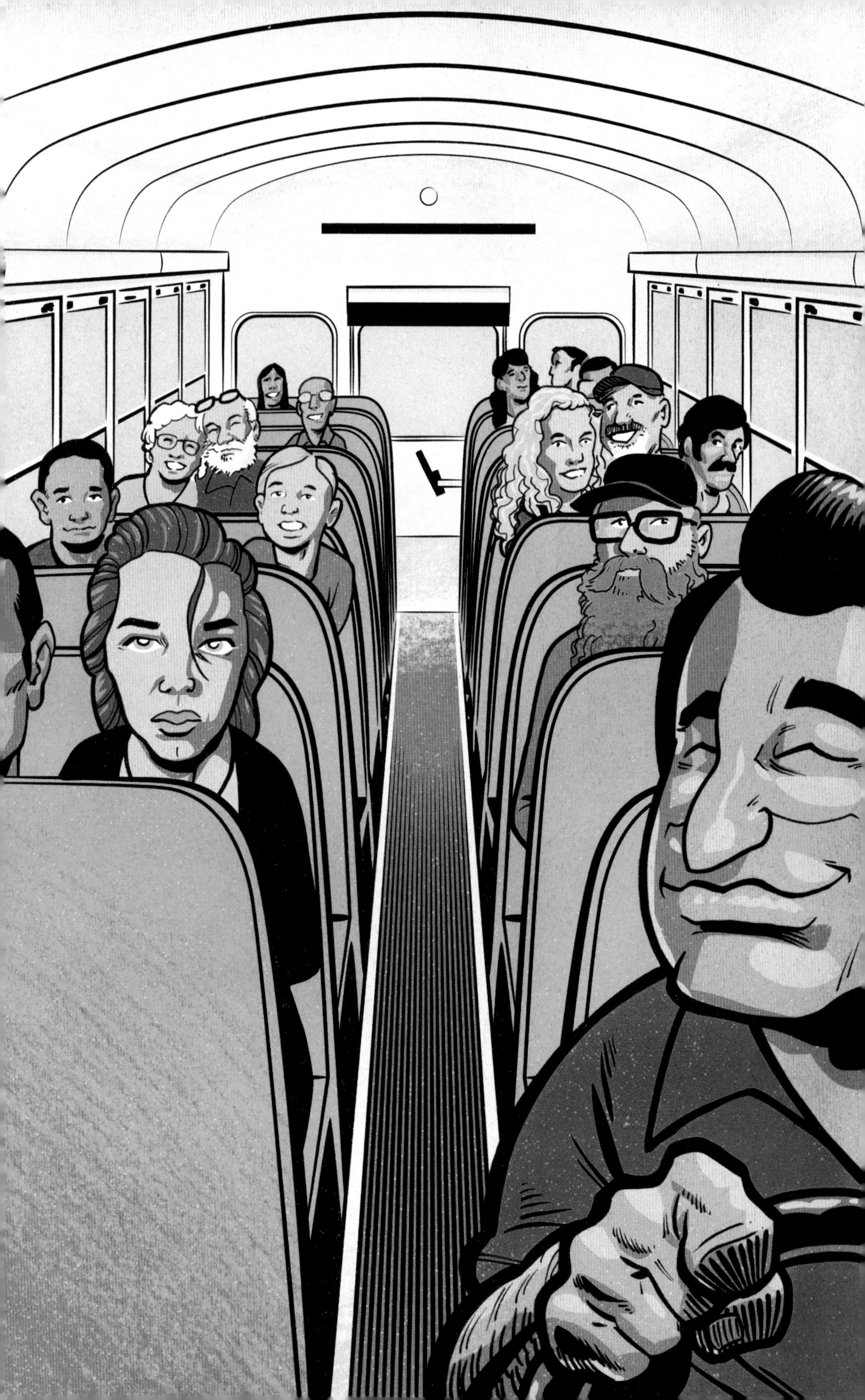

CHAPTER THREE:

YES WE DID!

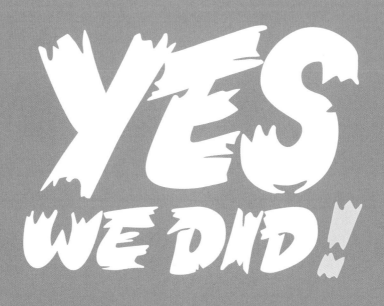

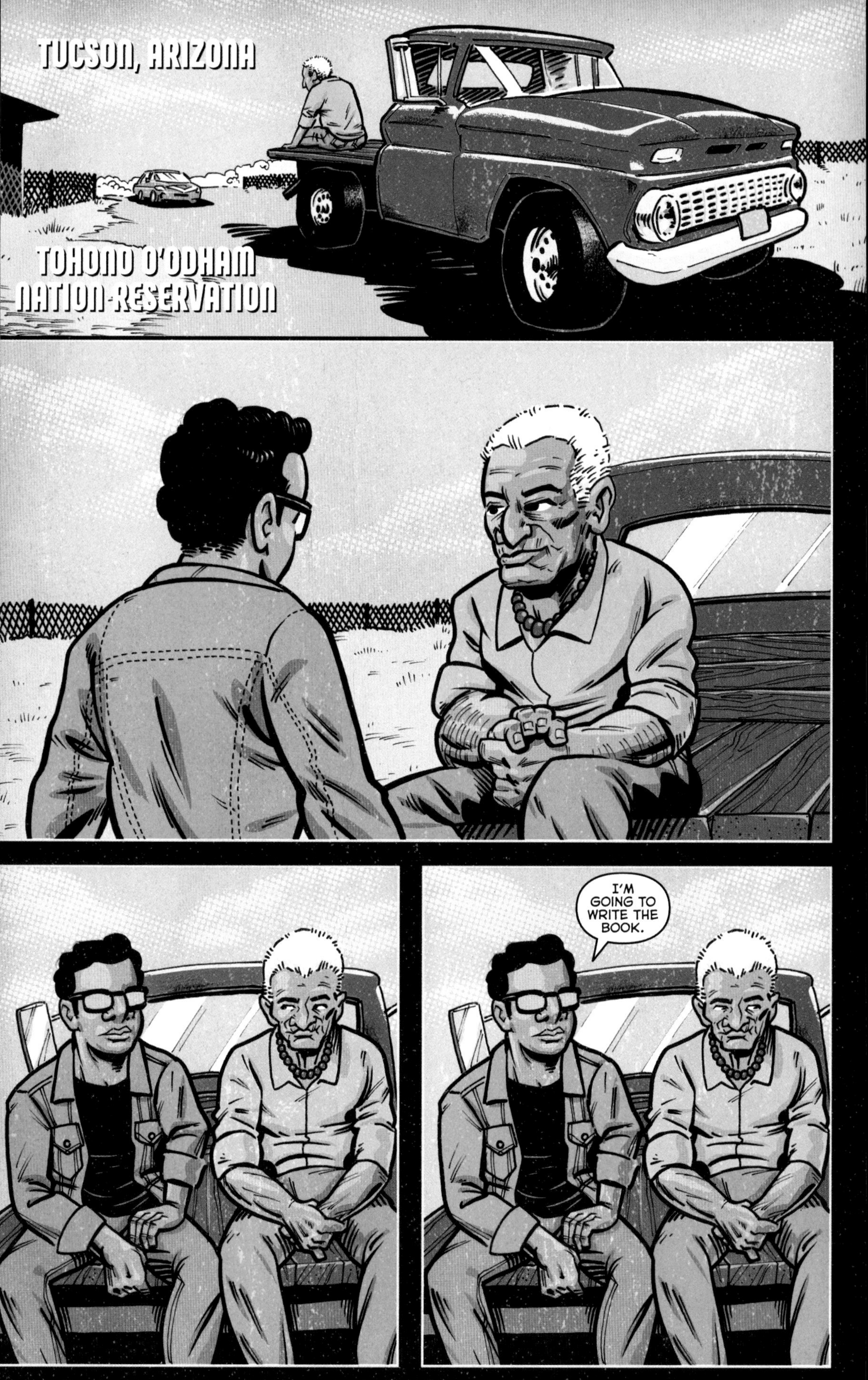
TUCSON, ARIZONA
TOHONO O'ODHAM NATION RESERVATION
I'M GOING TO WRITE THE BOOK.

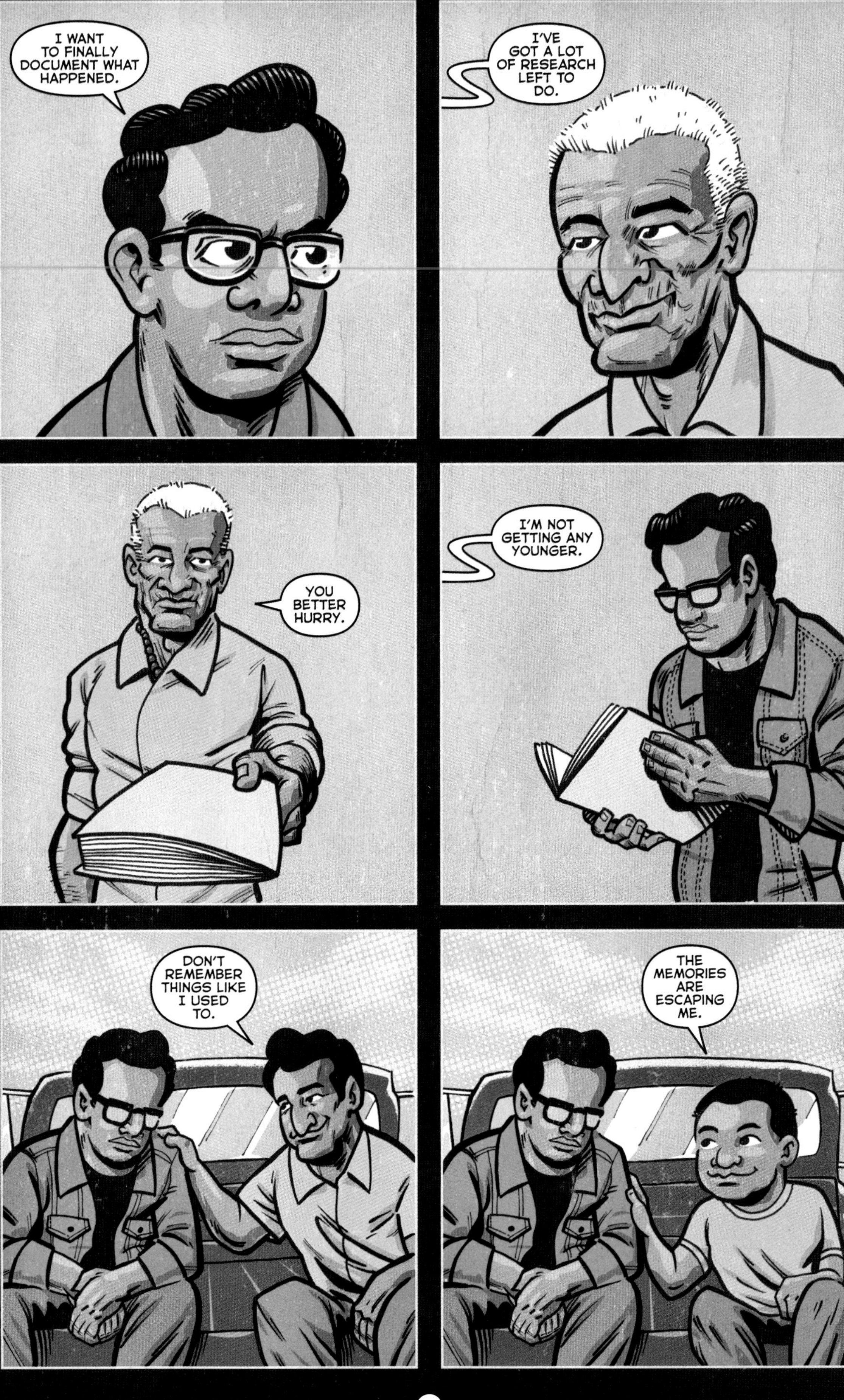
I WANT TO FINALLY DOCUMENT WHAT HAPPENED.
I'VE GOT A LOT OF RESEARCH LEFT TO DO.
YOU BETTER HURRY.
I'M NOT GETTING ANY YOUNGER.
DON'T REMEMBER THINGS LIKE I USED TO.
THE MEMORIES ARE ESCAPING ME.

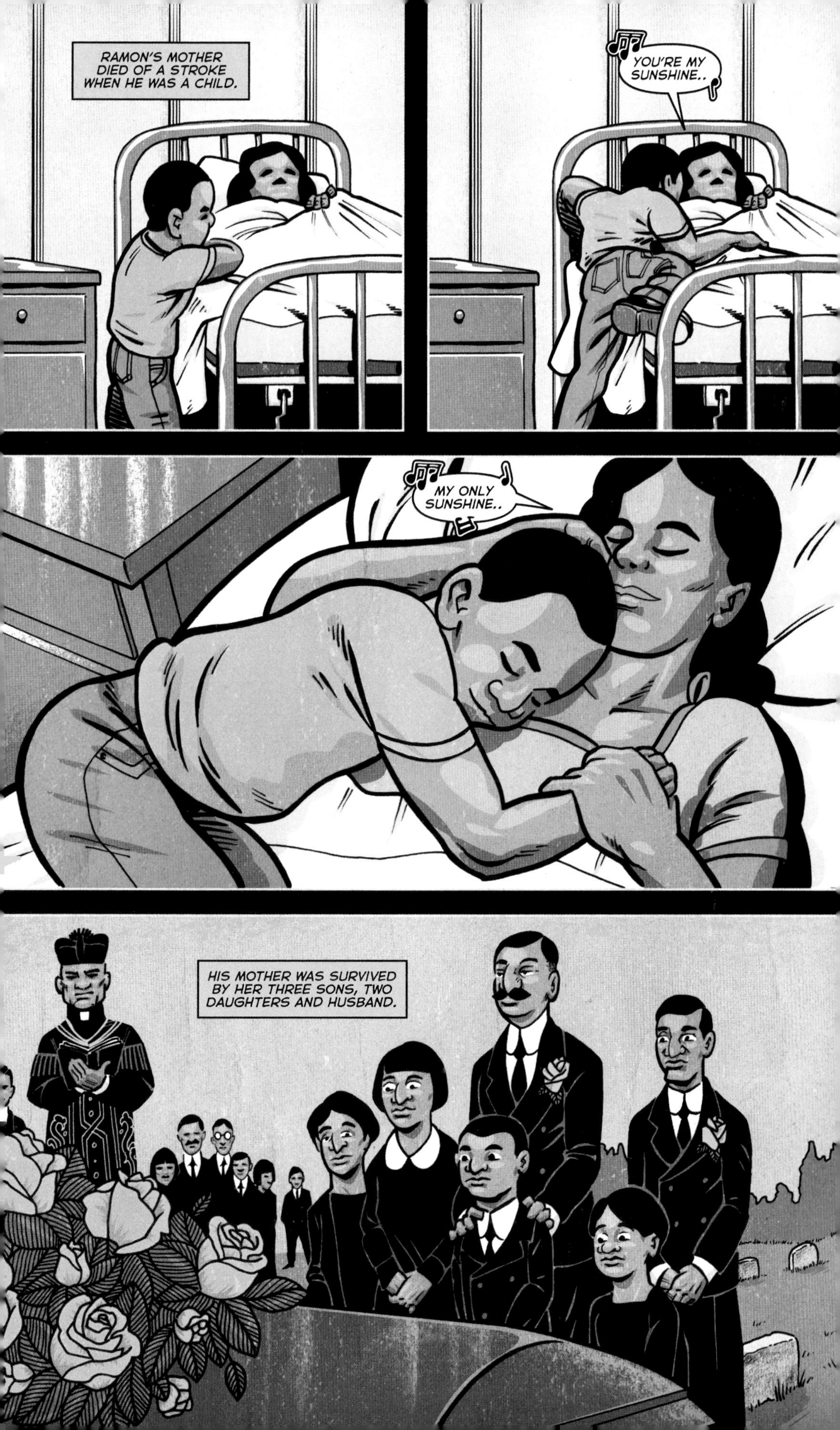
RAMON'S MOTHER DIED OF A STROKE WHEN HE WAS A CHILD.
YOU'RE MY SUNSHINE..
MY ONLY SUNSHINE..
HIS MOTHER WAS SURVIVED BY HER THREE SONS, TWO DAUGHTERS AND HUSBAND.

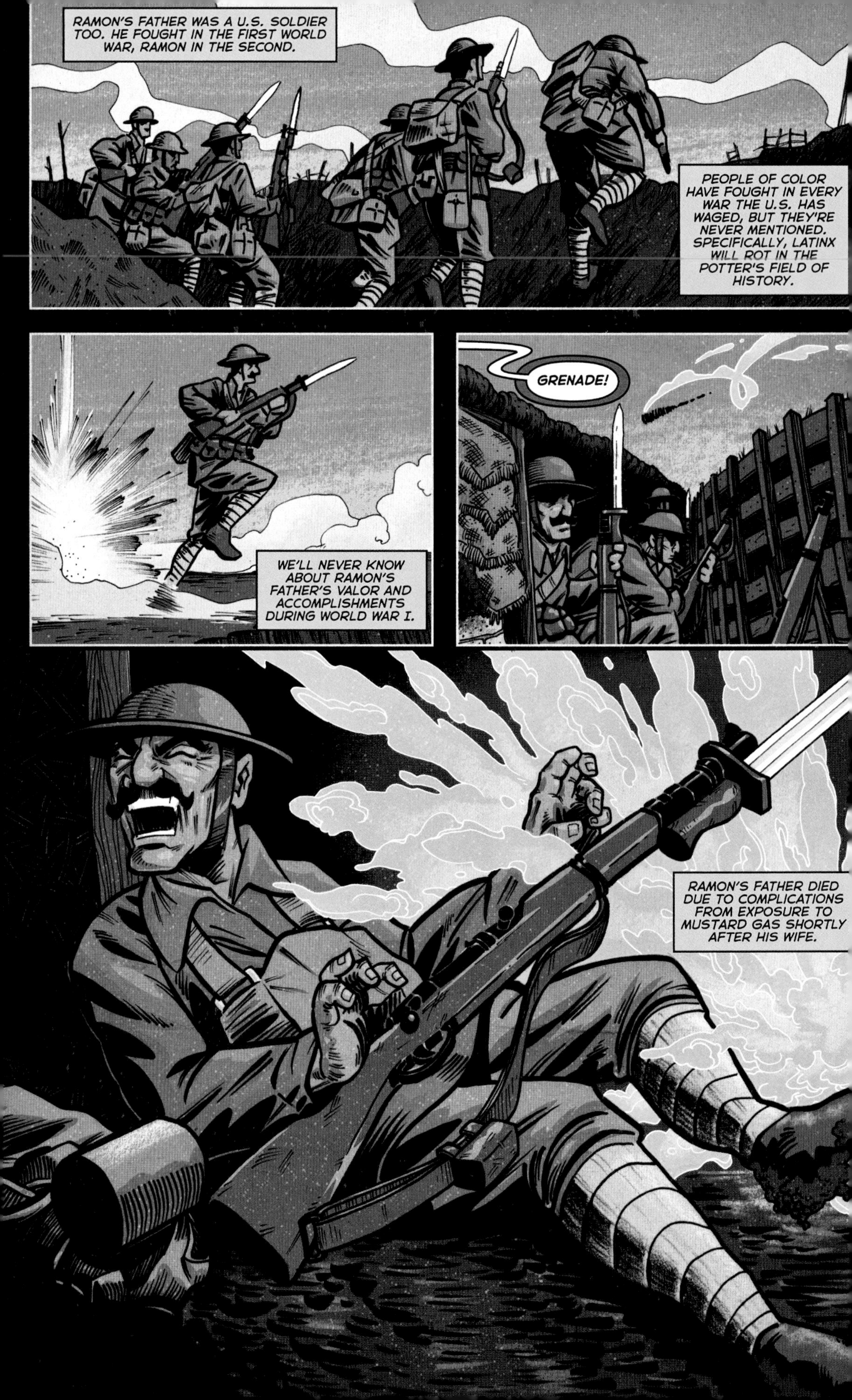
RAMON'S FATHER WAS A U.S. SOLDIER TOO. HE FOUGHT IN THE FIRST WORLD WAR, RAMON IN THE SECOND.
PEOPLE OF COLOR HAVE FOUGHT IN EVERY WAR THE U.S. HAS WAGED, BUT THEY'RE NEVER MENTIONED. SPECIFICALLY, LATINX WILL ROT IN THE POTTER'S FIELD OF HISTORY.
WE'LL NEVER KNOW ABOUT RAMON'S FATHER'S VALOR AND ACCOMPLISHMENTS DURING WORLD WAR I.
GRENADE!
RAMON'S FATHER DIED DUE TO COMPLICATIONS FROM EXPOSURE TO MUSTARD GAS SHORTLY AFTER HIS WIFE.

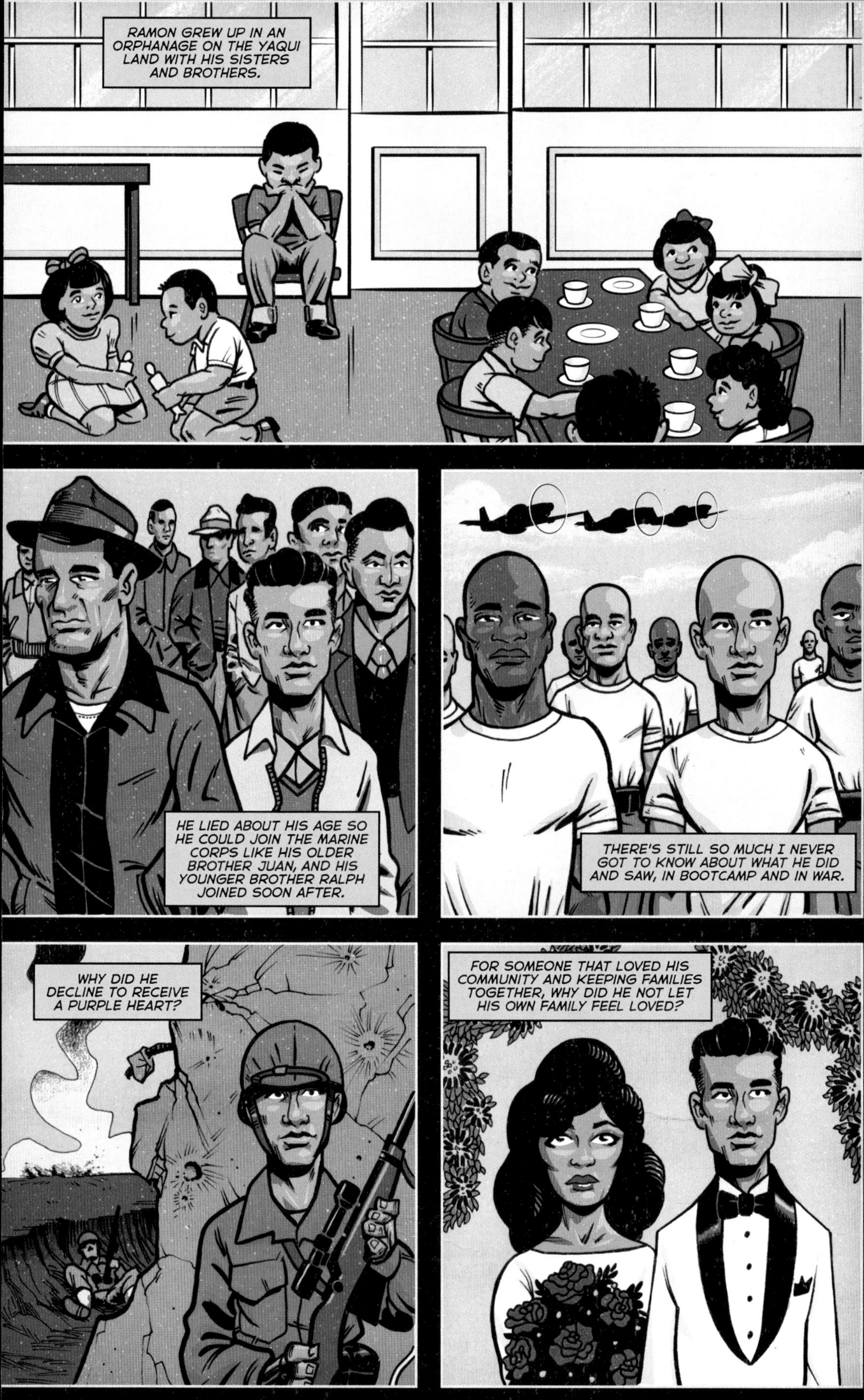
RAMON GREW UP IN AN ORPHANAGE ON THE YAQUI LAND WITH HIS SISTERS AND BROTHERS.
HE LIED ABOUT HIS AGE SO HE COULD JOIN THE MARINE CORPS LIKE HIS OLDER BROTHER JUAN, AND HIS YOUNGER BROTHER RALPH JOINED SOON AFTER.
THERE'S STILL SO MUCH I NEVER GOT TO KNOW ABOUT WHAT HE DID AND SAW, IN BOOTCAMP AND IN WAR.
WHY DID HE DECLINE TO RECEIVE A PURPLE HEART?
FOR SOMEONE THAT LOVED HIS COMMUNITY AND KEEPING FAMILIES TOGETHER, WHY DID HE NOT LET HIS OWN FAMILY FEEL LOVED?

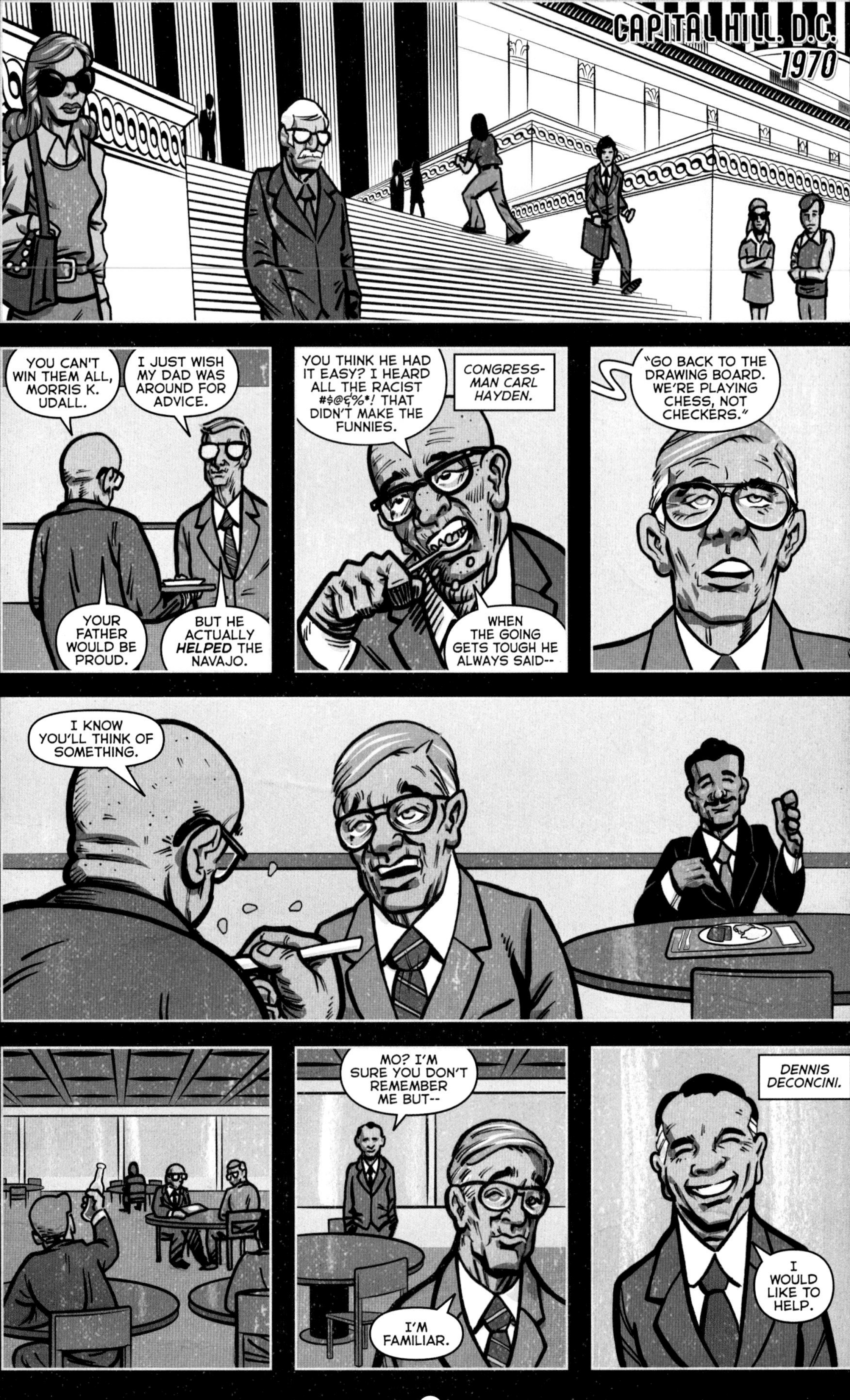
CAPITAL HILL, D.C. 1970
YOU CAN'T WIN THEM ALL, MORRIS K. UDALL.
I JUST WISH MY DAD WAS AROUND FOR ADVICE.
YOUR FATHER WOULD BE PROUD.
BUT HE ACTUALLY HELPED THE NAVAJO.
YOU THINK HE HAD IT EASY? I HEARD ALL THE RACIST #$@€%*! THAT DIDN'T MAKE THE FUNNIES.
CONGRESS-MAN CARL HAYDEN.
WHEN THE GOING GETS TOUGH HE ALWAYS SAID--
"GO BACK TO THE DRAWING BOARD. WE'RE PLAYING CHESS, NOT CHECKERS."
I KNOW YOU'LL THINK OF SOMETHING.
MO? I'M SURE YOU DON'T REMEMBER ME BUT--
I'M FAMILIAR.
DENNIS DECONCINI.
I WOULD LIKE TO HELP.

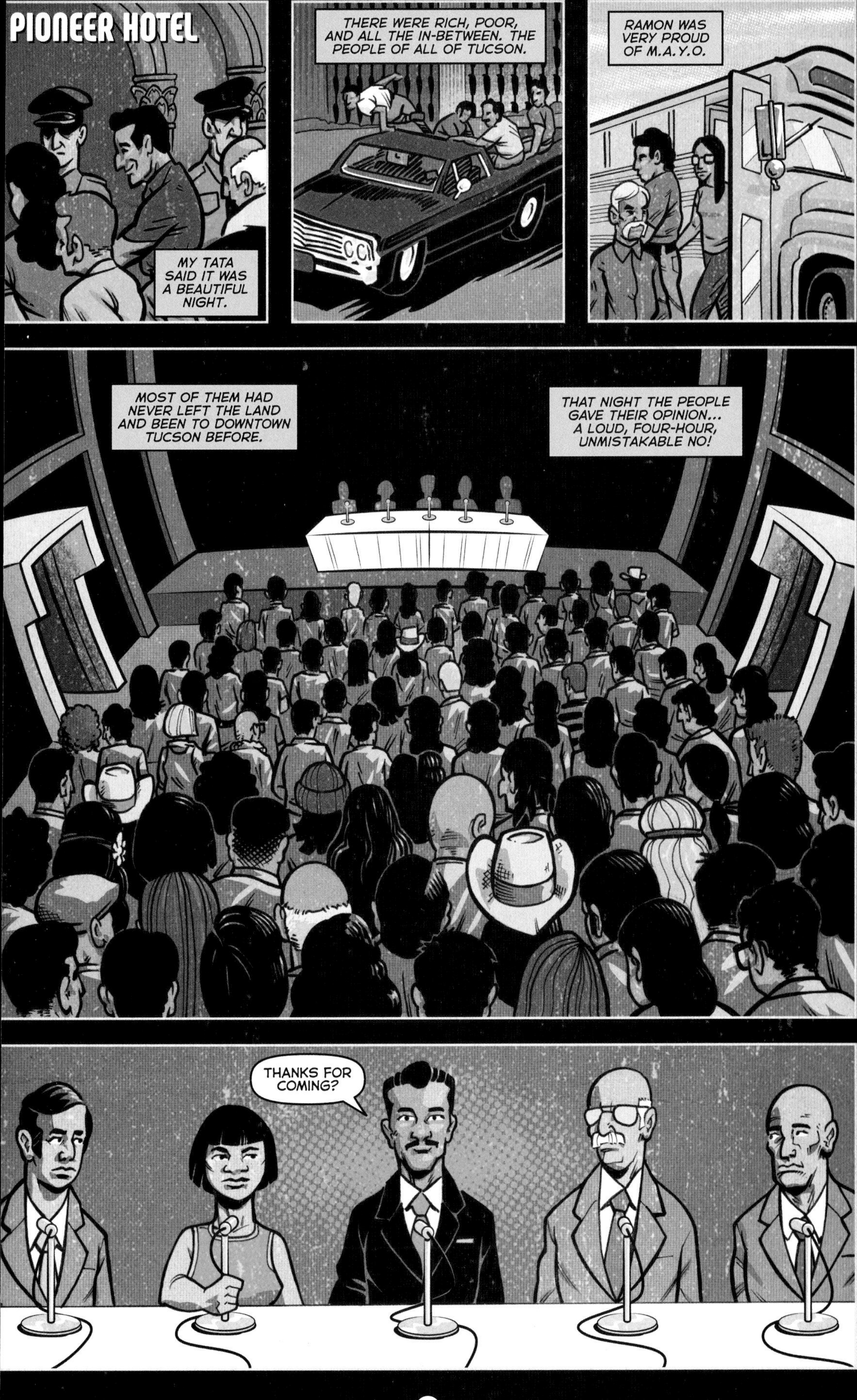
PIONEER HOTEL
MY TATA SAID IT WAS A BEAUTIFUL NIGHT.
THERE WERE RICH, POOR, AND ALL THE IN-BETWEEN. THE PEOPLE OF ALL OF TUCSON.
RAMON WAS VERY PROUD OF M.A.Y.O.
MOST OF THEM HAD NEVER LEFT THE LAND AND BEEN TO DOWNTOWN TUCSON BEFORE.
THAT NIGHT THE PEOPLE GAVE THEIR OPINION... A LOUD, FOUR-HOUR, UNMISTAKABLE NO!
THANKS FOR COMING?

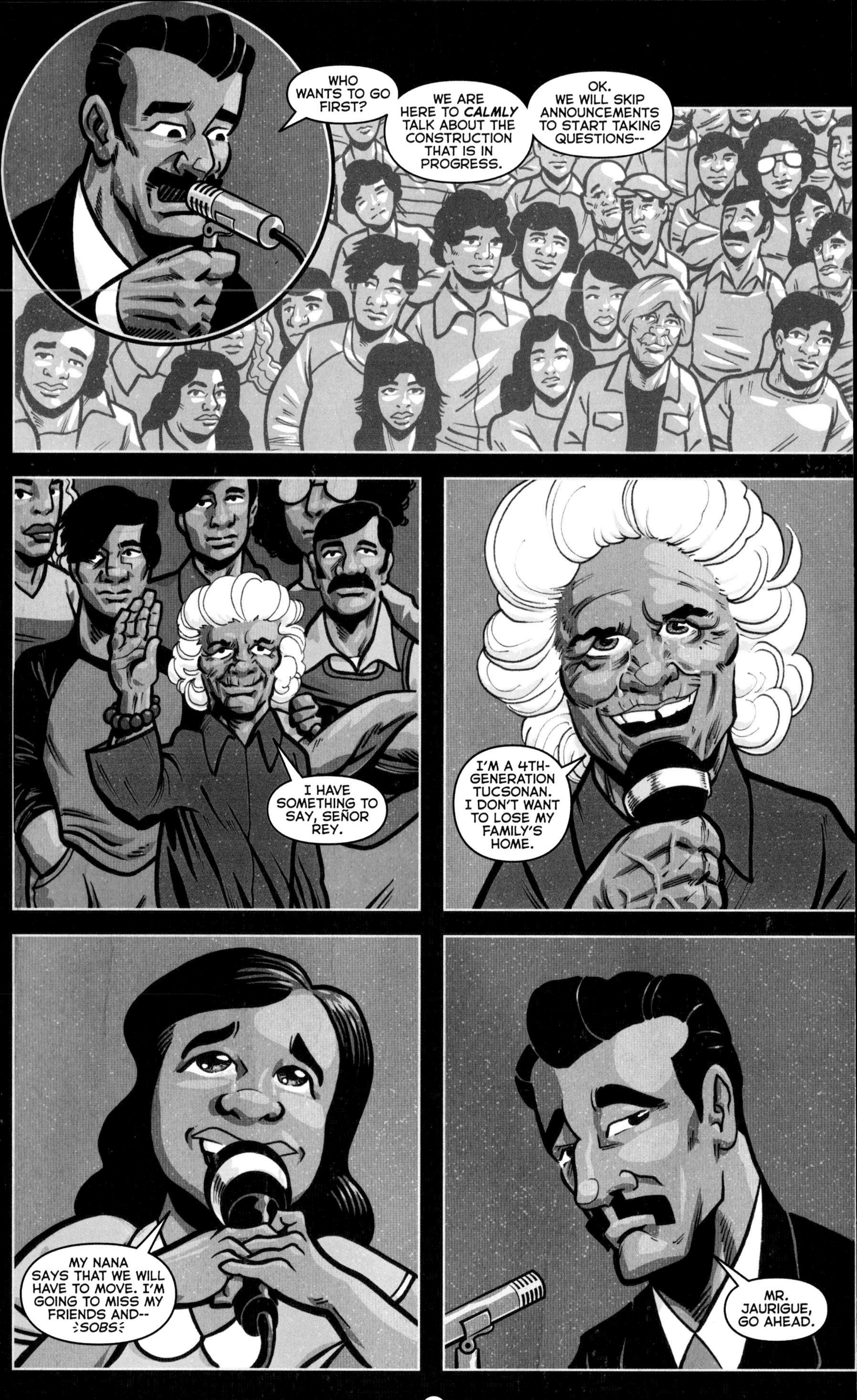
WHO WANTS TO GO FIRST?
WE ARE HERE TO CALMLY TALK ABOUT THE CONSTRUCTION THAT IS IN PROGRESS.
OK. WE WILL SKIP ANNOUNCEMENTS TO START TAKING QUESTIONS--
I HAVE SOMETHING TO SAY, SEÑOR REY.
I'M A 4TH-GENERATION TUCSONAN. I DON'T WANT TO LOSE MY FAMILY'S HOME.
MY NANA SAYS THAT WE WILL HAVE TO MOVE. I'M GOING TO MISS MY FRIENDS AND-- SOBS
MR. JAURIGUE, GO AHEAD.

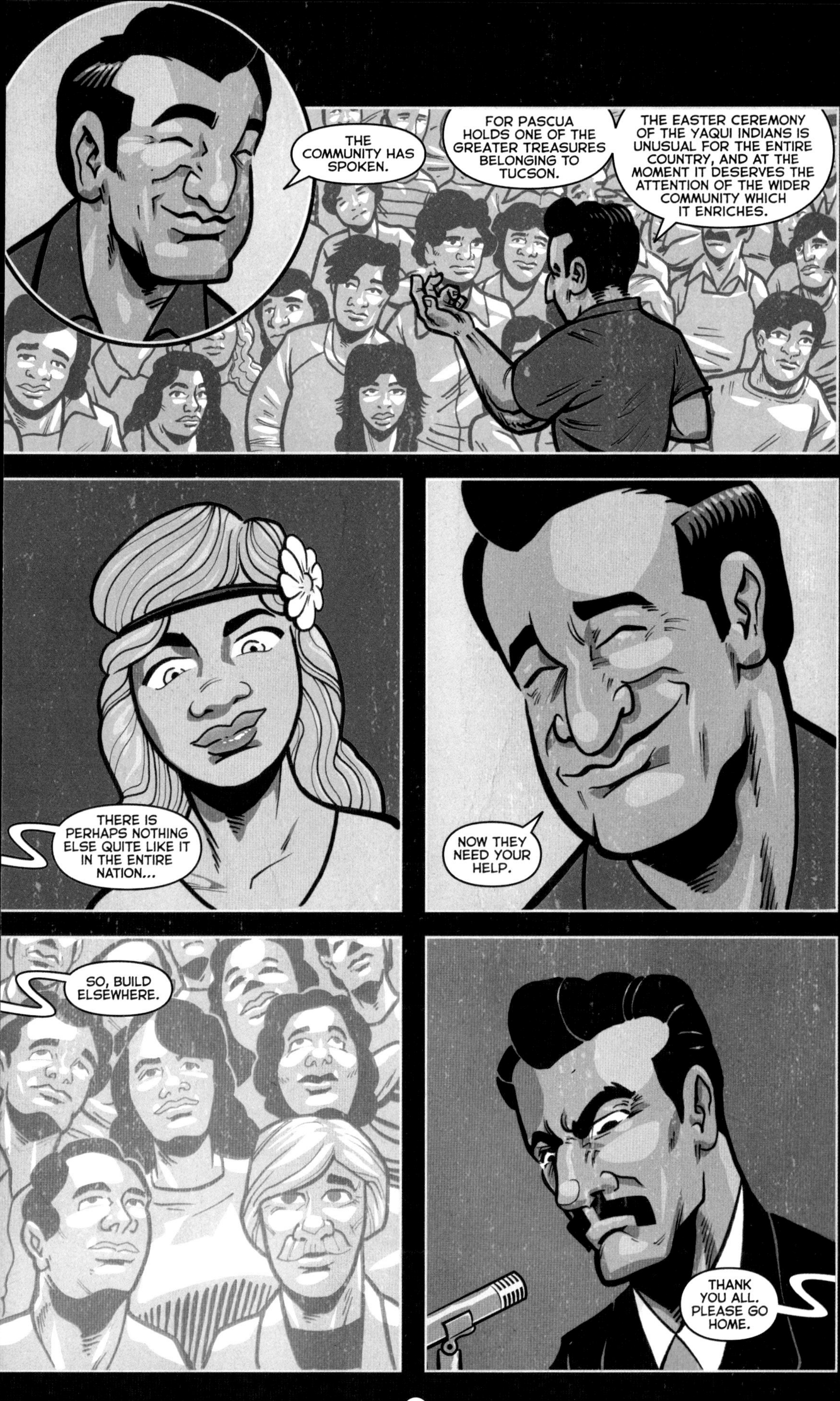

THE COMMUNITY HAS SPOKEN.
FOR PASCUA HOLDS ONE OF THE GREATER TREASURES BELONGING TO TUCSON.
THE EASTER CEREMONY OF THE YAQUI INDIANS IS UNUSUAL FOR THE ENTIRE COUNTRY, AND AT THE MOMENT IT DESERVES THE ATTENTION OF THE WIDER COMMUNITY WHICH IT ENRICHES.
THERE IS PERHAPS NOTHING ELSE QUITE LIKE IT IN THE ENTIRE NATION...
NOW THEY NEED YOUR HELP.
SO, BUILD ELSEWHERE.
THANK YOU ALL. PLEASE GO HOME.

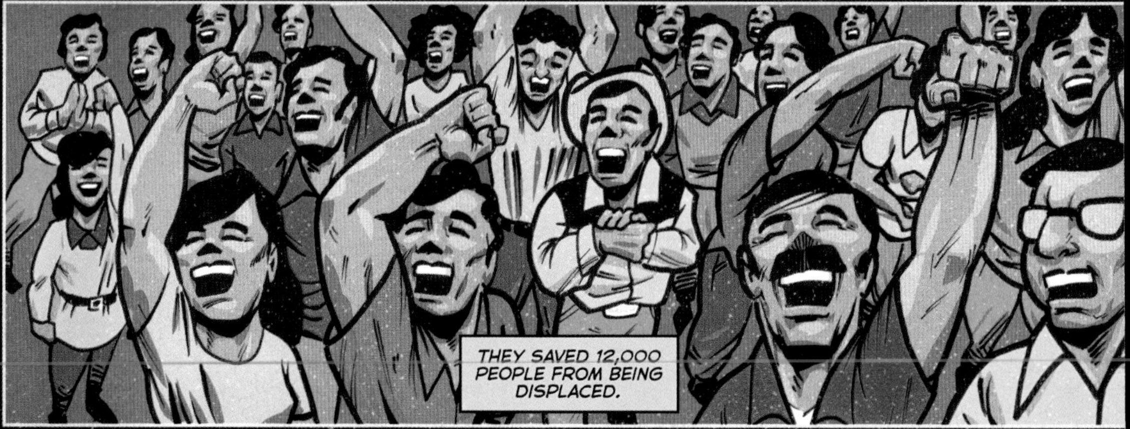
THEY SAVED 12,000 PEOPLE FROM BEING DISPLACED.

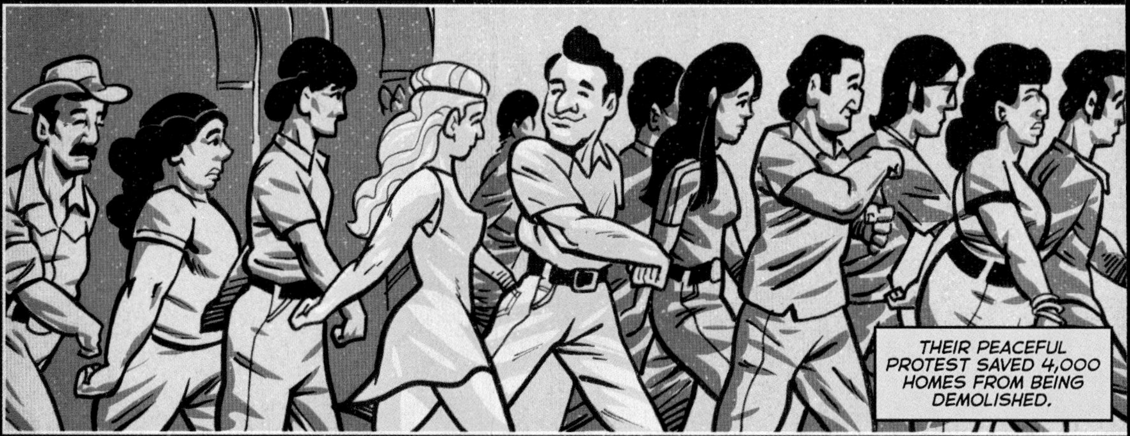
THEIR PEACEFUL PROTEST SAVED 4,000 HOMES FROM BEING DEMOLISHED.

EL TIRADITO

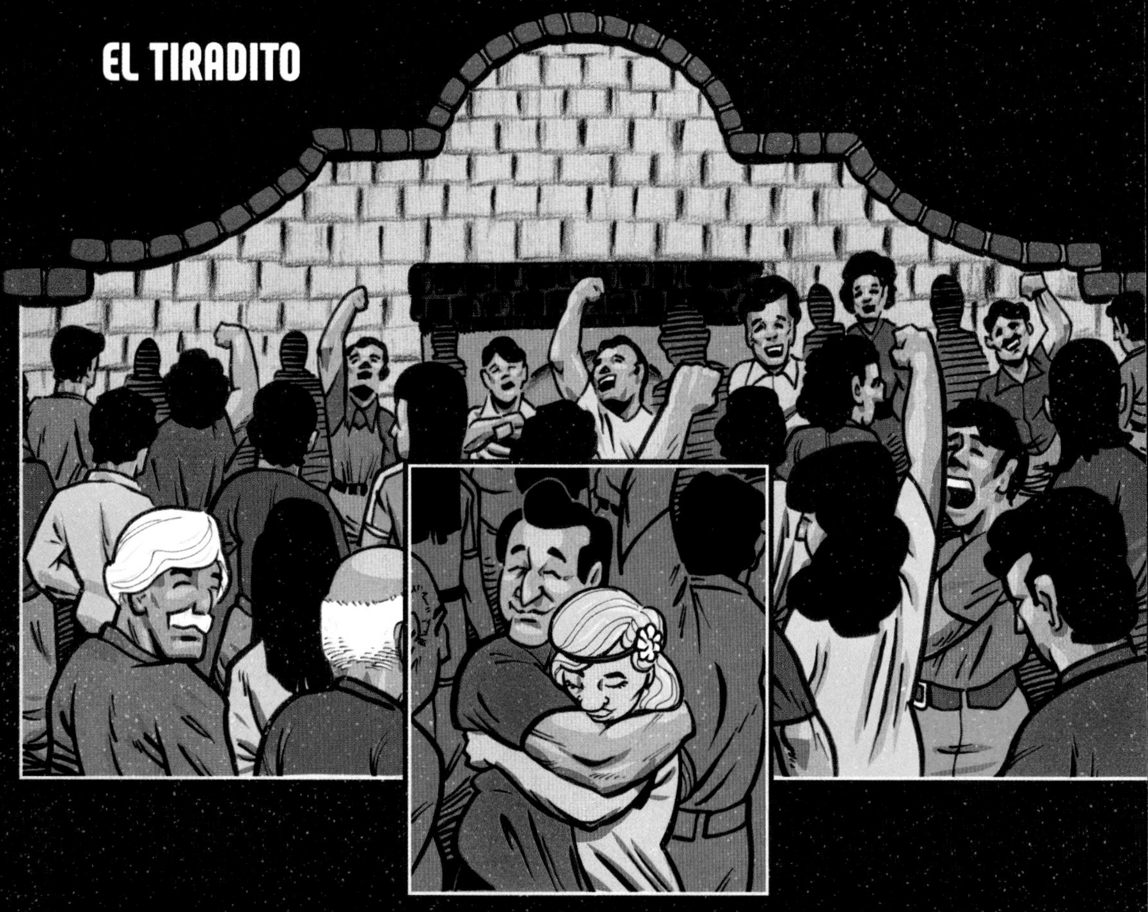

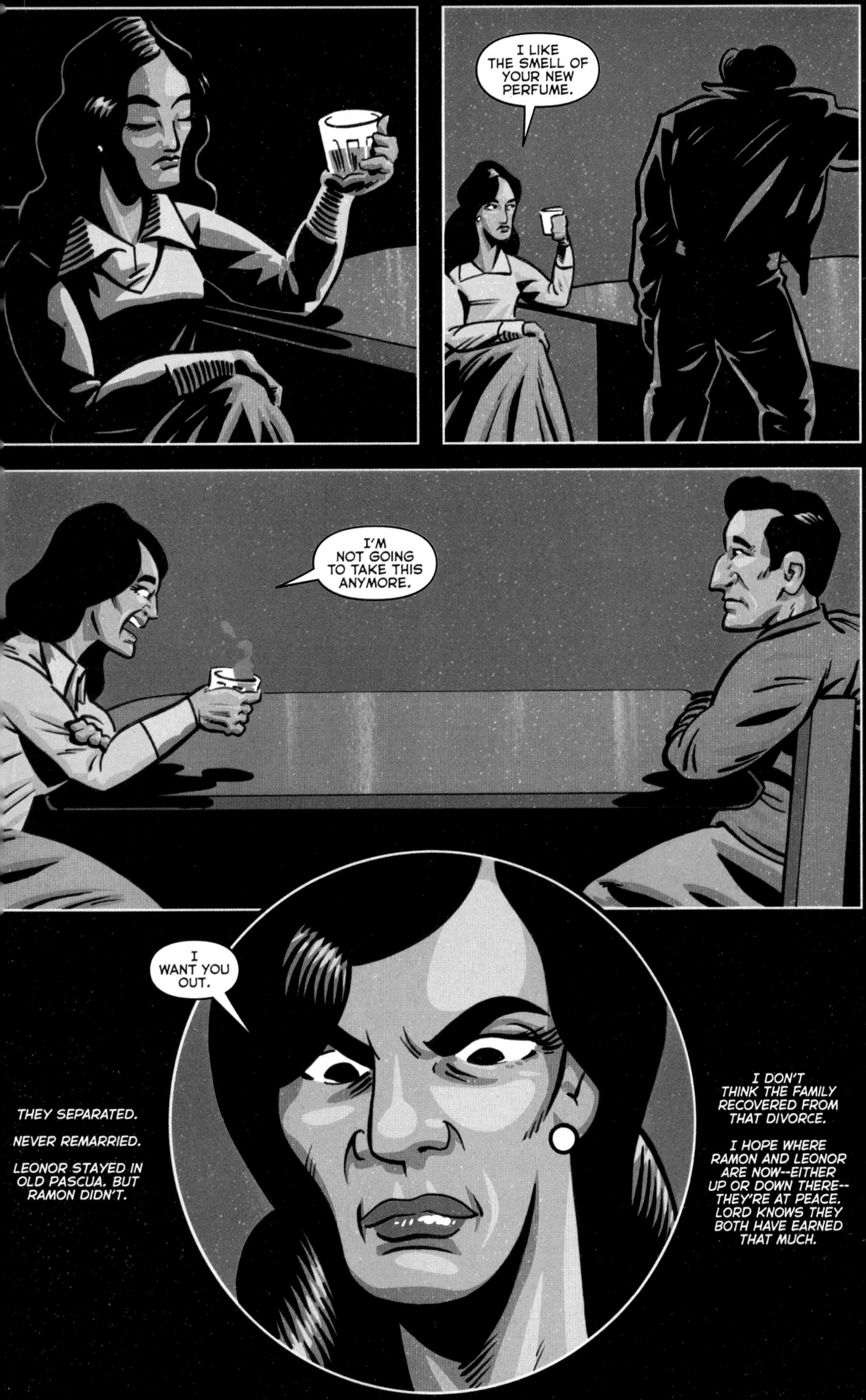
I LIKE THE SMELL OF YOUR NEW PERFUME.
I'M NOT GOING TO TAKE THIS ANYMORE.
I WANT YOU OUT.
THEY SEPARATED.
NEVER REMARRIED.
LEONOR STAYED IN OLD PASCUA. BUT RAMON DIDN'T.
I DON'T THINK THE FAMILY RECOVERED FROM THAT DIVORCE.
I HOPE WHERE RAMON AND LEONOR ARE NOW--EITHER UP OR DOWN THERE--THEY'RE AT PEACE. LORD KNOWS THEY BOTH HAVE EARNED THAT MUCH.

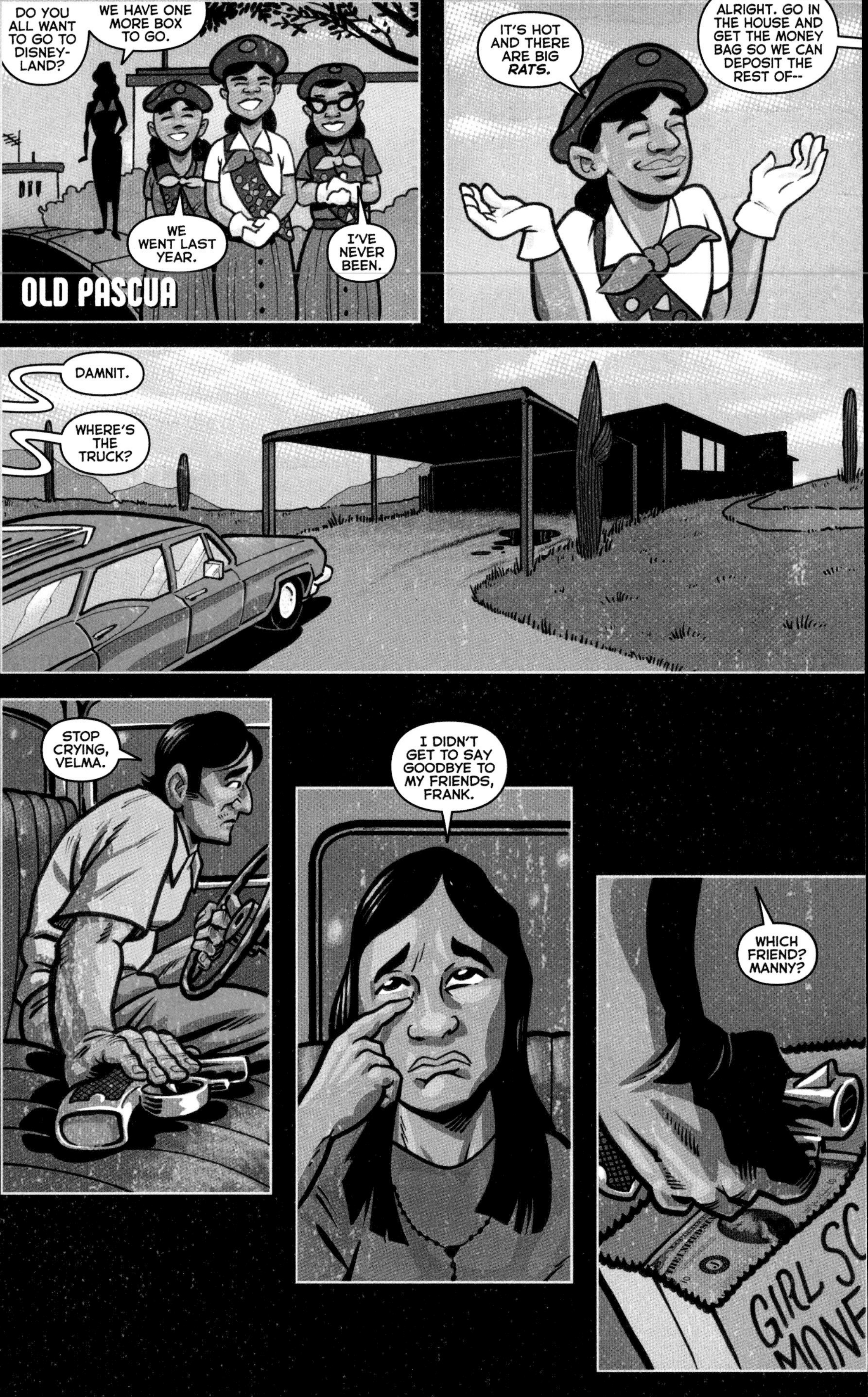
DO YOU ALL WANT TO GO TO DISNEY-LAND?
WE HAVE ONE MORE BOX TO GO.
WE WENT LAST YEAR.
I'VE NEVER BEEN.
OLD PASCUA
IT'S HOT AND THERE ARE BIG RATS.
ALRIGHT. GO IN THE HOUSE AND GET THE MONEY BAG SO WE CAN DEPOSIT THE REST OF--
DAMNIT.
WHERE'S THE TRUCK?
STOP CRYING, VELMA.
I DIDN'T GET TO SAY GOODBYE TO MY FRIENDS, FRANK.
WHICH FRIEND? MANNY?
GIRL SC
MONE

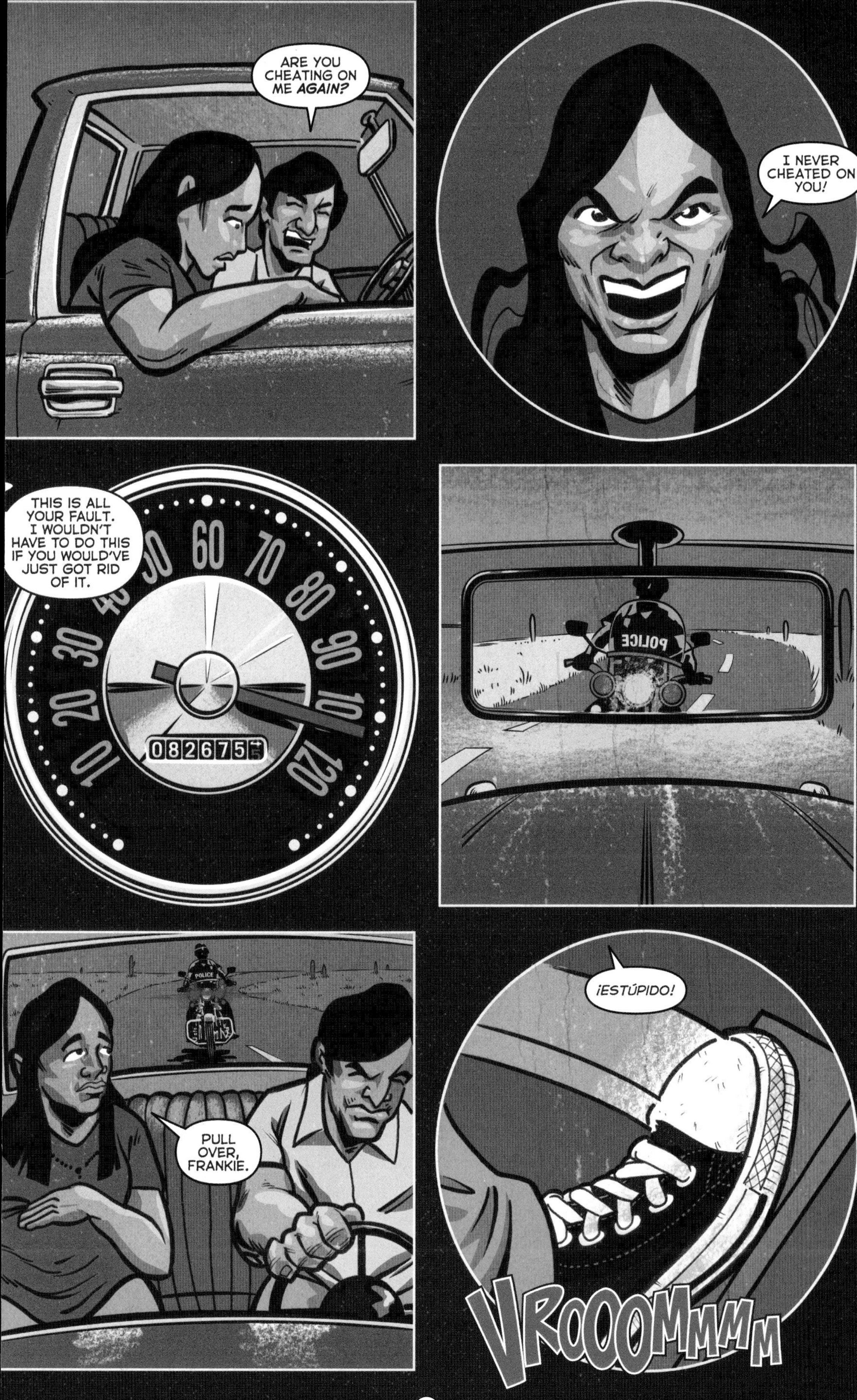
ARE YOU CHEATING ON ME AGAIN?
I NEVER CHEATED ON YOU!
THIS IS ALL YOUR FAULT. I WOULDN'T HAVE TO DO THIS IF YOU WOULD'VE JUST GOT RID OF IT.
POLICE
POLICE
PULL OVER, FRANKIE.
¡ESTÚPIDO!
VROOOMMMMM

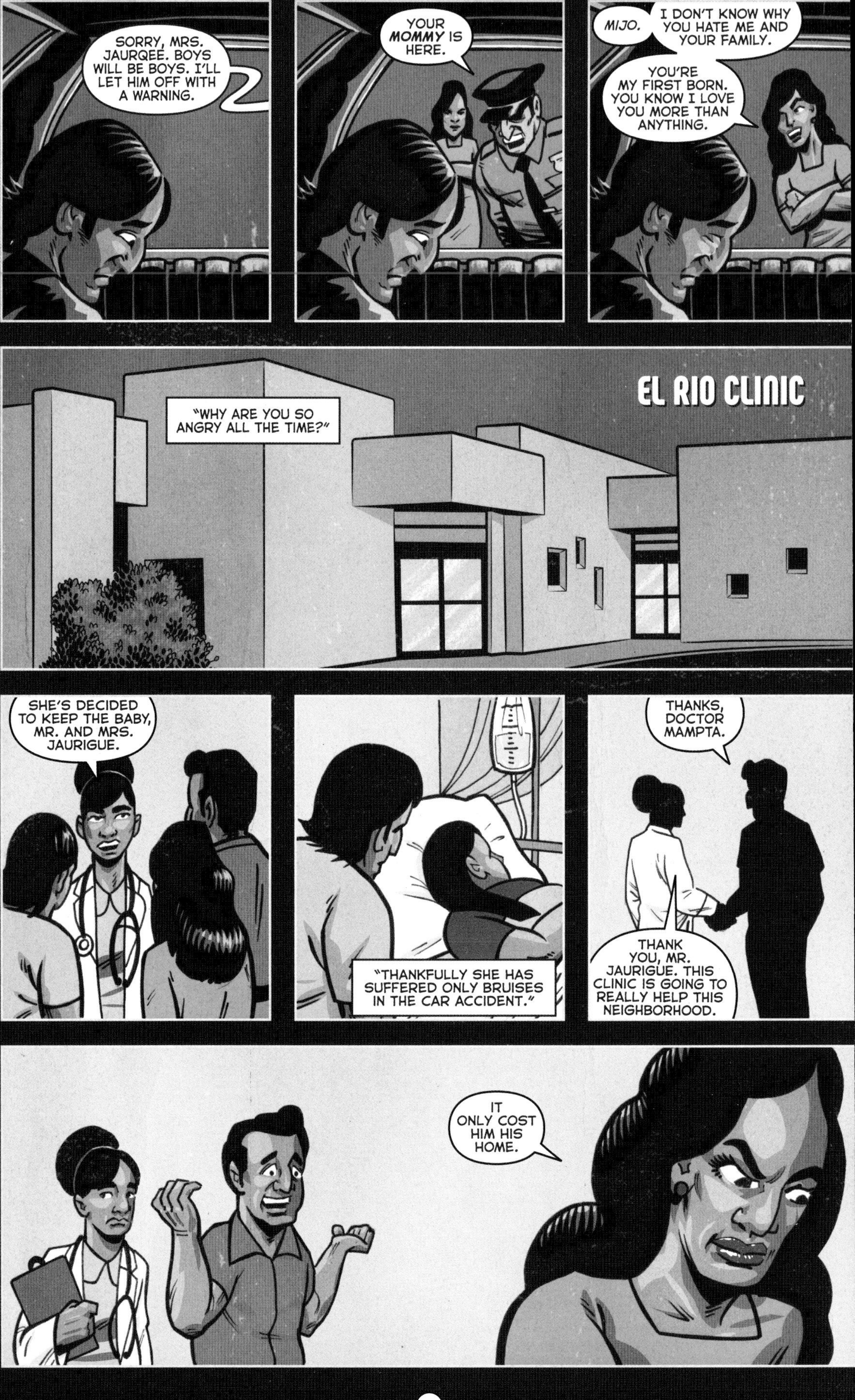
SORRY, MRS. JAURQEE. BOYS WILL BE BOYS. I'LL LET HIM OFF WITH A WARNING.
YOUR MOMMY IS HERE.
MIJO.
I DON'T KNOW WHY YOU HATE ME AND YOUR FAMILY.
YOU'RE MY FIRST BORN. YOU KNOW I LOVE YOU MORE THAN ANYTHING.
EL RIO CLINIC
"WHY ARE YOU SO ANGRY ALL THE TIME?"
SHE'S DECIDED TO KEEP THE BABY, MR. AND MRS. JAURIGUE.
"THANKFULLY SHE HAS SUFFERED ONLY BRUISES IN THE CAR ACCIDENT."
THANKS, DOCTOR MAMPTA.
THANK YOU, MR. JAURIGUE. THIS CLINIC IS GOING TO REALLY HELP THIS NEIGHBORHOOD.
IT ONLY COST HIM HIS HOME.

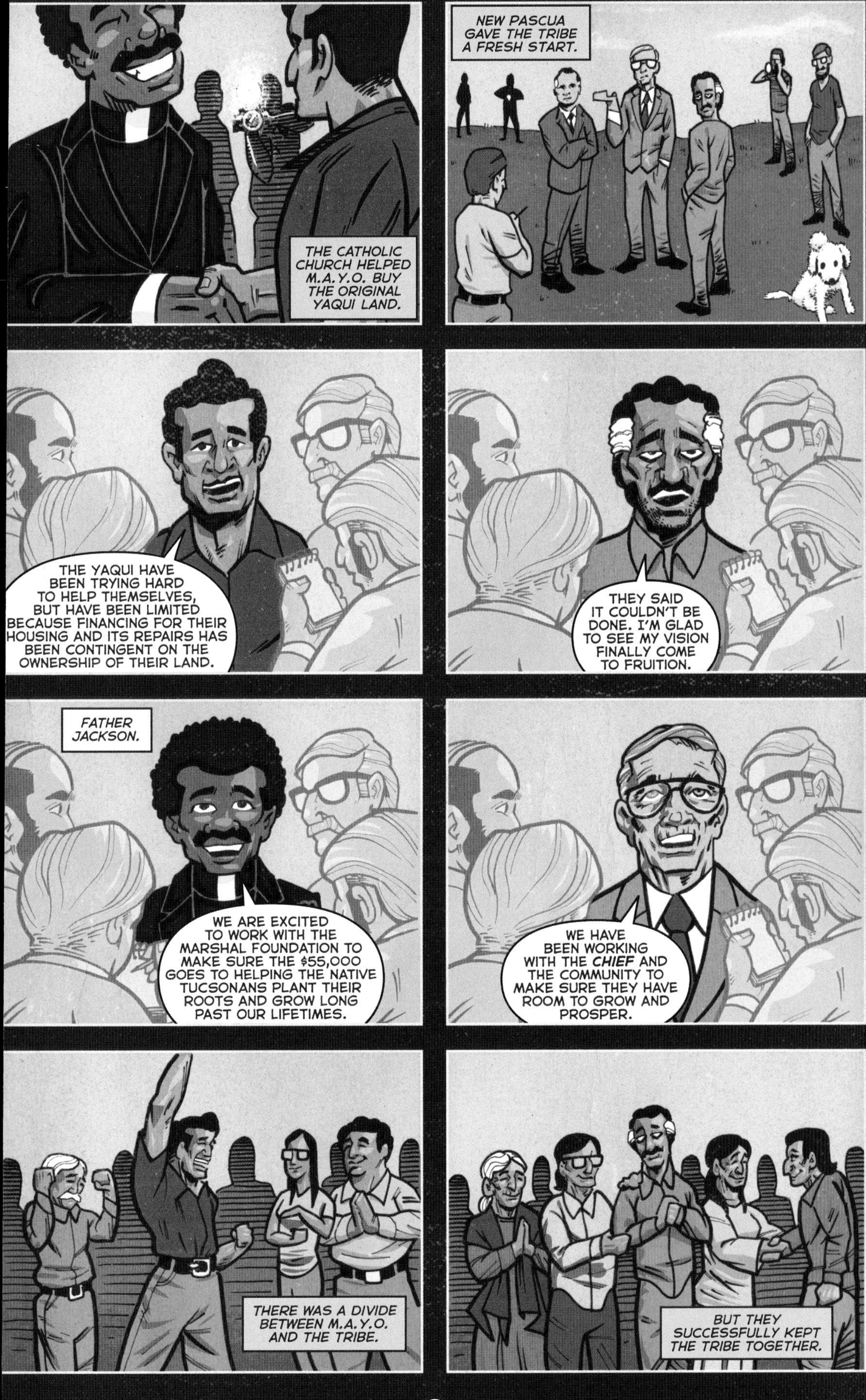

THE CATHOLIC CHURCH HELPED M.A.Y.O. BUY THE ORIGINAL YAQUI LAND.
NEW PASCUA GAVE THE TRIBE A FRESH START.
THE YAQUI HAVE BEEN TRYING HARD TO HELP THEMSELVES, BUT HAVE BEEN LIMITED BECAUSE FINANCING FOR THEIR HOUSING AND ITS REPAIRS HAS BEEN CONTINGENT ON THE OWNERSHIP OF THEIR LAND.
THEY SAID IT COULDN'T BE DONE. I'M GLAD TO SEE MY VISION FINALLY COME TO FRUITION.
FATHER JACKSON.
WE ARE EXCITED TO WORK WITH THE MARSHAL FOUNDATION TO MAKE SURE THE $55,000 GOES TO HELPING THE NATIVE TUCSONANS PLANT THEIR ROOTS AND GROW LONG PAST OUR LIFETIMES.
WE HAVE BEEN WORKING WITH THE *CHIEF* AND THE COMMUNITY TO MAKE SURE THEY HAVE ROOM TO GROW AND PROSPER.
THERE WAS A DIVIDE BETWEEN M.A.Y.O. AND THE TRIBE.
BUT THEY SUCCESSFULLY KEPT THE TRIBE TOGETHER.

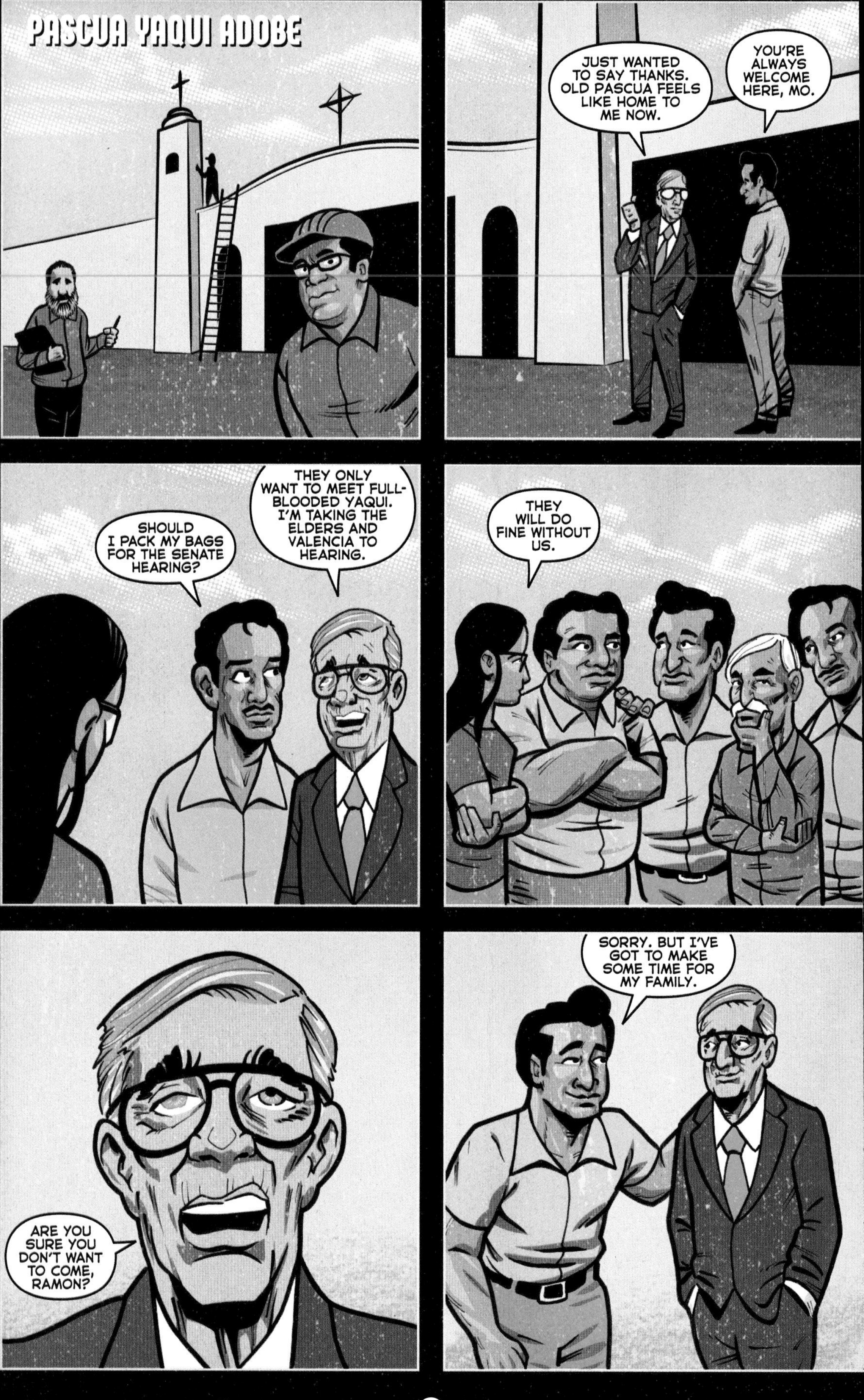
PASCUA YAQUI ADOBE
JUST WANTED TO SAY THANKS. OLD PASCUA FEELS LIKE HOME TO ME NOW.
YOU'RE ALWAYS WELCOME HERE, MO.
SHOULD I PACK MY BAGS FOR THE SENATE HEARING?
THEY ONLY WANT TO MEET FULL-BLOODED YAQUI. I'M TAKING THE ELDERS AND VALENCIA TO HEARING.
THEY WILL DO FINE WITHOUT US.
ARE YOU SURE YOU DON'T WANT TO COME, RAMON?
SORRY. BUT I'VE GOT TO MAKE SOME TIME FOR MY FAMILY.

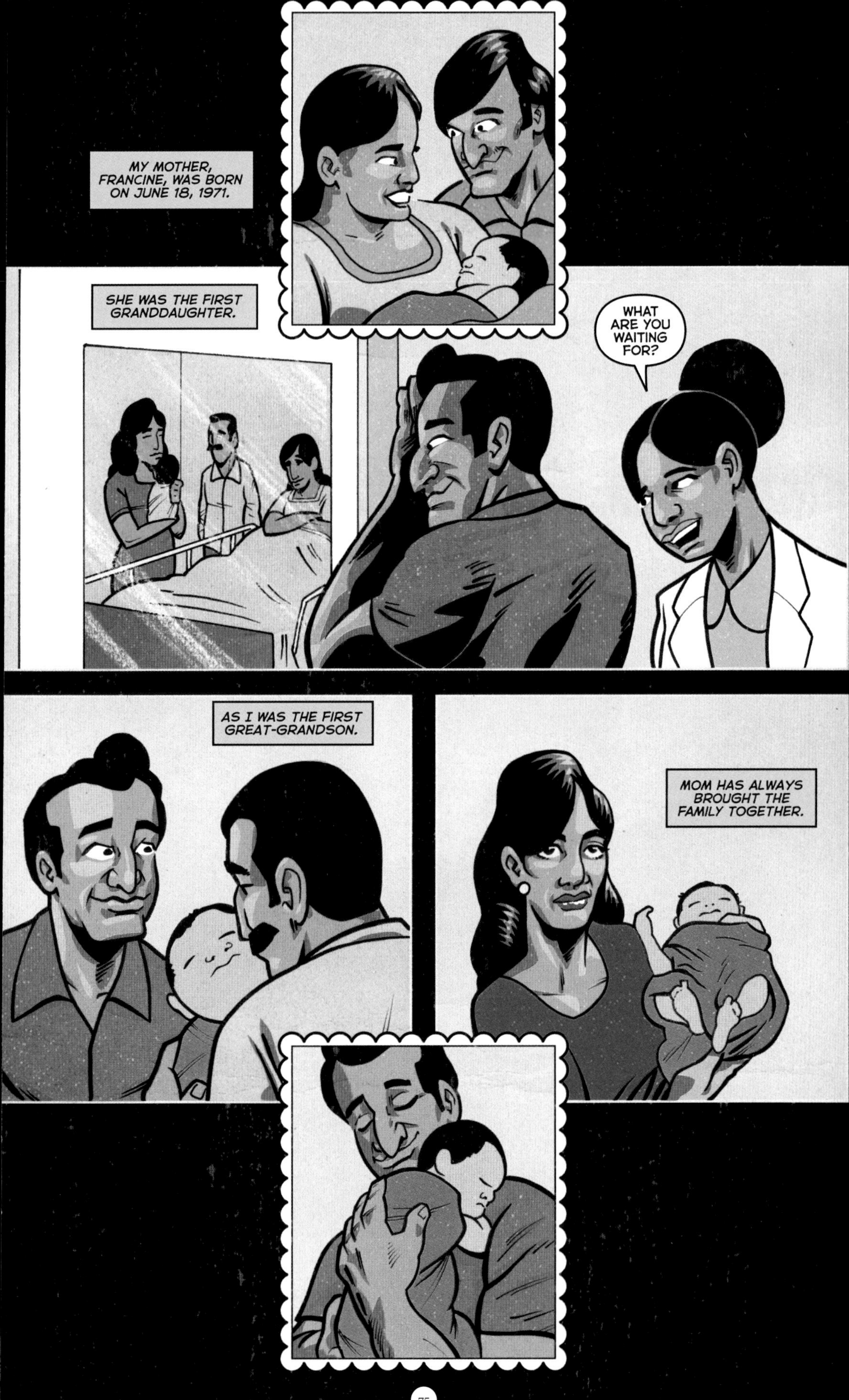
MY MOTHER, FRANCINE, WAS BORN ON JUNE 18, 1971.
SHE WAS THE FIRST GRANDDAUGHTER.
WHAT ARE YOU WAITING FOR?
AS I WAS THE FIRST GREAT-GRANDSON.
MOM HAS ALWAYS BROUGHT THE FAMILY TOGETHER.

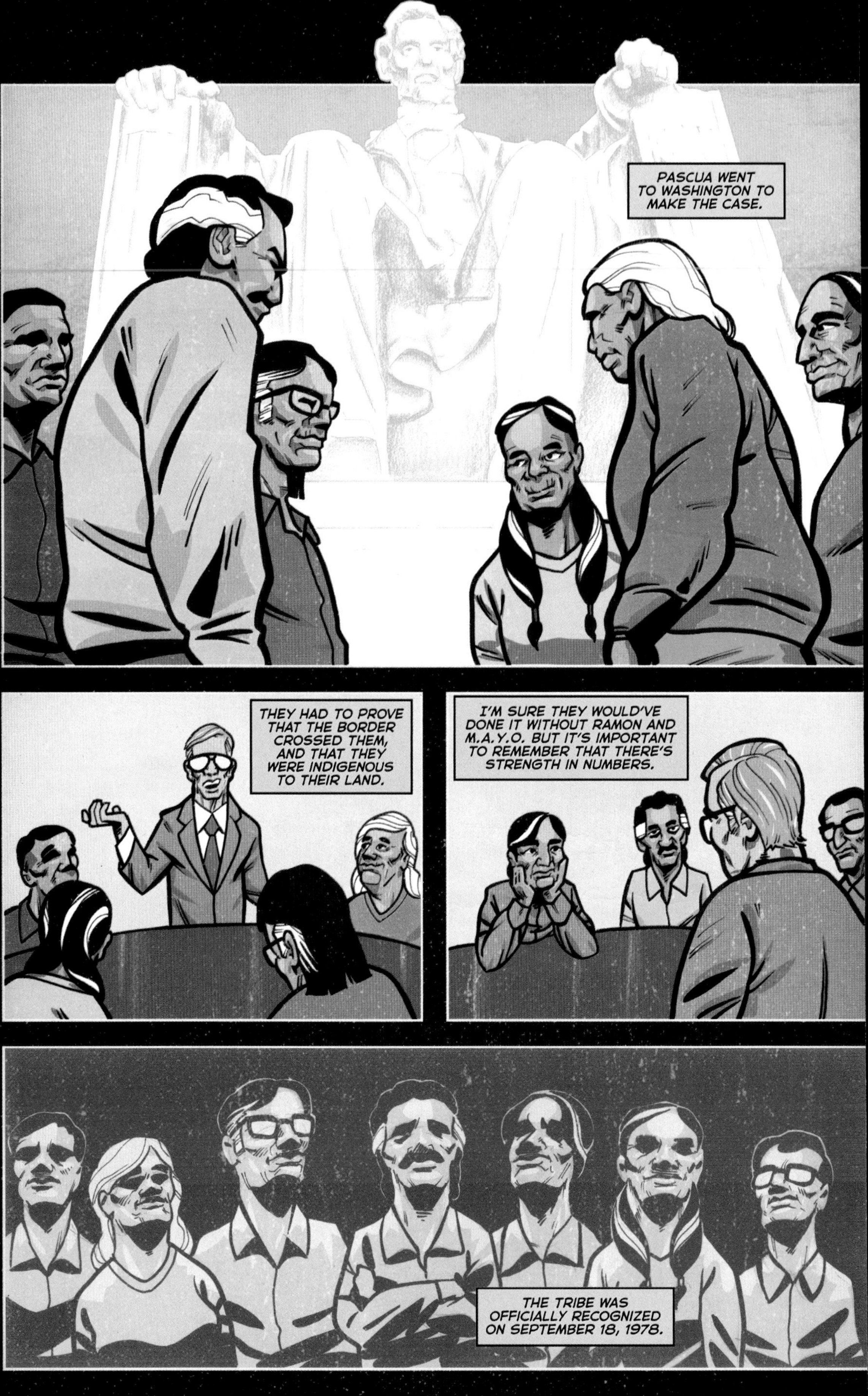
PASCUA WENT TO WASHINGTON TO MAKE THE CASE.
THEY HAD TO PROVE THAT THE BORDER CROSSED THEM, AND THAT THEY WERE INDIGENOUS TO THEIR LAND.
I'M SURE THEY WOULD'VE DONE IT WITHOUT RAMON AND M.A.Y.O. BUT IT'S IMPORTANT TO REMEMBER THAT THERE'S STRENGTH IN NUMBERS.
THE TRIBE WAS OFFICIALLY RECOGNIZED ON SEPTEMBER 18, 1978.

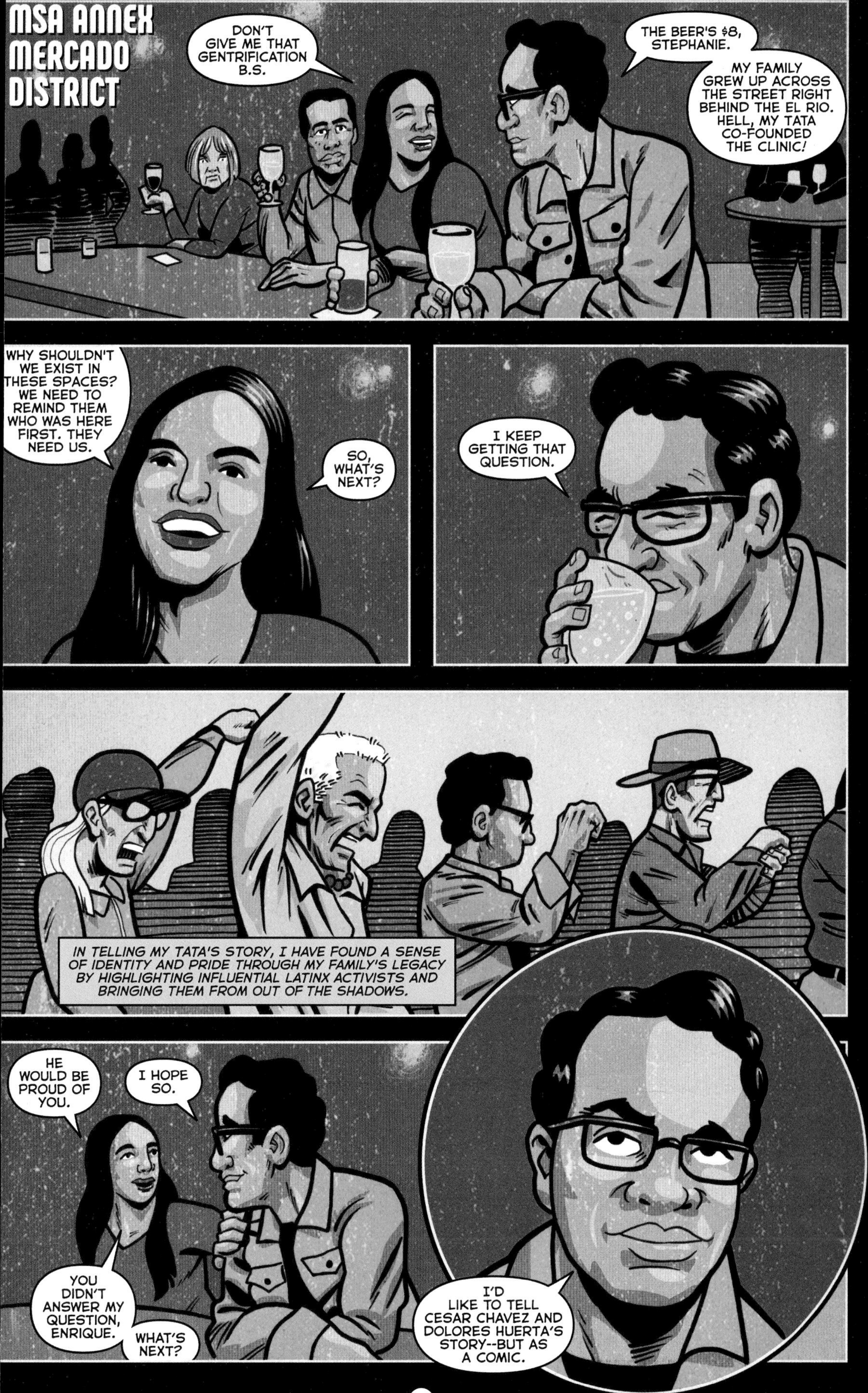
MSA ANNEX MERCADO DISTRICT
DON'T GIVE ME THAT GENTRIFICATION B.S.
THE BEER'S $8, STEPHANIE.
MY FAMILY GREW UP ACROSS THE STREET RIGHT BEHIND THE EL RIO. HELL, MY TATA CO-FOUNDED THE CLINIC!
WHY SHOULDN'T WE EXIST IN THESE SPACES? WE NEED TO REMIND THEM WHO WAS HERE FIRST. THEY NEED US.
SO, WHAT'S NEXT?
I KEEP GETTING THAT QUESTION.
IN TELLING MY TATA'S STORY, I HAVE FOUND A SENSE OF IDENTITY AND PRIDE THROUGH MY FAMILY'S LEGACY BY HIGHLIGHTING INFLUENTIAL LATINX ACTIVISTS AND BRINGING THEM FROM OUT OF THE SHADOWS.
HE WOULD BE PROUD OF YOU.
I HOPE SO.
YOU DIDN'T ANSWER MY QUESTION, ENRIQUE.
WHAT'S NEXT?
I'D LIKE TO TELL CESAR CHAVEZ AND DOLORES HUERTA'S STORY--BUT AS A COMIC.

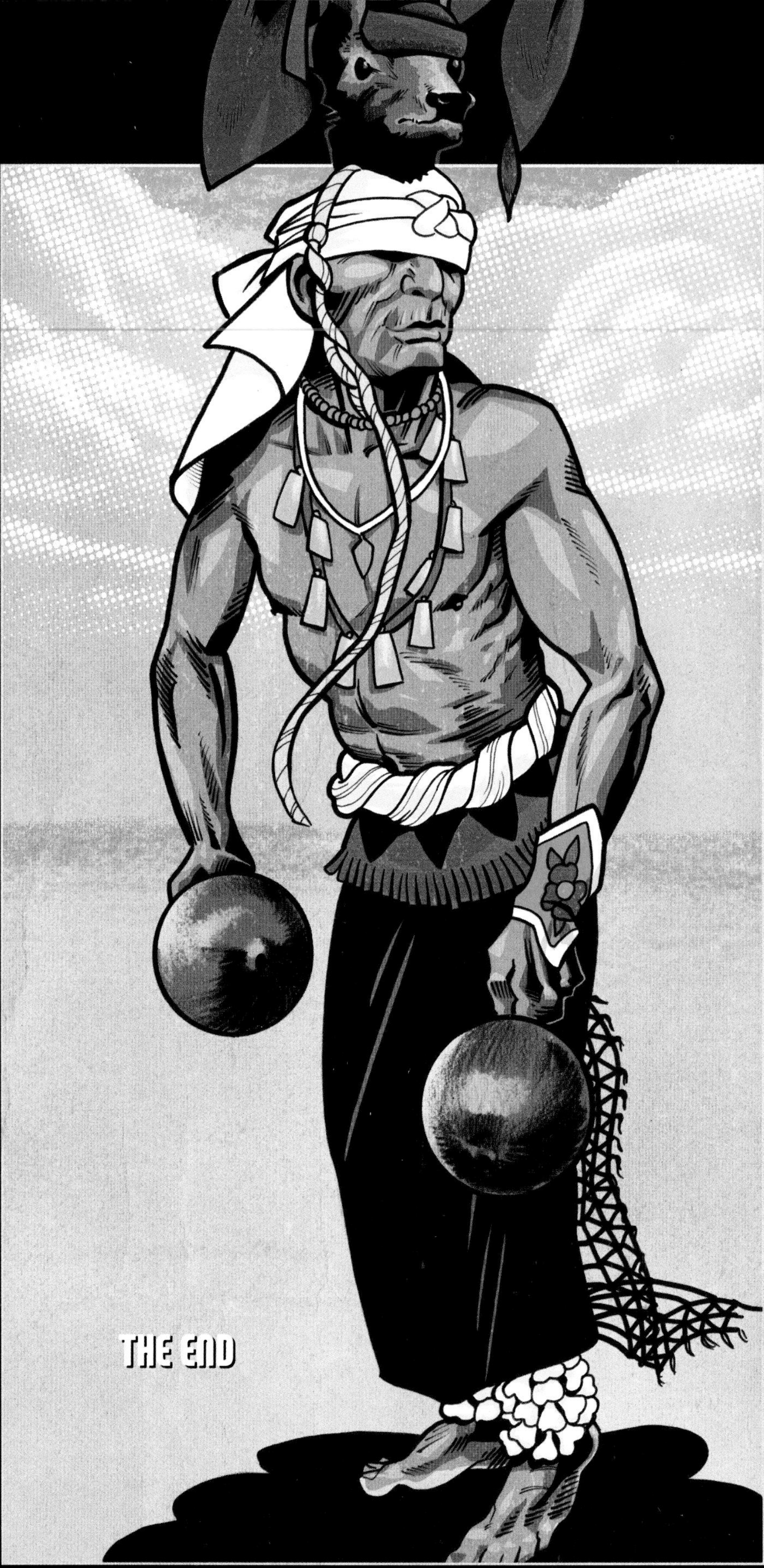
THE END

EPILOGUE

It was important to me to amend history.

I spent countless weekends and summers in Old Pascua. This particular part of Tucson is home to some of its indigenous residents, refugees who fled to a fertile barrio of the southern border, the same border that had crossed them as the US grew larger. My great-grandmother, Leonor Jaurigue, raised my sister and me when my parents were too busy working 9-to-5. Even though Leonor was a great-grandma we called her Nana, but everyone else called her Ma. She was a beautiful woman who loved to laugh, drink Zima, curse like a sailor, and watch wrestling. Bob Marley would play from the mini CD player she played in her garden. She was tough as nails and didn't take shit from no one.

Her parents were Yaqui, so that made her full blood. She would insist we all go down to the Fariseos every year. We would accompany her to the Yaqui Community Center on the weekends to watch the Fariseos and Matachinis dance and honor the death and resurrection of Jesus Christ. The Fariseos have been and remain open to be public for anyone to witness, and are one of the country's most beautiful rituals. The sight is almost as if you're witnessing a gathering of ghosts, their legs dressed in shells that clap at every step, their identities shielded with elaborate handmade masks with cartoon-like facial features, or covered with white fur. Participation is a responsibility passed down from generation to generation.

I used to play card games with Nana to pass the time. She would brew coffee when it was time to read the newspaper. She only wanted to read obituaries and handed me the rest. "I want to see which one of my friends died today," she would joke every single time with a big laugh. I would read the whole paper front to back and keep the comics. My mother would get the paper delivered to our house so I could continue this morning ritual. When I got the job offer to work for that same daily paper, Leonor was on her deathbed. She was the only one in my family who encouraged me to quit my job and take a lower paying one in order to follow my dream of becoming a journalist. My first day working for *The Arizona Daily Star*, I had to enter her name in the death listings. While this book is a tribute to the M.A.Y.O. organization, this comic is really for her.

It was always for Nana.

HENRY BARAJAS
September 2019

I'll be honest: this comic wasn't easy to write. The storyteller in me had a blast trying to put myself in these situations and creating logical scenes that are exciting enough to recreate for the page. But the journalist on my shoulder wanted the facts. Most of my days were spent in various libraries around Tucson, University of Arizona museums, touring around Old and New Pascua to get a lay of the land, and talking to people that were actually there. My family always had a love-hate relationship with Congressman Raul Grijalva. The Congressman will go down as one of the most influential lawmakers from Arizona in history. He is a staunch supporter of immigrants, environmental issues, and Native American rights. My family used to tell me stories about how he used to come to my Tata Rambo looking for support and advice. They felt that Grijalva never gave Ramon enough credit for all the help and guidance when he started his lifelong commitment to civil service. I couldn't find any documents that showed Grijalva at the events, but it was important for me to see if he can validate some of my findings and answer a few questions. I wanted to get the Congressman's account of what he remembered about what kind of leader Ramon was to his community, M.A.Y.O.'s work, and Anselmo Valencia's contributions to his people.

After numerous emails with Ms. Becerra, Grijalva's colleague, I finally secured a meeting at his southside office.

HERE ARE EXCERPTS FROM THAT INTERVIEW.

Raul Grijalva: Ramon was a leader in the sense that he would work with City Council, Mayor Corbett, and the late Rudy Castro who was on the council at the time. I was just getting started myself.

Henry Barajas: What were you doing back then?

Raul: I ran a neighborhood center: El Centro Aztlan. I was going to the University (of Arizona) and served as the president of the Latino Student Organization. Ramon helped me with my campaign to served as a school board member for TUSD.

Henry: What do you remember from the Interstate 10 development that was intended to go through the Yaqui's land?

Raul: There was a resistance, because it would've wiped out two-thirds of that neighborhood.

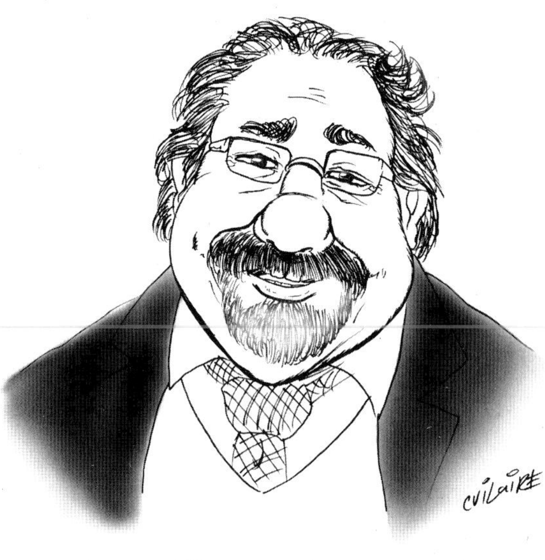
CVILAIRE

Raul Grijalva illustration by Christian Vilaire

Henry: Approximately 12,000 people.

Raul: The city felt that it was a weak community and they didn't really vote so [the City] wanted to run [the road] through there. The people living on the northern and southern side of the tribe didn't want it, so they wanted to go through Blue Moon. The resistance was very powerful. City Council and ADOT decided they were not going to do this. The State Legislators first were quiet and came out against it. That had a lot to do with Ramon and other leaders like [Anselmo] Valencia.

Henry: From my research, at a certain point, the community wanted to go to New Pascua. But there were people that wanted to stay in Old Pascua.

Raul: Once they were recognized as a tribe and given the land that became the rez. Then they received land in Old and New Pascua, Rillito, Guadalupe and a piece of all places in Scottsdale. I think that was a good move. [Valencia] thought it was a good move over (New Pascua). But people said "No. I've been here two, three generations—this is my home." I think much of the early leadership came from Old Pascua and it still does. Old Pascua is still a vibrant community. Keeping the loop from going (through OP) preserved Old Pascua and more importantly, I think it stabilized the neighborhood. It made it possible for them to build the community center and grow.

Henry: Tucson is a post-WWII city; the growth got to the point that Tucson started building around the Yaquis.

Raul: The arteries of traffic grew around them. They were the last to receive sewer systems and real lighting. Even though they were residents of the city, they were separated economically in terms of infrastructure. Richie was built there just for them. When the federal court case litigated it was said that one of the schools [was] built just for the Yaqui kids so they wouldn't go to any other schools. Just like how Dunbar was primarily [a] black school. Manzo was the Mexican school.

Henry: Did you work with Mo Udall? From what I gathered he was a very funny guy.

Raul: He was very committed to Native American issues. The Odam dearly love him. He was the chairman of the committee that I'm on, Natural Resources, he lead the charge to federally recognize them. He's the one who probably [more] responsible than anyone else—on a national level—to get this

---

"MOST TRIBES IN THE UNITED STATES THAT ARE RECOGNIZED HAVE TREATY RIGHTS. THE YAQUIS DIDN'T HAVE ONE, SO THEY HAD TO PROVE IT A DIFFERENT WAY."

---

done. I think it was his close, deep-felt commitment to native people who he felt that have been neglected and exploited most of their lives in this country. That effort was community-wide.

Henry: Valencia wasn't mentioned in any of the M.A.Y.O. documents I have. How impactful was Valencia back then?

Raul: He was an elder then—fierce defender of the Yaqui, a traditionalist, and as such had a great support of his people. I dealt with him two or three times. He was more centered in the village. He didn't interact with elected officials. I think his greatest contribution was keeping the traditions and culture alive. He was a very proud man.

Henry: There's a photo of Ramon with Cesar Chavez. It's something my family looks back on fondly.

Raul: Cesar came during the great boycott—that I was very involved in—they met at a church. They talked.

Henry: Based on the M.A.Y.O. newsletter, I think they were both supporting each other's causes. M.A.Y.O. supported the migrant farmworkers and (Chavez) supported the Yaqui's recognition.

Raul: That seems like a logical conclusion.

Henry: I spoke with someone at the tribe. For some reason, M.A.Y.O.'s efforts were omitted from their history. I can only find a mention of Ramon and M.A.Y.O. in a book titled Tribe Forgotten. The Yaquis show that they settled in Tucson and were federally recognized in 1974. Do you have any idea why they would glaze over (M.A.Y.O.)?

Raul: I don't know. The process—that's a really interesting group study because you had to do a census of tribal members, and you had to show the historic link to your presence in the country to become a federally recognized tribe. Mo Udall was carrying that strongly. Once you start that process—I hate to call it application—for the federal recognition it takes anywhere from two to three years to go through that whole study.

Henry: It looks like it took five years from what I have been able to gather.

Raul: Right now a tribe trying to get recognized is taking a decade, a decade-plus. The tribe is responsible for writing documentation about their presence; historically, that this was at one point a part of their ancestral land. That whole process for any tribe is tough. Especially if they don't have a treaty. Most tribes in the United States that are recognized have treaty rights. The Yaquis didn't have one, so they had to prove it a different way.

Henry: Do you know what happened to Ramon? Did he fall into obscurity?

Raul: I don't know. He kinda faded at the peak. He faded in the sense that he wasn't a public figure anymore.

THANK YOU! · ¡GRACIAS!

to the following Kickstarter backers for their support

Jann Jones	Consuelo Solorio	Hannah Barnes	Chuck Roman
Umer Qazi	Emilee Moeller	Arnie Bermudez	Andrew Raub
Maremonti Fund	Javier Cruz Winnik	Astrid Lovette Martinez	Richard Defazio
Andrew Leamon	Tony Parker	Randall Nichols	Stefano Zamboni
Andrew Clemson	Pornsak Pichetshote	sebastian	Sarah Sammis
Adelina Jaurigue	Ivan Salazar	Christopher Bravo	R Wauneka
Alex Segura	Alex	Bryan Conner	Seattlite of Love
Amber Benson	Jason Dewland	David Kinsel	Kim
Andrew Connor	David Fitzsimmons	Dennis Culver	Fosterocalypse
Brian Schirmer	Caden	Zoë Quinn	XABIER ETA MARTIN
Courtney Mock	Julia Tranchina	Maria Ludwig	ETXEBERRIA
Dan Gibson	Isaac Goodhart	Joe Musich	Alexa Dickman
eric laster	jacobcox	Shawn Demumbrum	Pete Pfau
Ernest Romero	Hermilo Guzman III	Andrew Nisbet	Edward Haynes
Hannah Rose May	Juan Morales	Daniel Petersen	Wendy B
Jeff Lemire	Sina Grace	JIMMY PALMIOTTI	Hope Nicholson
Jillian Adams	Richard Cardenas	Vince Hernandez	Michael Macropoulos
Marisa Stotter	Malcolm Johnson	Zack Kaplan	Heidi MacDonald
Nicole Rudick	Kristof Schmurtz	Kevin Church	Eric Palicki
Rob Feldman	Amber	Vincent Kukua	kristyq1
The Creative Fund	Max Cannon	sarah gaydos	Jon Obuchowski
Elliot Glicksman	Lou Lopez	Rodney Hedrick	Schraderopolis
Kristen Cook	Frank Beddor	CarolineLayne	Timmy Martin
Stephanie Bermudez	Ramon Olivas	Tom Prezelski	S Bazan
Palmers	Carissa Planalp	David Clarke	Dwayne Farver
Omar Spahi	Steven Yanez Romo	Mike and Barb Myers	Inclusive Press
Joe Rauch	Raphael	DANA LORENZO	Carlos Giffoni
Maryelizabeth Yturralde	Jericho Davidson	Patrick White	Ramon Marcus Villalobos
Eddie deAngelini	Jared R. McKinley	Erin Cavanaugh	Troy Peteri
Andy Liegl	Yvonne Ervin	Alexis Favis	Franky DeJesus
Comadres y Comics:	Carol Hayman	Christine Davis-Corona	Thomas Keith
Kristen, Sara, y Jen	Ronnie Green	jonathan	George Caltsoudas
Deborah Barajas	Robert Acosta	Isobela <3	Tony Fleecs
Eric Manch	Ben Abernathy	Andrew Brown	Ernie Estrella
Brian Michael Bendis	Jenn Corella	Eduardo Cordova	Jeff Miller
Kelly Sue Deconnick	christian Vilaire	Paul Trinies	Jimmy s. Jay
Cafe con Leche Nerds	Luis Jaime Pena	Alyssa Jackson	Colleen Doran
Enoch Chapman	Charlie Harris	Hernán Julin	Patrick Meaney
Jordan Rennert	David Hildebrand	Dan Stong	DoctorWhoCares
Frederick Luis Aldama	Raul Coto-Batres	Paul Gravett	David Sewell
Daniel Stone	Omar Padilla	Jesus Diaz	C. Elliott
Jacob Breckenridge	Danny Martin	Benjamin Mackey	Barbara Randall Kesel
Meg & Sprocket	Michael McKisson	Kory	zack
Sami Anz	Kate Newton	Ernest Allred	Daniel Park

LA VOZ DE M.A.Y.O. TATA RAMBO™

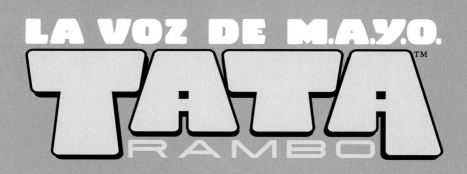

THANK YOU! · ¡GRACIAS!

to the following Kickstarter backers for their support

Ton Gloudemans
Ben Reichman
Megan Purdy
Marjory Duncan
Vernon Miles
Anjelina Belakovskaia
Rodrigo Vargas
Ryan Cady
Brigitte Davila
Michael Burns
Catfish
Joey Hernandez
zanniew
Matt Ziemak
Lizzie Napier
Terrance Grace
Tia Vasiliou
Danny Djeljosevic
Anthony C Mackaronis
Simon Birks
paul d jarman
Steve Mandel
Jason Wood
Jonathan Burgers
Austin Allen Hamblin
Phillip Sevy
drmidnight32
Lucia Fasano
Nicholas Prom
joepi
Logan Naugle
eric mengel
Rob Staeger
Nick Fagerlund
Kelly Fitzpatrick
Brendan Wright
Ted Contreras
Levi Fleming
Dave Friedman
Donald Claxon

Katie Daubert
J Kurtz
Robin
Jefferson Workman
Julio Rodriguez
Jason Inman
Lance Rund
Brittany Matter
Creatively Queer Press
Matt Smith
Jeff Barbanell
Luis F. Carrasco
Jason Pittman
Kristen Simon
John Layman
Kyle Rose
joshdogge
Frank Gidlewski
Javier Hernandez
Josh Shalek
Albert Ching
Ashley Johnson
Mariana Dale
David
Alexandre Piacsek
Stefan V
Kris K
Pouriya
J Lugo Miller
Alex Olsen
Sylvia Moon
Jeff
Andrea Gibbons
Tom Barnett
Vitas Varnas
Robert L. Vaughn
Alinna Stinnett
Rodrigo Diaz
Don Gleason
David Lasky

Nesher Asner
graham r beer
Jenn Baumgartner
Richard Wahl
Scott Wesely
Kent Heidelman
Barry Schneier
Chris Phillips
Eric M. Esquivel
Tanya
Sam Williams
Stephen Morris
Craig A. Taillefer
John Kivus
John Ward
Andy
Alex Chung
Elizabeth Brei
Kees Ribbens
David Pepose
Holly Aitchison
Adam P. Knave
James R. Crowley
Anthony
Ellen Power
Jay Lofstead
Josh Crews
Rich Douek
Shaun Manning
Ryan Cody
Jon Morris
James Leask
Skye Kilaen
Lucas
Jon Moisan
Vince
Sequart Research & Literacy Organization
Elena Salcedo
Rant Howard

Tyler McPhail
Mark Alexander Martínez
Alexander Lu
Ken Mora
Zach Roberts
Chad Lehrman
Farah Ismail
Omar Morales
Wisse
Julia Fung
Aleph Craven
Eric Zawadzki
Grace Gordon
Meagan Chriswell
Folarin Akinmade
Jameelah Lee
Matt Vieyra
Benjamin Wilkins
Romek van Litsenborgh
Heather Kenealy
Rhys L Griffiths
Mike Olivares
Erin Subramanian
Matt Hawkins
Sami Lehrman
Samanfur
William Carranza
Toby Canto
Kettle Glazed Doughnuts
Mark Byzewski
Jason Hammons
Joe Crawford
David Young
Kyle Beard
Chris Gore
Willie Esule
Ralph Jaurigue
Erin Jaurigue
Francine "Mom" Jaurigue

continued on next page

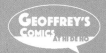

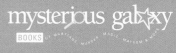

LA VOZ DE M.A.Y.O. TATA RAMBO™

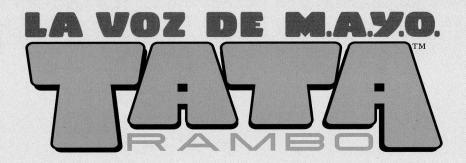

THANK YOU! · ¡GRACIAS!

to the following Kickstarter backers for their support

Izzy and Evye Georgiades
Luke Martinez
Meg Clark
Enoch Chapman
Hannah Rose May
Linda Ray
Spencer Strasmore
CHUNK
Jeff Lemire
Startup Unidos
Dan Alvarez
Ernest DeSpain
angel butierez
Benjamin James Gaska
Freddie Iboy
Tim Bentley
Eddie Botello
Molly
Deborah Barajas
Maryelizabeth Yturralde
Eddie deAngelini
Regine L. Sawyer
Scott Mantooth
Gabriel Hernandez
Simone Bianchi
H.S. Crow
Sam Oriach
Amber
Ellen Power
Steph Cannon
Michael Macropoulos
Rodrigo Diaz
Elizabeth Brei
Ken Mora
Sequart Research & Literacy Organization
Phillip Sevy
Jillian Adams
Craig A. Taillefer
John Ward
Sam Williams
Samanfur
Elaine Lee
Stephanie Phillips
Anthony
Rebecca Bateson
Swag Patrol
NangijalaIF
Farah Ismail
Jay Lofstead
David Crocker
Alex Chung
Gabrielle Lyon
Rant Howard
Christie Shinn
Terrance Grace
Tony Parker
Andy
Ernest Allred
zanniew
Lou Lopez
Ashley Johnson
Erin Subramanian
Sylvia Moon
Austin Hamblin
Lucas Devine
Thomas Keith
Jordan Robert Clark
Levi Fleming
Maria Sosa
Loria Mendoza
Rex Co.
Logan Naugle
Kara Prior
James Peter Alexakis
Micheal D Hart
David Schrader
Isaac Goodhart
Robert L Vaughn
Scott Wesely
Genna Ford
C. Elliott
Asher Powell
Joe Illidge
Carlos Giffoni
Nesher G Asner
Carol Hayman
Quinn Lajoie-Higgins
Chad Wrataric
Raul Coto-Batres
Josh Shalek
Morgan Hampton
Paul trinies
Megan Purdy
Robin Feins
Jean-Pierre Vidrine
Jeffrey Workman
Bryan A Conner
David Kinsel
Brent
Adelina Jaurigue
Patrick Meaney
Eric Palicki
Rob Staeger
Javier Cruz Winnik
Hernán Guarderas
Matt Smith
Barbara Kesel
Kate Newton
Javier Hernandez
Robert Wauneka
Sarah S. Sammis
Paul Gravett
Albert Ching
Terence Dollard
Stephen Seigel
Kent Heidelman
John Seven
Jack Baur
Geoffrey + Amanda
Paul Lai
Jenny y Owen Blacker
Greg Matiasevich
Kat O.
Nick Allen
Adam Ferris
Blaine Jordan
Thom Allard
Anthony Rubin
Anne Kaufer
Chris Callahan
Kiel Phegley
Nola Pfau
Donald E Claxon
sarah gaydos
Isabel Ann Castro
paul meyer
Danny Djeljosevic
steve mandel
Alexa R Dickman
Randall Nichols
Jenn Corella
John Kyritsis
Andrew Connor
Theresa N. Rojas
David Sewell
Bea Melnarowicz
Andrew Brown
Catfish Baruni
Ryan Lofty
Lauren Bonetti
Rod Hedrick
Carmen Marin
Cynthia Gerriets
Paul D Jarman
Joe Crawford
Kim Lowe
Omar Padilla
Erin Cavanaugh

LA VOZ DE M.A.Y.O. TATA™ RAMBO

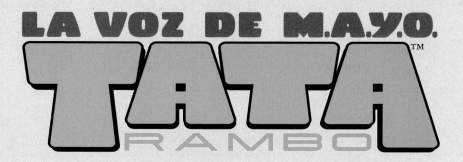

THANK YOU! · ¡GRACIAS!

to the following Kickstarter backers for their support

Andrew Nisbet
Michael DeLong
Jonathan Marks Barravecchia
Ernie Estrella
Hernán Julin
Steven Scott
Michelle Davis
Alyssa Jackson
Jorge Garza
Chris Foster
Chuck Roman
David Hildebrand
Hope Nicholson
Vince Hernandez
ted contreras
christian vilaire
Jesus Diaz
Richard Cardenas
Hector Rodriguez
Ivan Salazar
Daniel Petersen
Julia Tranchina
Shawn Demumbrum
Alexander Jones
Luis Carrasco
Lori Matsumoto
William J Dennis
John Andrew Raub
David Clarke
Jann Jones
Franky J DeJesus
Patch A Perryman
Hanna Schoenberg
Kristy Quinn
Nadia Uhl
Brittany Matter
Hermilo Guzman III
Colleen Doran
Kristen Simon
Scott Koblish
Robert Acosta
Stephen Mejia
Antoinette Abeyta
pigletbunny
Mark Byzewski
Jarred Allen
Holly Aitchison
Natasha
Heidi
Elliot J. Landry
Scott Phelps
Jacob Breckenridge's Parents
Pedro Russo
Shannon
Cassidy
Jim Chadwick
Ivan Moore
Leanne Georgiades
Chris Campbell
Mark Roslan
Erik
Jeff Simpkins
Bobby Dean Bentley
Chido Comics
Hannah Gaber
Cindy Womack
Cait Murphy
Enrique Campos Nanez
Moniqa Aylin
Gerardo
rachel elliott
Glynna Allen
Raul Gonzalez
Fred Higgins
Lisa Zinkie
Jetamors
Danny Robinson
Linda Laird
Terry Mayo
Poppy Carpenter
Melanie
Jody Culkin
Denise M Lopez
Veronica Cruz
Joey Esposito
Rinske
Matt Hawkins
Elena Salcedo
Jacob Cordas
Leo A. Flores
Giraldo L Alvare
Miguel Ziranhua
Carlos Ruiz
Teresa Reyes
Mike Olivares
Victoria Lawless
Deku Imagination Studio
The Erik
Daniel Vera
Jacob Breckenridge
Judy Valentine
Bridgitte
David Wilkerson
Masked Republic
Zack Kaplan
Omar Spahi
Theo Kipnis
Joe Rauch
Jacob Cox
Charlie Harris
Larz anderson
Juan Morales
Chip Mosher
Matthew Kremske
Sara W. Bazan
Isabel Quintero
Jimmy Palmiotti
Tamara Ochoa
Jandro Gamboa
Louis Valenzuela
YnCComics
Calvin Reid
Arnoldo G Rivas
Ernest Romero
The Creative Fund by BackerKit
Neil Kight
Kristen Cook
Andrew Leamon
Maura M. Lynch
Danny Martin
Rawnzilla
quinngonzalez
Jacqueline Fortin
Timothy Doyle
Theresa Mary Fischer
Nick Palmer
Christy Sawyer
Comadres y Comics

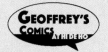

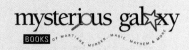

La Voz De MAYO
Newsletters

Before Ramon passed away, he passed down to me copies of the newsletter he self-published at the Santa Rosa Church and Ritchie Elementary. La Voz De M.A.Y.O. was written by the Mexican American Yaqui Organization to keep the community informed. The lost texts you're about to read will be brought back to print for the first time in 50 years. The group reported the news, church function listings, poetry, editorials, and propaganda.

LA VOZ DE MAYO

LA VOZ DE LOS BARRIOS DE PASCUA, ADELANTO, Y ORACLE PARK (BLUE MOON).... 2075 N. CALLE CENTRAL..... TUCSON, ARIZONA 85705

VOL. 1, NUMBER 1   MEXICAN AMERICAN YAQUI ORGANIZATION (MAYO)   *********   OCTOBER, 1969

NOMBRE NUEVO Y VOZ NUEVA

El nombre es MAYO...Mexicanos Americanos Y Yaquis Organizados. El nombre es nuevo, como este periódico, la voz de la organización,es nuevo tambien.

Pero la organizacion misma nació la noche de 28 Avril, 1969. Esa noche los barrios de Pascua, Adelanto, y Oracle Park (Blue Moon) quebraron el silencio de formalidad en City Hall, y protestaron, con una voz, su exclusion del programa Ciudad Modelo. El nombre MAYO aparece ahora, como el nombre nuevo de una organizacion que ha estado creciendo mas y mas desde Avril 28.

La organizacion que nació como participante en Ciudad Modelo ahora se ha extendido para tocar a todas partes de la vida de estos tres barrios. Mientras Ciudad Modelo sigue siendo una parte muy importante de la organizacion, la organizacion misma es sobre todo una union de residentes organizados para usar todos los metodos posibles para ir adelante.....ahora!

Una junta de los representantes elegidos - un dia entero de discusiones en Picture Rocks - se fijó en la palabra sencilla: ORGANIZACION. Toda la idea, todos los propositos, todas las posibilidades de MAYO se resumen en el grito: ORGANIZENSE!

Consejos y apoyo vienen de afuera, por ejemplo, de CEO, de OEO, de Servicio Social Católico, etc. Pero la sangre en las venas de MAYO es la participacion de los residentes organizados.

LA VOZ DE MAYO tiene que ser la voz de estos residentes. Todos los residentes estan invitados a escribir articulos y cartas, y si Dios es servido, LA VOZ aparecera cada mes. Si seguiremos comunicando, seguiremos organizandonos. Adelante!!!

ITO NAU JICKAINE

por Manuel Alvarez

O-owim nau llajaco senu we-en tu tebae junen a-ane, Ca vingua Tuc inica te vittaite einee aju neilla jaubu Ca llumaisi taa jackak ini etejoria, Ciudad Modelo. Vetana, Welle eme ataane vetchivo junensu. Sestul a jicca uchia ajicca ataane ajuneilla-ne, Kechi, inivetchivo Wa-ami em ructe eme ica llac, bempo emchim utteata vitne junen a vovicha bempo.

Jivasu emomae etejo peagua, nau etejoca nau teguipanuaca emo jiccaine jivatua jitasa intoco junu-u jiva.

The name is MAYO...Mexican American Yaqui Organization. The name is new, just like this paper, the voice of the organization.

But the organization was born the night of April 28, 1969. That night the barrios of Pascua, Adelanto, and Oracle Park (Blue Moon) broke the silence of formality in City Hall, and protested with one voice their exclusion from the Model Cities Program. The name MAYO appears now as the new name of an organization that has been growing since that night.

The organization that was born as a part of Model Cities has now been extended to all aspects of the life of these three barrios. While Model Cities continues to be an important part of the organization, the organization itself is above all a coalition of residents organized to use all possible methods to move ahead now!

A meeting of the elected representatives - a day of discussion at Picture Rocks - zeroed in on the simple word ORGANIZATION. The whole idea, the whole purpose, all the potential of MAYO is summed up in the cry: ORGANIZE!

Advice and support come from outside, for example from CEO, OEO, Catholic Social Service, etc. But the blood in the veins of MAYO is the participation of the organized residents.

The VOICE OF MAYO has to be the voice of these residents. All residents are invited to write articles or letters, and God willing, THE VOICE OF MAYO will appear each month. If we keep communicating, we will keep getting more organized. Let's keep moving ahead!

MISA CON MUSICA

CADA DOMINGO A LAS NUEVE

EN SANTA ROSA

—

¡TODOS INVITADOS!

ESCUCHE KXEW 1600

LUNES 3 P.M.   DISCUSIONES

MIERCOLES 3 P.M. CIUDAD MODELO

STUDYHALL EMPIEZA

Gracias a unos representantes de MAYO, a Sra. Jolivet, y Sr. Sam Polito, la escuela Richey se esta usando cada noche de Lunes a Jueves para un studyhall. Tommy Celaya esta abriendo las puertas a las siete, y se cierran a las nueve.

El proposito es tener un lugar (la biblioteca de Richey) donde los jovenes pueden concentrar y estudiar en silencio. Solamente los que vienen a estudiar en serio estan admitidos, y cada noche hay dos supervisores presentes.

Muchos jovenes ya se han aprovechado de este studyhall, y esperamos que su numero va a crecer. Los supervisores son:

Manuel Alvarez, Felipe Olivas, Rafael Gomez, Pete Lopez, Dolores Sanchez, Cecilia Valencia, Eddie Flores y P. Ricardo Elford.

> STUDYHALL OPEN
> Richey School Library
> For Grades 7 thru 12
> Monday thru Thursday
> 7 to 9 PM
> Adult Supervision

ROMERO CANDIDATO

Martes, el dia 7 de Octubre, hay elecciones para la mesa directiva escolar del distrito numero uno. Este año tenemos un candidato Mexicano-americano.

Este candidato es Ruben Romero. Señor Romero nacio en Douglas hace 34 años. Ha vivido en Tucson desde 1952, y graduo de la THS y la UA. Es un veterano de la Fuerza Aerea y un miembro de la catedral de San Agustin. Ha tenido mucha experiencia, entrenamiento, y participacion en asuntos civicos. Se ha dedicado a la eliminacion de condiciones que niegan la oportunidad igual para todos los niños a recibir la misma educacion. Y se ha dedicado al mejoramiento de la cualidad de la educacion dada.

Todo votador registrado en el Distrito Escolar Numero Uno puede votar. No necesita ser dueno de propiedad. Puede registrarse hasta el dia de la eleccion.

Dos de las escuelas en que la gente puede votar son la escuela Menlo Park y la escuela Safford.

Tuesday, the 7th of October, there are elections for school district number one. This year there is a Mexican-American candidate.

He is Ruben Romero. Mr. Romero was born in Douglas 34 years ago. He has lived in Tucson since 1952, and graduated from THS and the UA. He is an Air Force veteran, and a member of the Cathedral Parish. He has had much experience, training, and participation in civic affairs. He is dedicated to eliminating conditions that deny the equal opportunity for all children to receive the same education. And he is dedicated to the improvement of the quality of the education given.

Every registered voter in School District Number One can vote. It is not necessary to be a property owner. You can register right up until the day of election.

Two of the schools in which the people can vote are Menlo Park school, and Safford School.

AGENCIAS

by Pete Lopez

Me encuentro con dificultad para empezar relatar lo siguiente porque mi creencia es en accion, no en palabras. Primeramente la unidad de tres barrios esta incluido en el nombre MAYO. Esta organizacion empezo con las agencias de las Enfermeras Visitantes. Varias personas han sido recomendadas a doctores y al hospital del condado. El nombre de esta agencia es Visiting Nurses Association. La segunda agencia es los Boy Scouts of America. Le doy las gracias al Senor Duane Weidler por el tiempo que nos ha prestado para organizar el comite y un sin numero de chicos de once a trece anos de edad que han ingresado en los Boy Scouts de America.

El comité esta compuesto por algunos hombres de esta organizacion, que son los siguientes:

Ramon Jaurigue	Pres. de Comision
Pete Lopez	Vice-presidente
Ralph Gomez	Chairman of the BSA
Jorge Salgado	Scoutmaster
Manuel Alvarez	Tesorero y Comite
Peter Alvarez	Comite
Rudy Romero	Comite
Ignacio Elenez	Comite
Richard Flores	Assistant Scoutmaster
Eddie Flores	Assistant Scoutmaster

GRAPE BOYCOTT

by Rosie Jimenez

Several young people from MAYO have taken part in protests against stores that sell table grapes. This, along with bumper-stickers seen in the area, has caused people to ask what it is all about.

Four years ago in California, under the leadership of Cesar Chavez, the grape fieldworkers demanded their right to organize be recognized. They wanted a union so that they would be paid justly and have all the protections the other workers in this country have had for so long. The ranchers refused so the workers went on strike. The whole country learned the word: HUELGA!

The first ranches to be struck grew wine grapes, and before long they accepted the union. But when the table grape growers were struck, they brought in outside help to pick the grapes - busloads of workers from Mexico.

Since the strike was no longer enough, Chavez and the Farmworkers'

Union turned to boycott. A new expression was heard all over the US: BOYCOTT GRAPES, do not buy grapes. People everywhere were asked not to buy grapes till the Union was recognized.

The table grape ranchers are still holding out. The boycott would have brought total success by now if so many grapes were not sent to Vietnam. But they are so the HUELGA & Boycott still go on.

Here are some of Cesar Chavez' words: "We are men and women who have suffered and endured much and not only because of our abject poverty but because we have been kept poor. The colors of our skin, the languages of our cultural and national origins, the lack of formal education, the exclusion from the democratic process, the numbers of our slain in recent wars--all these burdens generation after generation have sought to demoralize us, to break our human spirit. But God knows that we are not beasts of burden, we are not agricultural implements or rented slaves, we are men. We are men locked in a death struggle against man's inhumanity to man."

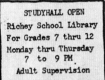

ELECCIONES

La noche de 12 Junio, 1969, eligimos nuestros representantes en MAYO, y ellos sirven tambien como la mesa directiva de Ciudad Modelo aqui. Son:

Ramon H. Jaurigue
Padre Antonio Sanchez
Ted Valenzuela
Rosie Jimenez
Felipe Olivas
George Salgado
Joaquin Burruel
Felipe Gastelo
Gloria Tona
Ignacio Elenez
Cecilia Valencia
Rudy Romero
Dolores Sanchez
Pete Lopez
Agustina Gallardo
Juan Alvarez
Teodora Acuna
Basilio Olivas
Delfina Soto
Joaquin Bracamonte
Manuel Alvarez
Richard Flores
Natalia Cocio
Eddie Flores
Ralph Gomez

En la junta de 17 Junio, 1969, en el centro de Santa Rosa, estas personas eligieron los siguientes miembros ejecutivos:

Chairman: Ramon H. Jaurigue
Co-Chairman: Pete Lopez
Secretary: Joaquin Burruel
Asst. Sec: Rosie Jimenez
Treasurer: George Salgado
Asst. Trs: Teodora Acuna

Estas 6 personas forman la Mesa Ejecutiva, de MAYO y de Ciudad Modelo.

The former group was elected as MAYO and Model Cities representatives at Richey School, June 12, 1969. They elected the latter six as the executive board on June 17, 1969, at Santa Rosa.

        A N D . . . .

On Sept. 10, 1969, the following members of MAYO were named to the Model Cities proposed task forces:

Economic Development:
        Ralph Gomez
        Ramon Jaurigue

Employment Opportunity:
        Pete Lopez
        Ramon Jaurigue

Transportation:
        Pete Lopez
        Basilio Olivas

Health:
        Dolores Lopez
        Dolores Sanchez

Social Welfare:
        Natalia Cocio
        Delfina Soto
        Cecilia Valencia

Crime Reduction:
        Manuel Alvarez
        Felipe Olivas

Education:
        Cecilia Valencia
        Gloria Tona

FUTURE EVENTS

Our readers are reminded that MAYO general meetings are held at Richey School the first Wednesday of each month. Each person's attendance benefits the whole neighborhood, and it would be great if those who have been attending would bring along a neighbor who has not. Meetings begin at seven-thirty.

*****
***
*

Bulletin: As we go to press, we have learned that the young people's meetings have been moved to Monday nights, same time, same station. It's too late to make the change in Ceci Valencia's article, so readers please take notice! Monday's the nite!

*****
***
*

In our next issue we hope to give you a detailed listing of hours and days when the different agencies are present. Also, a look at our Scouts' near future. Anyone else who would like to announce events in this column.... see one of the editors soon!

*****
***
*

Another bulletin: Fr. Cote announces that there will soon be Sunday afternoon catechism for the children, given by university students under the direction of Fr. Malizia from the U. Newman Center. More details on this soon also.

REDACCION - EDITORIAL BOARD

Redactores:
        Ramon Jaurigue
        Pete Lopez
        Teodora Acuna
Youth Editor:
        Cecilia Valencia

LA VOZ DE MAYO is published each month by the Mexican American Yaqui Organization of the Barrios of Pascua, Adelanto and Oracle Park, Tucson, Arizona.

CARTAS

To the Editor:

I am making my plea to the people of my neighborhood...I am a member of your Model Cities Program.

This program if utilized by the people of this community will be the best thing that the Federal Gov't. has done for the people here in the Southwest where it is needed the most....

A lot more information is available to us if we can start coming to the meeting scheduled once a month for the residents of Oracle Park, Adelanto and Pascua. Please give two hours of your time so that we can talk to you and explain this program. It is here now, the foundation has now been laid out, the people in Washington have given us the OK. We can go ahead with our plan.... Take advantage of this, don't be left out. People have a habit of waiting to see how things will work out, and then if they do, they will go ahead. Do not be the ones that are always left out... the smarter people are attending the meetings at Richey School, to get all the information now, not later.....

I myself believe this program to be a very good one. If the people on my Committee, the Federal Gov't, the state and the city believe it too, who am I to say that it will never make it. I wholeheartedly support this program, but do not take my word for it...find out for yourself. A reminder will be sent to you when our next meeting will be held.

                Joaquin Burruel
                1224 N. 14th
                Oracle Park

The following letter recently appeared in the Tucson Daily Citizen.

To the Editor:

An article in the Aug. 21 Tucson Daily Citizen mentioned that the "mayor and City Council proposed expansion of the Model Cities Program for the inclusion of the Pascua Village area."

It should be pointed out that there are two kinds of proposals: those that are free and voluntary and those that are made after considerable pushing by someone else.

The day the mayor and council became aware of the worthwhileness of proposing the expansion on behalf of Pascua village, over 200 residents of the village, along with a number of other concerned persons, were present in and about the City Hall council chambers. A great deal of work to further this proposal had been done prior to that date by persons of the Manzo Area Council.

So while it is true to say that the mayor and council proposed the expansion, it is also true, in the interests of accuracy, to state that the proposal was somewhat forced by the push of others -- the ordinary citizens and property users who felt left out and now find themselves in.

                JOHN SHAUGHNESSY
                410 South 6th Ave.

TEEN ACTION

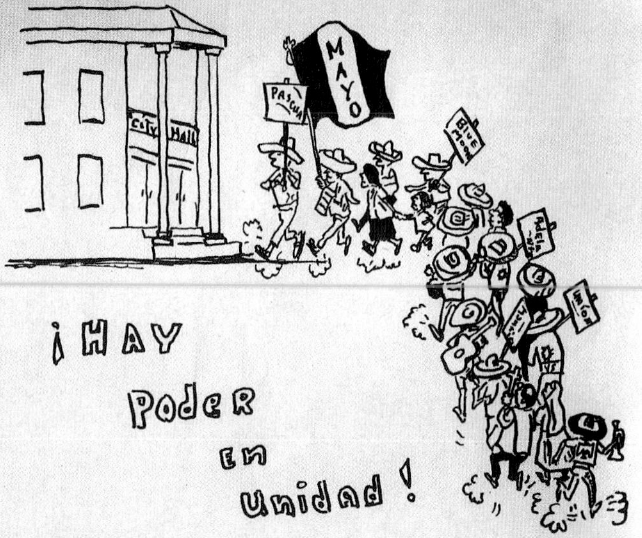
City Hall
MAYO
PASCUA
¡HAY
Poder
en
Unidad!

by Cecilia Valencia

The young people of MAYO now have a teen group going. Santa Rosa church is their gathering place. For the past four months the teenagers have been working very hard on projects to raise funds for present and future needs for themselves as well as others. They involve themselves not only with work but also enjoyment. The kids are now planning a Halloween party for the youngsters.

We are so proud to have these teens interested in doing something for their barrio and being part of the Voice of MAYO. Like the kids said one time: "Since we've been living and brought up here, we have not yet seen any action going, and we believe it's about time we start doing something about it." They may be a quiet group, but their work is loud and clear.

Any teenager who wants to be part of what's happening in his barrio is welcomed to the meetings every Tuesday night, at 7:30 at Santa Rosa Church.

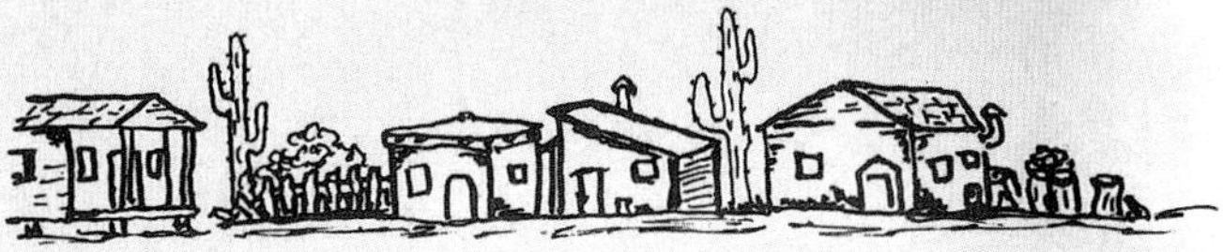

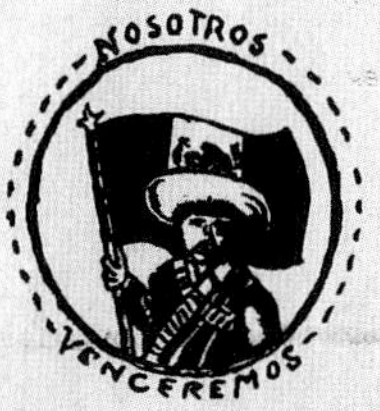
NOSOTROS
VENCEREMOS

RECENT HAPPENINGS OF INTEREST TO US IN PROJECT MODEL CITIES......

by P. Juan Shaughnessy

Among the on-going activities of the Model Cities program thruout the whole district these days are two covered by the project that are of particular interest to us, and for that matter to everyone involved in the project:

1. The continuing formation of the groups to be known as the Study Groups. (These groups are also called the Task Forces.)

These are groups made up of at least two persons from each of the Model Cities Units -- along with the people of the various agencies concerned with and knowledgeable in the problems under discussion in connection with the various Model Cities Units.

From our unit here for example, we have the people listed on page two on the study groups concerned with Medical Care and Services, and with Employment Opportunities.

You may recall at one time or originally there were ten large problem areas that were going to be studied. By combination and ongoing progress, these have been reduced to fewer categories or Task Forces, which will still study with various sub-committees all of the various ten original problems.

(continued next column)

You are welcome to put yourself as available to serve on these. Talk to one of the board members now or at the next general meeting.

2. The other big step and bit of progress underway is the continuing information being gotten out by the Block Captains and other people gaining better understanding of the program as they participate.

If you are a block captain, get in touch with the meetings and the local president of our unit (Ramon Jaurigue), so the program may continue gaining ground in our unit... especially by participating in the Block System, so vital to the program.

(Father Shaughnessy is a memmber of the Inner City Apostolate or Apostolado de los Barrios. Many of our readers have heard him on the Monday afternoon (at 3 p.m.) Model cities program on radio station KXEW. Ed.)

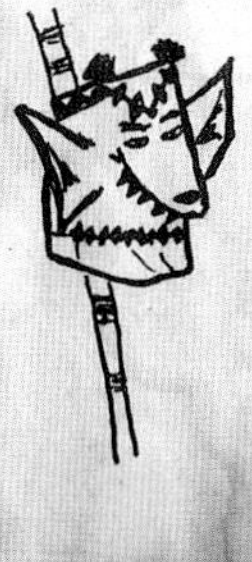

HERE & THERE

by Ramon Juarigue

He's way over in L.A. but we know P. Antonio Sanchez will be glad to see LA VOZ. No one's forgetting all Padre Pancho Villa did for us and as one of us last year. Wish we could see him again levantando revolucion in the middle of a meeting.

*****

Lots of action around Sta. Rosa in recent months owes thanks to Father Cote for launching the happenings around the church. And to the many agencies who accepted invitations to come in...nurses, Scouts, Catholic Social Service and others.

*****

Maybe the biggest (and loudest) action was the summer school. A repeat of thanks to Amy, the ladies who cooked every day and our NYC girls!

*****

Someone else we miss is (Tiny) Tim Klein, who's studying in San Francisco now. Another face we'd like to see back around here, bigotes and all!

*****

Maybe the most exciting event of the summer was the Fiesta de Santa Rosa. All the preparation work of young and old paid off, and the crowds of people taking part didn't hold back any enthusiasm. Fr. Cote's partner in the concelebrated Mass was Fr. Vicente Soriano.

*****

A big pat on the back to the kids who are always willing to pass out all those meeting notices (and other stuff) from door to door.....

*****

Don't forget anyone who is an area resident is invited to write articles and letters. We're shooting for once a month.

EDITORIAL

Here in the barrios we are not asleep.

Wide awake, we can see that progress is still only half-real.

We know that we have made a lot of progress during the past year. For example, the new El Rio Santa Cruz Health Center. But we also know that there would be much, much more progress, if it were not for the stupidity of a lot of people.

Awake, we wonder why so many people worry much more about elephants and cages than they do about people and housing.

Awake, we wonder why so much money and human effort are wasted on useless paper work.

We wonder how a young policeman could come saying he wished he had permission of his chief to carry a shotgun in our barrio.

And why a county employee has to meddle in the decisions of a consumers' council.

We do not understand all this.

But then we do not understand either why a drunken binge in the barrio is just a drunken binge, while in a fancy motel a drunken binge is a social event.

Who knows? We cannot understand everything, right?

We just continue organizing ourselves.

Aqui en los barrios no estamos dormidos.

Despiertos, podemos ver que el progreso todavia es solamente una media-realidad.

Sabemos que hemos progresado mucho durante el utimo año. Por ejemolo, el nuevo centro de salud. Pero tambien sabemos que habria mucho, mucho mas progreso, si no fuera por la estupidez de mucha gente.

Despiertos, nos preguntamos porque tantos se preocupan mucho mas sobre elefantes y jaulas, que con humanos y casas.

Despiertos, nos preguntamos porque tanto dinero y tanto esfuerzo humano se gastan para papeleria inutil.

Nos preguntamos como un policia joven pudiera venir diciendo que quisiera tener permiso de su jefe para llevar una escopeta a nuestro barrio.

Y porque una empleada del Condado tiene que meterse en las decisiones de un concilio de consumidores.

No comprendemos todo esto.

Pero tampoco comprendemos porque una borrachera en el barrio es simplemente una borrachera, mientras en un motel elegante una borrachera es un evento social.

Quien sabe? No lo podemos comprender todo, verdad?

Solamente seguimos organizandonos.

"Despues de la Procesion en honor de Santa Rosa......."

PELÍCULAS MEXICANAS

La Biblioteca de la ciudad de Tucson esta presentando gratis las siguientes peliculas mexicanas:

NOSOTROS LOS POBRES con Pedro Infante y Evita Muñoz. Biblioteca Valencia Martes el 16 de Febrero y biblioteca central Miercoles el 17 de Febrero.

USTEDES LOS RICOS con Pedro Infante y Evita Muñoz. Biblioteca Valencia Martes el 16 de Marzo y biblioteca central Miercoles el 17 de Marzo.

PEPE EL TORO con Pedro Infante y Joaquin Cordero. Biblioteca Valencia Martes el 20 de Abril y biblioteca central Miercoles el 21 de Abril.

LAS TRES CALAVERAS con Joaquin Cordero y Lucha Villa. Biblioteca Valencia Martel el 18 de Mayo y biblioteca central Miercoles el 19 de Mayo.

Las bibliotecas tendrán funciones a las siguientes horas:

BIBLIOTECA VALENCIA
a las 10 de la mañana
a la 1 de la tarde
a las 4 de la tarde

BIBLIOTECA CENTRAL
a las 10:30 de la mañana
a las 6:30 de la noche

CENTRO DE SALUD

El Rio Santa Cruz Neighborhood Health Center (Centro de Salud está ofreciendo ahora los siguientes servicios:

Tratamiento de enfermedades de adultos y niños, examinaciones físicas, servicios de enfermeras, Rayos-X, Servicios de nutricion, transportacion, farmacia, clínica para niños, servicios antes de nacimiento, servicios sociales y para enfermedades emocionales.

Quien puede usar el centro? Residentes dentro la region Ciudad Modelo en Tucson, especialmente esos residentes qu no tienen suficientes recursos para recibir servicios médicos Pero si su familia ya tiene médico, se la pide que continúe bajo su cuidado.

El costo? Se basará en lo que la persona pueda pagar.

Las horas de consultas son las siguientes: Los lunes, miercoles, y viernes - de 9 a.m. a 9 p.m. Los martes y jueves - de 9 a.m. a 6 p.m. Y los sabados - 9 a.m. a 12 mediodia.

Pase o llame ahora mismo para hacer una cita. Registre a su familia. El Rio Santa Cruz Neighborhood Health Center (Centro de Salud) - 332 S. Freeway, Teléfono 792-9890.

Para mas informes llame ahora mismo. Proteja a su salud y la de su familia.

For more information on the Neighborhood Health Center, call 792-9890 now.

"Water, anybody?...."

LA VOZ DE MAYO

THE VOICE OF BARRIOS PASCUA, ADELANTO, AND ORACLE PARK (BLUE MOON)   2075 N. CALLE CENTRAL TUCSON, AZ. PHONE 622-5680

VOLUME 1, NUMBER 2   MEXICAN AMERICAN YAQUI ORGANIZATION (MAYO)   NOVEMBER, 1969

LIMPIEZA PROGRESANDO

por Ramon Jaurigue

El programa de limpieza en la comunidad es un programa de ayudarse uno mismo para limpiar el barrio. Consiste en que todos se envuelvan para hacer todo el esfuerzo de cada quien poner su parte en el mejoramiento de todo el barrio, desde la Grant hasta la Speedway.

Que casualidad es que todo el tiempo tenemos que andar pidiendo ayuda a gente de afuera para que venga a limpiar nuestra basura, que uno mismo ha dejado de hacerlo. No es justo que tengan que hacer esto para nosotros aqui en el barrio si aqui mismo hay el esfuerzo para poder hacerse.

Que casualidad que otra gente de afuera tenga que venir a nuestro barrio para ensenarnos a hacer la limpieza que nosotros mismos lo podemos hacer.

Y otra cosa.... no es justo que a las mismas gentes que se interan y quieren hacer algo por su comunidad les dejen todo el trabajo a ellos. Y tambien, no hay que criticar a esos que estan interesados en su barrio para poder hacer que su comunidad valga algo. Estas personas interesadas se critican como pendejos o como lambiones, porque andan ellos muy interesados en hacer ese trabajo para que levanten el prestigio de la comunidad en que viven ellos y ustedes. Asi es que no nomas se sienten y critiquen a la gente interesada...sino juntense y ayuden a esta gente, porque ellos necesitan su ayuda.

Dicen que el departamento de sanidad no ayuda y no tiene interes en nuestra comunidad, pero esto no es cierto porque tenemos a un buen amigo, el senor Tom Price del departamento mismo que esta haciendo todo el esfuerzo ayudandonos en la limpieza y haciendo posible que tengamos el equipo, los troques, etc. para que se haga nuestro programa posible.

Una cosa que dice Sr. Price es que no hay necesidad que hubiera tanta basura en nuestro barrio si sacaramos nuestra basura para afuera para que se la lleven los troques que vienen dos veces a la semana. Asi es que el dice que toda la basura que querriamos deshacernos podemos ponerla afuera para que se la lleven. Lo mismo

las ramas y las hojas y todo lo demas se lo llevan ellos se estan puestas en cajas o en los botes de la basura. Entonces hay que comenzar hacer esto para no tener tanta basura en nuestro barrio y tambien para no tener que estar tirando la basura en los callejones. No hay necesidad que la basura se tire todo el tiempo en las calles, callejones, plazita, o lotes.

Por eso hay que comenzar a poner nuestra basura afuera en frente de las casas.

Tambien el departamento de las calles los estan ayudando para que nuestro programa sea un buen exito, poniendo a nuestra disposicion el equipo y los trabajadores de su departamento, para que vengan a levantar la basura mas pesada y la basura que les estamos juntando nosotros cada Sabado.

Quizas ustedes hayan mirado ya esos troques levantando la basura. Asi es que no hay que decir que no nos estan ayudando ellos o que no tienen interes en nuestro barrio. Hay que ensenarles a ellos tambien que nosotros mismos tenemos el mismo interes para ayudarnos y hacer posible que nos sigan ayudando. Como dice el dicho: "Si hay unidad, hay poder!" Que viva la raza!

The clean-up program is a self-help community program which has to involve everyone in the barrio. It is important that everyone do their part and not wait for other people from outside to come and show us the way to clean up the mess we have neglected. And let's not leave the work to the same people who are always this

work to better our community. Let's all get together and pitch in, and not sit back and say, "Let those fools do it." The so-called fools are proud of what they are doing to improve their community and yours, so let's all get with it and make it a big success.

We have the help, from our good friend Tom Price from the Sanitation Department, who has made it possible for us to have the trucks, equipment, and drivers available so that we can do our thing. He also says that the trash collectors come into our community twice a week, so let's start putting our trash cans out to be hauled away. That means everything that you want to get rid of, like weeds, tree branches, just as long as they are put in boxes, trash cans, or in bundles no longer than three feet. So let's start putting the trash out, instead of throwing it out in the alley.

Let's not forget our good friends of the city Street Department who are coming every Wednesday and hauling away the bigger piles of trash and dirt that we are piling up for them every Saturday. They will come till we finish the clean-up, and we hope that they will continue coming.

We can't say that they are not helping or that they are not interested, so let's start showing that we residents are interested. Let's all come out on Saturdays to do the work, and not leave it to a few. Join in and make it a big thing.

****

PLAZA ONCE AGAIN CLEAR FOR USE BY THE RESIDENTS

The first area cleared by the MAYO clean-up project was the Plaza where the church of San Ignacio once stood. The men have placed logs around the outside to keep cars out, and they are watching closely so that this does not become a dumping place again. The residents are assured that this Plaza is now once again for their use. Father Richard Cantrell has given us a Ramada which will soon be put up in the Plaza. It is sincerely hoped that everybody - young and old - will cooperate to keep it clean and clear.

MAYO BY-LAWS PASSED

At the MAYO General Meeting of Oct. 16, 1969, at Richey School, the following by-laws were unanimously approved by the residents present:

BY-LAWS OF M.A.Y.O./UNIT NUMBER 6

ARTICLE I. Name. This organization shall be known as the Mexican, American, Yaqui, Organization.

ARTICLE II. Purpose. The purpose is to unite the residents of Pascua, Adelanto and Oracle Park area; to provide a means by which the residents' needs and problems can be communicated to public and private agencies, foundations, and groups and can be solved.

ARTICLE III. Membership Regulations and Restrictions. Membership shall be limited to residents of Pascua, Adelanto and Oracle Park Areas. Any person who is not a resident but who is interested in the Neighborhood can join the organization but not hold any elected office or vote in any action. Any resident 14 years of age and up is permitted to vote.

ARTICLE IV. Officers of the organization. The officers shall be President, Vice-president, Secretary, Assistant Secretary, Treasurer, and Assistant Treasurer; and whatever other officers this organization shall deem needful to carry out its objectives. The officers shall be elected for a period of one year.
Section 2. The Responsibilities of the officers.
a. President - to preside at or direct general meetings and to arrange for and call meetings.
b. Vice-president - to help president and serve as president in his absence.
c. Secretary - to take minutes, to keep records and correspondence.

d. Assistant Secretary - to help secretary and serve as secretary in his absence.
e. Treasurer - to keep financial records and administer funds.
f. Assistant Treasurer - to help treasurer and serve as treasurer in his absence.

Section 3. Recall of Officers.
Ten (10) member-residents of M.A.Y.O. or six (6) members of the Executive Board may petition the president to hold a special election. The president shall call such election within twenty-one (21) days after receiving such a petition in writing.

ARTICLE V. General Membership Meetings.
Section 1. General Membership Meetings will be the first Wednesday of every month unless under unusual circumstances.
Section 2. The President may call special meetings when he deems it necessary.
Section 3. Emergency General Meetings may also be called at the request of several residents and at the discretion of the Executive Board

ARTICLE VI. Executive Committee and Board of Directors.
Section 1. The Executive Committee will be composed of the President, the Vice-president, Secretaries, and Treasurers.
Section 2. The Executive Committee will be elected by the Board of Directors which is composed of twenty-five (25) members, who are elected in a general meeting of M.A.Y.O. Five members of the Board of Directors will be youths (under age of 21) and five will be over 50 years old. Thirteen will constitute a quorum for the Board of Directors.

Section 3. The President or the Executive Committee may appoint any standing or special committee that is needed. Such appointments will be subject to approval by the Board of Directors.

ARTICLE VII. Task Forces. The Board of Directors will select the delegates to the Task Forces.

ARTICLE VIII. Representatives to Other Board Levels of Model Cities. The Board of Directors will select representatives to the Model Neighborhood Council, the Conference Committee and the Policy Board. Of ever five (5) representatives to the Mode Neighborhood Council, one will be a youth and one an elderly.

ARTICLE IX. Conduct of Meetings. Meetings will be conducted informall by the President or Vice-president but in case of conflict, Robert's Rules of Order, Revised, will apply.

ARTICLE X. Amendments of By-Laws. These By-laws may be amended by approval of a two-thirds majority of th resident-members present at a genera meeting, provided the amendment has been circulated in writing at least fifteen (15) days prior to said meeting.

ARTICLE XI. Procedures for Replacing Representatives. In the event that a representative, elected or appointed at any level, does not responsibl do his job, the Board of Directors m appoint a replacement for the remainder of the term of office. Any representative proposed to be replaced shall be entitled at least five (5) days notice of the meeting of the Board of Directors at which such removal is to be voted upon and shall entitled to appear before and be hea by the Board of Directors at that meeting.

LA CAUSA

by Teddy Acuna

I'd like to give my views on what the minority groups are doing, especially the Mexican-American.

You know, sometimes we just take things for granted, and don't think much about it. There is so much propaganda about the Mexican-American, and we have to think about it very much.

Are we really different from the anglos? Color-wise, are we going to be rated as second-class citizens? Is there any difference if we are black, brown, pink, blue or white? The only real question is: will we be treated equally? Like if we all dyed our skin the same color.

We can't be blaming all anglos for the way some think. But we should fight for equality, for our just and fair rights, just like the blacks, Indians, Puerto Ricans and others have to fight. We can't let them change our culture.

They call us everything from militant radicals to communists who are trying to take over the USA. How long will we tolerate this kind of thinking? How long are the minority people going to take exploitation, abuse, colonialism? Will we as American chicanos and blacks and Puerto Ricans, etc. stand up for our rights? We have had enough, especially the Indian, who was here before Columbus showed up.

A lot of people give me their opinions. One girl told me she was completely against school walkouts, but still admitted she didn't know why the kids in one case walked out. She said if it happened at her school, she wouldn't walk out even if she believed it was right. A boy told me MALC was militant communism, and wouldn't achieve anything, and we're going to be rated second class citizens after all anyway.

Do they really think before they say things like this? We have so much to do, but first of all, everybody has to think very much!

ANIMADOS ACTUAN

by Cecilia Valencia

After seven months of hard work, Los Animados de Mayo would like to say that the Halloween party turned out a great success. They had in the vicinity of 200 children attending that night. Besides giving the youngsters the Halloween party, Los Animados have been busy selling candles to raise more funds, and have also helped with the MAYO clean-up campaign.

Los Animados are now planning their next project: a Thanksgiving dinner. They also have something going for Christmas.

This is a really busy group, and the hope to show their parents and other just what they can do in the future.

PERDON POR LA VERDAD

por Pedro Lopez

Sin querer ofender a nadie me veo obligado a poner estas cuantas lineas para abrir un poco el entendimiento. La oficina de MAYO esta abierta para ayudar a los residentes de MAYO a trabajar juntos no para prometer imposibilidades.

A lo que me refiero es que estamos dispuestos a ofrecer ayuda por consejos de las agencias para poder instruir a la gente como poder resolver algunos de sus problemas. Ustedes saben bien que lo que uno hace de por si, es de mas ventaja para si mismo.

Vamos abrir los ojos y fijarnos cual problema es el que necesita mas atencion en nuestras familias al presente. Ya sea falta de atencion o amor a nuestros hijos. Si fuera atencion: le ponemos importancia a lo que nuestros hijos o hijas necesitan: discusion con la madre o el padre tocante cosas materiales y personales. Tienen lo que necesitan? Principalmente amor de los padres?

Lo que los hijos hacen y necesitan es importante. Perdon por la verdad.

MODEL CITIES NEWS

Under the Technical Assistance Grant the Model Neighborhood Council has hired as laison director Mr. Richard Holmes, of Unit 1. Many of our readers know him from meetings, and know that he is Spanish-speaking and familiar with the problems of the Model Cities Area.....The Tucson Neighborhood Health Center will be the old Mother Higgins Juvenile Detention Center and will open in the spring. The project was begun by Dr. Abrams of the U., but many of the arrangements have been planned by the Model Neighborhood Council.....Of course there will be a lot more said about the Health Center in future editions of LA VOZ.

MAYO SCOUT TROOP RECEIVES AWARD

Our Mayo Boy Scout Troop #221 came up with a Blue Ribbon award at the Campo-ree Saturday the 8th of November.

Congrations to our own tropa loca and Scoutmaster George Salgado!!!

****
NO COMPREN UVAS !!! NO COMAN UVAS !!!

MAYO President Ramon Jaurigue and Vice-President Pete Lopez discuss Operation Clean-up with one of the drivers.

UCHIA

por Manuel V. Alvarez

1. Jabesa nocbaeteco quia nocne, tuisi amamatec anatene, inapo in cobapo in suagua ino nattemae: ¿ jagsaca o-owim ka itom jiccaja, ka itom yuem eiya? Itom tegui panuaum tui-i simem vetchivo, imi-i luturia ayucsime avicha; Ka gucpul o-ou aet teguipanua, apo u jamut kechi sime guepulavenasi eaca ka yumjojue, iani te tua bamse junu-u vetchivo enchim utteata te bovicha.

2. Jehui, eme ka nocak cave enchim jiccaine, eme a juneya itepo sime te guatia, caita te jipue; ka itepo jiba yorim mericano. Vecrom, sime junume polovem ito venasi, vempo vein tui jiapsi al-leaca teguipanua taa itoin utteata gua-ata, junensu, catem pacua tatagua naue teguiquipanuacci ito ta-ane itom jiapsim naue joiguane, yo but tula, itom pueplo tutulisi ya riana: Dios, itoin achai a ye jiocaine, tauguam itoin reuguac avitne.

3. Ka vinguatuc seenu tuc-capo, goj o baji ussi hiohuiam gojnaiki limetam jamta iminiaki itom, Escuela Richey. Jic-cayem ameu noca iliussim ussim ussihiohuim catem ussim majae vempo caita juneya. Yaura enchim acoparuane amambuiseco, enchimajunayatua chucula catem gomtine o asumeyane; 16 Oct. emou anocac, apo Ramon Jaurigue.

4. Into senu ahuc, sime Barriom te tutebae Pascua; Adelanto; Blue Moon, sime jume o-ouwim te gua-ata itom amane veychivo; batnatacay venasi enchim aguneyatua; yaura ka sancuata ka montone solarpo, ca-llempo: Bu-u jiosay cajam ahuc sancuata, amet eriane; lunes into jueves, trok iat na huehuama.

by Ramon Jaurigue

Thanks to Mrs. Concha Ruiz and Miss Dolores Sanchez for providing a wonderful lunch for the clean-up workers.
*****
Let's not forget the mothers' club and the wonderful job they are doing with the rummage-sale money. They have bought shelves for the books kept in the hall, and have other projects in the church.
*****
Para LOS ANIMADOS DE MAYO: a big hand goes out for the bunch of kids who have not only shown interest but have been getting things done for themselves and others. Their Halloween party was a big success.
*****
At Richey School: thanks to Mrs. Ana Jolivet for helping to make the study hall available for our kids, and all the other activities.
*****
What's wrong at John Spring? They say that our kids are not making it to school. What about it, parents...are you just going to sit back and not do anything about it or let the school officials do your part too?
*****
Gracias to Fr. Cote for the new roof that is on the hall. Even tho his time is taken up at Holy Family, he is here with us launching the happenings around the church.
*****
From over in L.A., P. Antonio Sanchez sends his regards to all, and his heart is here with us. So let's not disappoint him; like he always said, hay poder en unidad. So let's get with it and not let him down. He is trying to come and visit us as soon as he can.
*****
Porque hay poder en unidad, let's start coming to our monthly meeting at Richey school the first Wednesday of each month. That way you all can know what is going on in our community and in the Model Cities Program.
*****
Once again some last minute bulletins are coming in just as we go to press. For one, the Sunday afternoon catechism classes are now going to take place every Sunday at Santa Rosa. The time is the same: 2 till 3 p.m., and remember: for children 6 thru 11 years. Mil gracias to our four U. students who work with our kids in this project.
*****
We just now heard the good news that there will be classes in basic English and G.E.D. each week, 7 to 9 p.m., at Richey School. Opening night will be Thursday, Nov. 13. We'll have a lot more to say on this in the next issue.
*****
A reminder: on KXEW Mondays at 3.... charlas informales con los Padres del Apostolado de los Barrios. Sundays at 10 a.m. on channel 13: Mass for shutins, y el primer domingo de cada mes esta misa es en espanol.
*****
Once again, we remind you that all residents are invited to write articles for LA VOZ. You can give them to Pete Lopez any morning at the Center (or call him: 622-5680). Or you can give them to one of the other editors.

CARTAS

(The following letter comes from Mr. Howard Rouch, director of Catholic Social Service, who has done much for MAYO.)

Editor of LA VOZ DE MAYO:

The name is LA VOZ DE MAYO, the voice of the people of barrios Pascua, Adelanto and Oracle Park; a voice which has already broken the silence of the people of these barrios. Is it to be only a voice of these barrios? It is a voice of LA RAZA, the people of Mexican and Indian heritage. But is it only the voice of LA RAZA?

LA VOZ DE MAYO must be the voice of the people, all people who share with the many residents of these barrios, and barrios throughout our land, the burden of poverty, the burden of hunger, the burden of poor health with poor medical care, the burden of being cold on a bitter, chilling night..... It must be the voice of the aged, left lonely, sick and weakened by lack of food, the aged who live in the barrio in a lonely little shack, in apartments in areas where their neighbors are seeing better times. It must be the voice of the many young women who are expecting babies, the young barrio girls, the daughters of rich men who find themselves alone expecting a child who has no legal father, the black girl the anglo girl - all the young girls who do not receive good medical care.

The people of the barrios are awakening from a long sleep...a long period of silence. They know pain, all the pains of mankind. They are demanding release from pain, a fair chance in what can be a great society. Will these people demand only for themselves? By themselves? No. The people of the barrios are sympatico with their fellow man be he black, white, or brown. The people of the barrio must not fight alone but must join hands with others of all races and all creeds.

Sincerely,
Howard Rouch

Editor:

The Huriasim is the essence of the Yaqui way of life. Without tradition the Yaqui culture would die.

The Comite Yaqui de la Fe, 417 W. 39 St., Tucson, was formed by Maestros Juan Flores and Thomas Valuenzuela, Sr. in 1959 for the purpose of preserving Yaqui tradition. The specific programs established were:
1) Build a brick church to serve as a permanent basis for Yaqui life, & 2) Build a communal kitchen to handle the needs of the people during religious and fiesta time.

These were the two main goals of the founders of the Comite. The first goal has almost been completed while the second plan is in the development stage.

Since 1968 there has been an expansion of the goals of the Comite. They now wish to buy a school bus for work and religious obligations. Eventually the Comite would like to form a busline which would provide low-cost transportation for the working poor. They would also like to form a "job-skills school" for Yaqui men and women, to learn trades and revive Yaqui traditional arts and crafts. These are but a few of the dreams that the Yaqui people of the Barrio Libre hope to accomplish in the years ahead.

Sincerely yours,
Mike Turner

Editor of LA VOZ DE MAYO:

I would like to address myself to our brothers in the barrios about assisting our young.

Are you fed up? Are you sick and tired of the life we live in the barrios? Look around you -- How many of us are going nowhere? At our jobs we work hard for a skimpy paycheck. Do you know that our women still work for 65¢ an hour and some for 14 dollars a week? That our older people are rotting in adobe shacks? That they are sending our children to Fort Grant to be trained for prison later? How many of you have jobs where there is no insurance, vacations or sick pay, and they work you weekends too. The fact of the matter is they make you quit so they won't have to give you any of this. How many of you know chuck steak and round steak when it comes to eating meat? Really, we know more about sopa, beans and potatoes.

Go to any school in our barrios any time and you see 30 to 40 Mexican-Americans that are called retarded, putting together clothes hangers, and while you are there let the tears rain down from your eyes and tell yourself we are not a sick people. And go to the high schools to see how they make dropouts and how they tell our children they can never go to college.

How many wrecks do we have parked out on the streets and in our front yards? The used car lots take us for suckers every time we buy an old car. How many times are we turned down for a loan from a bank? You know very well that we go to the only place in town that will give us a washing-machine on time, but they charge us 100 dollars more for it. This man has been doing this to us for years. There is also a clothing store downtown.......

When has your landlord ever done anything about repairing his house? Instead, the roof leaks, there is no fence for your children, the plaster cracks and babies eat it.

Now, let's ask ourselves -- do we want to keep on living like this? --that is, like rats in a trap where there is no chance of escaping? Look around and see our old people -- see how they were never to escape. Our own people that have "made it" have never helped us. Instead, they stay away from us as far as they can and put cream and white powder on their ladies. The ones in politics give us only talk.

But you know there are over 25 thousand of us living in the Barrios and we cover the entire West Side of Tucson. By getting together we can become the strongest people in Tucson, and we can take action to better ourselves, to protect our women and children, to be strong in our bodies and to have pride in ourselves as a group and not just as a single person alone. Join with the Young-Mexican-American Association. We are among the very few who have opened this road. The YMAA is made of men who work as dishwashers, busboys, yardworkers, laborers. They are men who understand your way of talking, and that is Mexican-American Spanish. They are not Mexican American teachers, lawyers, and doctors who say they represent us but who have sold us out for big jobs.

Join now with the YMAA to start moving our people in the Barrios, y que VIVA LA RAZA EN LOS BARRIOS DE TUCSON

To join or contact the YMAA, call me at 624-3198, or see Albert Miranda at 5007 S. Liberty Ave, or write to the YMAA, P.O. Box 2054, Tucson, Az.

Sincerely,
Frank Gonzalez Wood

HELPMOBILE MAKING WEEKLY VISITS

by Dolores V. Sanchez

For many weeks the National Council of Jewish Women has provided a bus t help the women of the area to learn how to sew, how to use surplus commodities, first aid, crafts, and numerous things of interest to the women.

The National Council of Jewish Women is a nationwide organization. It is run by donations and contributions, and funds are also raised by fashion shows, dinners, etc.

For example, here at MAYO we have ha sewing, food preparation, and flower making. At the present time we are making Christmas decorations for the church. All the materials are being supplied by the Jewish Women and the donate their time to come and teach how to make things.

A cordial invitation is extended to each and every one of you who is interested. Let us all show the Jewis Women that we are interested in thei services. We will be expecting you every Wednesday morning at ten (till 12 noon).

BURRUEL VOTED IN

At the November 5 general meeting of MAYO, Mrs. Jolivet asked if one person from the area might be a member of the group of Mexican-Americans that will go to discuss problems with School District Number One. The members present proceeded to elect Joaquin Burruel, 1224 N. 14th who is also secretary of the Executive Board of MAYO.

All the residents should feel free to give their ideas and opinions to Joaquin, since the problems to be discussed are so very important and so close to all of us.

REDACCION - EDITORIAL BOARD

Redactores:

Ramon Jaurigue
Pete Lopez
Teddy Acuna

Youth Editor:

Cecilia Valencia

LA VOZ DE MAYO is published each month by the Mexican American Yaqui Organization of Tucson, Arizona.

LA VOZ DE MAYO

THE VOICE OF BARRIOS PASCUA, ADELANTO, AND ORACLE PARK (BLUE MOON) 2075 N. CALLE CENTRAL TUCSON, AZ. PHONE 622-5680
VOLUME I, NUMBER 3   MEXICAN AMERICAN YAQUI ORGANIZATION (MAYO)   DECEMBER, 1969

NUEVO ATAQUE CONTRA LOS BARRIOS

A new attack against the barrios has again been started through the Dept. of Community Development of the City of Tucson. They have prepared a plan called the Community Renewal Program to acquire a lot of land in the Model Cities Area which at present has many people living on it. And then they plan to change the zoning to industrial, and make an industrial park out of it.

I am speaking mainly about Old Pascua. If they succeed in doing this, we have had it!

Now they have come up with a new program which is the proposed East-West freeway (and the Butterfield freeway) which are planned to cut through the Model Cities Area. As proposed they will be very disruptive, and will destroy many homes and will destroy many schools and will erect tremendous additional barriers in the barrios. If freeway plans are passed, we have had it, even if building does not begin soon. People will be displaced in our barrios and other barrios. The total freeway plan would displace about 12000 people, 4000 homes and many schools. We must act now and protect ourselves against this unethical way of trying to get rid of our barrios!

They say that the Community Renewal Program was undertaken by the City with citizen participation and was supported by city staff and consultants, but as far as we know the citizens are the last ones to know what is being done for them, or shall we say what is being done to them. How much do we actually need freeways unless we need them to make a quick getaway from the actual problems that are present and have been for many years. Do you people think that this is the way we are going to save our barrios from further deterioration?
I doubt that our neighbors on the East & North sides like to see money spent on these big freeways when taxes are so high and there are so many people who need food, health care and better homes. I do not think the citizens of Tucson will approve of us losing our land and our homes if they are really informed.

NUESTROS BARRIOS

IN SAILAM
por Manuel Alvarez

Senu o ou tuii cobaco jita junevahae-tuco jibasu tabuic batoita anattemaine hua ajuneiyatuane. Buume o-ouwim chea jita juneiya, tequil, nocpo, jiosiapo ajioste o tui cobata jipueu, chuipia, ta inichupia ca sime agueiya, mamni tacam batoim nasuc, guepula teune amacsan, junuen vetchivo, tuisi vejee senu o ou tutulita sugua jipuetuco. Ta itepo quia o ouwim jibba: ?Cabe itom mastac jitasa te a awene? Catem jainea sime inime, yorim, mericano, necrom, itom aniane itepo jun aneta-neco. Ta ini ama ayuc naue te tequi-panuane, ca oviachi itomac anne ca nochaec ca nocne quia guene itomac culp-ti, ica te jiccaine (hacer bola, huitti eme ke ajiccaja) Catem majae o ousi em ane itom asoam simeta ji-pune; empo o ou caita ajoa enchi amastane, teguil, oficio, entureu caita vejetuane.

Nechem jiocole, ochalim, malam, ussi hiohuim ini ne netane: sancuata te lleutoibay imi itom joarapo, Adelanto, Blue Moon, itom emania. Emou ne Lios boania utteasi.

Un nuevo ataque contra los barrios se ha empezado por el Departamento del Desarollo de la Comunidad de Tucson. Ellos han preparado un plan que se llama Community Renewal Program para conseguir mucho terreno en el area de Ciudad Modelo que ahora tiene muchos habitantes. Y quieren cambiar el zonamiento para hacer un parque industrial.

Estoy hablando principalmente de Old Pascua. Si ellos tienen éxito, ya se ha acabado todo para nosotros!

Ahora tienen un programa nuevo que es el propuesto freeway este-oeste (y Butterfield) que correrían por el area Ciudad Modelo. Van a destruir muchas casas y muchas escuelas, y levantarán nuevas y tremendas barricadas en los barrios. Si pasan los planes, todo se ha acabado, aunque la construccion no empieze muy pronto. Gente sera desemplazado en nuestros barrios y otros barrios. El plan total desemplazara aproximada-mente 12,000 personas, 4000 casas, y muchas escuelas. Tenemos que actuar inmediatamente, para protegerno contra este modo inmoral de quitarnos de nuestros barrios!

Se dice que el Community Renewal Program fué empezado por la ciudad con la participacion de los ciudadanos y fué apoyado por staff y consejeros de la ciudad, pero a nosotros nos parece que los ciudadanos son los últimos para oir que se está haciendo por ellos, o diremos contra ellos. ¿Cuanto nece-sitamos los freeways a menos que se usaran para escaparse de los problemas actuales? ¿Creen ustedes que en esta manera vamos a salvar nuestros barrios de mas deterioracion?

Dudo que nuestros vecinos del norte y este de Tucson quieren ver dinero gas tado en grandes freeways cuando los impuestos estan tan altos y hay tanta gente en necesidad de comida, ayuda medica, y casas. No creo que los ciu dadanos de Tucson aprobarán de nosotros perdiendo nuestro terreno y nuestras casas, si ellos estan bien informados.

Ramon Jaurigue
Editor

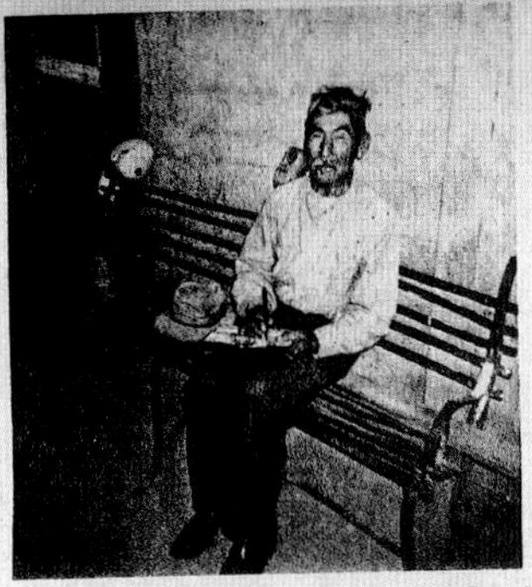

Don Manuel Alvarez, sitting in front of his home, works on one of his monthly contributions in Yaqui to LA VOZ DE MAYO.

AROUND MAYO

Most of you know by now that Pima County Adult Basic Education classes are taking place at Richey school Mon. to Thurs. 7 - 9 pm for English and GED. There are now 50 students in basic English and 70 studying for their GED. We give our thanks to the people who are making this program possible.....

A new member has been chosen to join the group that will discuss problems with School District 1: Mrs. Eleanor Jimenez. Feel free to give your ideas to her and to Joaquin Burruel.....

At the last MAYO meeting, after discussion, the members decided to do away with the old studyhall system, and now the studyhall is open to adults, and also to youth when the adults are using it.....

Porque hay poder en unidad, let's start getting more people to our monthly meetings. There were 73 at the last meeting, a big drop from our first meeting with 300 Remember: meetings at Richey School the first Wed. of every month at 7:30 pm......

Again we thank Mrs. Concha Ruiz and Miss Dolores Sanchez for providing a wonderful lunch for the cleanup workers. And thanks to those who help serve. Let's all KEEP COOPERATING IN THE CLEAN-UP PROJECT.....

Thanks to Station KTKT for the toys for the December 21 kids' party! and to J. C. Penney for the Santa Claus outfit.....

Doctrina classes with our friends from the UA Newman Club will begin again Sunday January 4th...

****

Scouts See Archie Moore

Our Tropa Loca, MAYO Boy Scout Troop #221, had three representatatives at the luncheon with world champion boxer Archie Moore. The luncheon took place at the Pioneer Hotel on Thursday, Dec. 18th. Our three MAYO reps were Ricky Cocio, Rudy Sigueiros, and Ralph Jaurigue.

CARTAS

To The People Of MAYO:

You and your friends throughout Pima County have been concerned for a number of years about getting prompt medical care at the Pima County Hospital. Professionals at the hospital and others have also been concerned. The Pima County Board of Supervisors have started to take action. There has been improvements but no statement of public policy so that you are really sure about what is going on.

On Saturday, December 6, 1969 a group met at the YWCA. They are calling themselves the Citizens' Coalition for Social Action. There were representatives from various groups in town including Ramon Jaurigue and Ralph Gomez from MAYO. A delegation will be asking the County Board of Supervisors to make a public declaration of policy about admission proceedures and to take a stand on improving the entire hospital particularly the emergency room.

The group was concerned about all people needing prompt medical care including people with emotional problems. There was also concern about non-citizens, especially Mexican citizens and concern about rich or poor who may have to suffer unnecessary pain waiting for help.

The representatives at the group were not looking for and did not ask for free medical care for everybody. The request to be made is that people be treated first and billed later and say what they can afford.

Many people have said we should not ask. The county doesn't have the money. The county does spend money on many other things. Which is more important, people's health or costly county roads? Others have said some people are dishonest and will try to get free care. Are the people who use the county hospital anymore dishonest than other people? Are the people of the barrios, poor people anymore dishonest then anyone else? The federal government simply has everyone make out a report of what they earned for income tax forms and then checks later. Everyone knows from the federal government experience there are dishonest people - rich, middle class and poor. There are dishonest Yaquis, Mexicans, Blacks, Anglos... The federal government still relies on the word of the man making out his income tax form because MOST PEOPLE ARE HONEST.

We think most people are honest about needing medical care. Let's get behind Ramon, Ralph and the other who are trying to fight for a better county hospital where they treat you first and ask questions later.

Howard Rouch

Senor Redactor:

Soy residente del barrio que cae dentro de la Unidad Ciudad Modelo Número 1.

Algunos creen que el nombre de nuestra Unidad es "El Rio - Manzo." Por medió de esta carta deseo expresar que la Unidad se llama sencillamente "El Rio" porque ya no somos tan mansitos como antes. Puede que algun día nos demos el nombre de "El Rio Bronco," o "El Rio Bravo."

Atentamente,
Ricardo Luis

READERS of LA VOZ:

By now you have at one time or another heard of Y.M.A.A. In order to bring everything there is to know about it we have prepared this letter. We ask you to take time to read it so that you may know Y.M.A.A., and what it can do for you - should you decide to join us.

As a group it has already done for you such things as cleaning up barrios, demanding better parks, more and better paying jobs, better schools and many other things that the young Chicano husband needs to provide the best for his family. Less Chicano youngsters are now getting arrested and sniffing glue; while older Chicanos are teaching them not to break the law.

Y.M.A.A. protects the Chicano family as a group and will do for a member things like tell the renter to send a professional roach killer to spray the house, fence the yard for the safety of children, to discount rent if members paint and repair his house.

We also have connections which will solve many problems directly. If it be collections, social security or back wages, we as a group, will get fast results.

Although this may sound like talk that politicians and others give, we want you to know that we have been doing this for three years and it is because Y.M.A.A. is made up of people such as yourself.

They are drop-outs, have an arrest record, and are poor. Y.M.A.A. is not a religion. They are just Chicanos from Los Barrios helping each other. For fun and play the Y.M.A.A. has soft ball games, carne asadas and parties.

In order that a young Chicano will have a chance to become someone, we of Y.M.A.A. are against bad schools, bad jobs, bad police, bad courts, bad housing, and bad parks. So - if you are ready to stand up and be part of a proud group - join us NOW and be counted.

Three months ago Y.M.A.A. rented a building for its Center at 902 North Main - across from John Spring School We have a second-hand store where members will buy at half price; an office to take care of problems, a backyard to repair broken cars - as soon as we get some big tools.

As you see we really work for LA RAZA so don't you think it's time we stop cutting up each other in bars and learn to fight the real enemy? You are welcome to our Center open on week-ends, to get more information. No need to dress up to come, as you will be among your own people.

Todos Juntos, Adelante
Frank Gonzales Wood
YMAA Tu Sabes

LA VOZ DE MAYO is published each month by the Mexican American Yaqui Organization of Tucson, Arizona.

MERRY CHRISTMAS
TO OUR READERS

HISTORIA DE LAS POSADAS

por Felizardo Valencia

LAS POSADAS son una novena navideña que recuerda las jornadas de José y María de Nazaret a Belén en anticipación del nacimiento del Niño Jesús. La palabra POSADA significa alojamiento, y LAS POSADAS conmemoran en particular la búsqueda de alojamiento por José y María cuando estos nobles esposos llegaron a Belén para cumplir con el edicto del emperador Romano, César Augusto, que todo el mundo se empadronara. Los Santos Esposos venían de Nazaret, una ciudad en Galilea, a Belén, una ciudad en Judea, por ser José de la casa y familia de David. María estaba encinta, y pronto daría a luz a su hijo primogénito, a quien le llamarían Jesús.

En el año de 1587, un fraile agustiniano, Fray Diego de Soria, O.S.A., introdujo la novena, LAS POSADAS, en la iglesia de Acolman en México con el fin de combatir la costumbre pagana de los indios aztecas quienes solían honrar al dios guerrero, Huitzilopochtli, durante la temporada que corresponde a la Navidad en el calendario cristiano. La intención de este fraile fué de instituir una devoción cristiana que no solo le hiciera las debidas honras al Niño Jesus en su adviento, sino que también sirviera para contrarrestar o por lo menos minimizar la atención que los indios le daban al rito pagano.

Poco se imaginaba este ingenioso fraile en aquel tiempo que sus dedicados esfuerzos perdurarían a través de los siglos. Hoy casi a los cuatrocientos años después, LAS POSADAS no solamente se han establecido como una tradición religiosa y cultural por todo México, sino que además se han extendido por el extranjero. Y en su amplia extensión, la celebración de LAS POSADAS ha producido un entusiasmo y fervor espiritual marcado en los participantes. No cabe duda que el agraciado Fray Diego de Soria con la invención de LAS POSADAS le dio al mundo hispanoparlante un instrumento de oración que sirvió para llenar el vacuo espiritual que ¡había existido al aproximarse la Navidad. En lugares donde LAS POSADAS se han acostumbrado, la gente espera con ansias porque únicamente con la celebración de LAS POSADAS habrá de tener la Navidad un significado completo para ellos. Por esta misma razón, se espera que en aquellos lugares donde LAS POSADAS

no se han verificado y cuando por primera vez se celebren, la gente exigirá que se continúen año por año.

¿A que se debe la popularización de LAS POSADAS en esta época moderna? Para darle contesta a esta pregunta, hay que recordar el motivo inicial que causó la introducción de LAS POSADAS. En aquel tiempo, los indios aztecas ni se interesaban ni mucho menos se preparaban para la llegada del Niño Jesus porque toda su atención la dirigían a la adoración del dios pagano. Cuando se introdujeron LAS POSADAS que son una historia netamente humana que está adornada con ceremonia y color, los indios de pronto rehusaron la costumbre pagana por darle preferencia a LAS POSADAS. Pues bien cabe hacer una comparación semejante en esta época moderna. Ahora en vez de ser un dios pagano el que atrae el interés de la gente al acercarse la Navidad, lo es el carácter comercialista que en muchos lugares ha substituido al tema espiritual que debidamente corresponde a la Navidad, una fiesta santa. Mucha gente se ha dedicado tan exclusivamente a dar y recibir regalos durante la estación navideña que hasta han perdido vista el origen religioso de este gran día. Desde luego que dar y recibir regalos no es cosa mala. Por lo contrario, puede ser obra de caridad y amistad. Sin embargo esta costumbre cesa de ser laudable cuando causa que uno olvide el espíritu navideño verdadero que en efecto es honrar a Jesucristo en su nacimiento. Y este viene siendo el propósito fundamental de LAS POSADAS -- HONRAR A JESUCRISTO EN SU NACIMIENTO.

✳ ✳ ✳ ✳ ✳

Peace, Love, and Freedom

The moon shines her glistening rays
over the endless desert.
The giant saguaros cast their tall
man-like shadows
Stretching their hands
toward the star-filled sky.

If you used your imagination
the saguaros can be men
stretching out their hands
in prayer,
begging God for

PEACE, LOVE
and FREEDOM

Gloria Jimenez

CESAR CHAVEZ EN TUCSON

Ramon Jaurigue, editorial staff of LA VOZ, speaks with Cesar Chavez at the Press Conference held at the Inner City Center on December 4th.

✳ ✳ ✳ ✳ ✳ ✳

El día tres de Diciembre fué un día muy importante en Tucson: César Chavez el líder de la Huelga y el Boicoteo de la uva vino a Tucson.

César vino a Tucson en la última parte de un viaje alrededor de todos los estados, con el propósito de buscar mas apoyo para el movimiento. Los huelguistas han luchado por sus derechos de tener una unión por 4 años ahora, pero los rancheros ricos permanecen tercos. Han traido esquiroles (scab workers) de Mexico, y la cosecha de la uva ha continuado. Por eso los campesinos en huelga están dependiendo completamente en el boicoteo. Cada persona que no compra uvas esta ayudando a la causa. La venta de uvas en Tucson ha bajado 33%, y los rancheros han perdido $25 millones, pero todavía se han rehusado a entrar en negociaciones con la Unión de Trabajadores. Y por eso la Huelga y el Boicoteo están continuando.

No compremos ni una sola uva, para ayudar a nuestros hermanos en los campos sin ninguna protección, mal pagados, y víctimas de patrones que se estan haciendo mas ricos con un sistema de esclavitud.

Viva César Chavez y Viva La Causa!

A "no" uttered from deepest conviction is better and greater than a "yes" merely uttered to please or what is worse, to avoid trouble.

Gandhi

YOUTH NEWS

by Cecilia Valencia

Lots of things going on lately among young MAYO people.....

On Sunday Dec. 14th, the gang from the Newman Center who teach the 6 to 11's gave the kids a Christmas party at the center.

And the next Sunday, Dec. 21, there was another Christmas party, this one presented by members of the old LINK staff, our own ANIMADOS, and LOS DORADOS.

Lots of young people in the Posadas each night too. At this writing, there are three more nights for throwing "confites y canelones pa' los muchachos que son muy tragones."

Richard Flores has retired as the President of LOS ANIMADOS. Many thanks to el ex-presidente for all that he did during his time in office. Who will be the new President?

LAS POSADAS

by Teddy Acuña

Something new in our MAYO barrios this year at Christmas time... the nine days of LAS POSADAS.

Right from the first there was fine participation, and everybody caught on to the songs quickly. There was terrific participation of guitarr-istas right from the first too. At this writing we've two nights to go, and we're sure they will be every bit as successful. Thanks go to all who helped in making these POSADAS successful....those who help-ed get the kids dressed up, control "traffic", etc., and those families to whose homes we went "pidiendo posada": Ramon Lopez, A. Gallardo, Teddy Acuna, Ceci Valencia, M.Moreno, G. Salgado, Pete Lopez, Josie Gas-telum, Tilly Ybanez, R. Jaurigue, J. Valenzuela, Mary Mendoza, Pete Al-varez, Concha Ruiz, Emilia Kron, Henrietta Womack, Felipe Olivas,and Emma Gallardo.

GRACIAS A TODOS!

RALph GOMEZ Resident Consultant

by Ramon Jaurigue

As you all know by now, the inter-viewing and hiring committee of MAYO met on the evening of Dec. 8 and in-terviewed six candidates for the pos-ition of resident consultant, follow-ing the procedure recommended by the Project Director Richard Holmes, for publicizing the opening, receiving applications, and conducting the interviews.

Following the interviews, the comm-ittee conferred to select the most qualified applicant.

We chose Mr. Ralph Gomez, 613 West Lester St., as the most qualified applicant, to begin work immediately. We also chose Miss Erlinda Galaz, 2040 N. Calle Central, to be the next most qualified, in case Mr. Gomez is unavailable to work.

At the hiring session, observers were present representing the Training and Technical Assistance Program (Richard Holmes) and the City Demonstration Agency (Michael Maloney). The Comm-ittee for Economic Opportunity was invited to send an observer, but he was not present.

MAYO wishes to thank the Model Neigh-borhood Council for their ready coop-eration to get our Unit on equal foot-ing with the other five units.

by Mrs. Dolores Lopez

I am the group leader of the Campfire Girls at Richey School. I have twenty four wonderful girls.

We had a successful candy sale. Thank you to Hope's Salon, La Fuente, China Palace and Tucson House for letting the girls come in and sell some of their candy.

We weren't allowed to sell candy at the Statler Hilton. But the manager says it is not impossible to get dona-tions for the girls.

There is a lot more to do, and we need all the help we can get.

Our children don't have the opportuni-ties the Anglo-Saxon has.

The Campfire Girls have the Law - the Objectives of the Campfire Girls.

We want the opportunity to make friends with other Campfire Girls. To do things in groups like camping, to go on hikes, to take a picnic lunch, crafts, hobbies, etc.

We need the parents help. And YOU out there to extend a helping hand, donations to help us fulfill our needs. Thank you.

A NEW DAY

The dawn kisses the earth with
the glow of warmth and love,
The dew sheds its glistening pearls
on a blushing rose,
The air smells of daisies as bright
as heaven above,
The frost is melting in the warm
rays of the sun of early morn.
The birds are singing their praises
as a new day is born.

Gloria Jimenez
Grade 6
Richey School

Progress in Operation Clean-up continues. Above left, Connie Jimenez and Elena Ruiz prepare food for the workers. In the center picture, truck driver Frank Gonzalez Wood talks with volunteers from the UA Newman Club. And at the right, four of our own MAYO workers gain strength before going back to work for the afternoon session. Come and join us next time!

LA VOZ DE MAYO

THE VOICE OF BARRIOS PASCUA, ADELANTO, AND ORACLE PARK (BLUE MOON) 2075 NORTH CALLE CENTRAL TUCSON, ARIZONA
VOLUME I, NUMBER 4 MEXICAN AMERICAN YAQUI ORGANIZATION (MAYO) JANUARY AND FEBRUARY, NINETEEN SEVENTY

SUPERVISORS FACE PEOPLE FEB. 3

There has been concern for a number of years about the immediate accessibility of medical care for persons seeking treatment at the Pima County Hospital. Residency requirements and financial eligibility red tape have frequently been the excuse for the hospital not providing necessary care to patients. Lack of space, inadequate staff, staff attitudes and other factors have resulted in problems in a system of county medical care which is degrading to its recipients and (without questioning the skill of the existing staff) is also providing inadequate treatment.

A report which called for immediate action on the part of the Board of Supervisors and County Hospital Administrators to study the situation was completed on June 10, 1967 by the Tucson Community Council. In June, 1969, requested by the Board of Supervisors, an Ad Hoc Committee report reviewing the Social Service Department also addressed itself to some of the hospital's problems. There has been token improvement at the hospital.

There is still much to be done.

On Saturday December 6, 1969, a group of concerned Tucsonans met at the Y.W.C.A. to discuss the Pima County Hospital. The group, known as the Citizens' Coalition for Social Action proposed that there is need for immediate action by the County Board of Supervisors to accept health care as a human right, and a human right that involves the preservation of the worth and dignity of the person receiving such care. Admission procedures must be based on medical need. Treatment should be in a facility with adequate space, adequate equipment, and adequate personnel. Eligibility should never be a barrier to the provision of treatment at this faacility in a situation wherein there is an acute need. The deployment of funds, facilities and personnel for excellent care of the sick should be the highest priority of the county.

Father Alberto Carrillo, of the Inner City Center, will address the Board of Supervisors on behalf of the Citizen's Coalition for Social Action on February 3 at 10:30 in the morning, at 131 West Congress, the 11th floor. Your endorsement of these recommendations would be most appreciated. A letter to the Board of Supervisors by your organization would be most helpful in solving the problem. A representative from your organization at the February 3 Board Meeting at 10:30 a.m. would be even more helpful.

Ramon Jaurigue

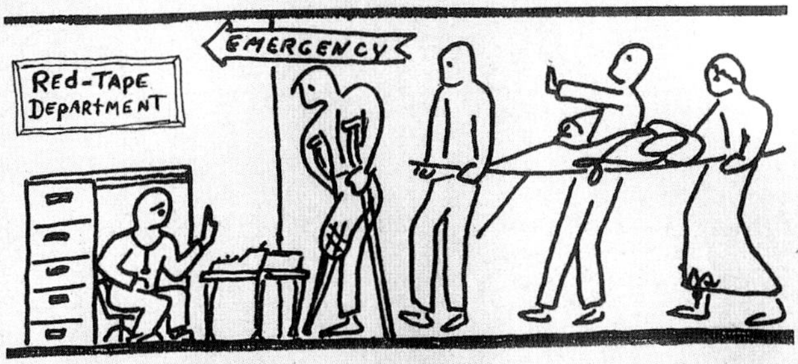
EMERGENCY
RED-TAPE DEPARTMENT

Por unos años ahora, la gente se ha preocupado sobre la accesibilidad inmediata de cuidado médico para las personas buscando tratamiento en el Pima County Hospital. Requisitos de residencia y elegibilidad financiera han sido frecuentemente una excusa para el hospital para no dar la ayuda necesaria a los pacientes. Falta de espacio, y personal, actitudes de personal, y otras cosas han resultado en problemas en un sistema de cuidado médico que degrada a los pacientes y (sin dudar la habilidad del personal presente) provee tratamiento inadecuado.

Despues de dos reportes, por el Tucson Community Council en 1967 y un Comité Ad Hoc en 1969, había un poco de mejoramiento. Todavía queda mucho para hacer.

Sábado, 6 Dec. 1969 había una junta de Tucsonenses preocupados, en la YWCA, para discutir el hospital del Condado. El grupo, nombrado Citizen's Coalition for Social Action, hizo la propoción que hay necesidad de accion inmediata de parte de la Mesa de Supervisores del Condado, para aceptar el cuidado médico como un derecho humano, y un derecho humano que envuelve la preservacion del valor y de la dignidad de la persona que está recibiendo dicho cuidado. Procesos de admision deben ser basados en la necesidad médica. Los tratamientos deben estar en facilidades con espacio adecuado, equipo adecuado, personal adecuado. Elegibilidad nunca debe ser un obstáculo a la provisión de tratamiento en esta facilidad en una situacion en donde haya una necesidad grave. La distribucion de fondos, facilidades y personal para el cuidado excelente de los enfermos debe ser la prioridad mayor del Condado.

El Padre Alberto Carrillo, del Apostolado de los Barrios, hablará a la Mesa de Supervisores en nombre de la Citizens' Coalition for Social Action el día 3 de Febrero, a las 10:30 por la mañana, en 131 West Congress, el piso once. **El respaldo** de todos ustedes para con estas recomendaciones sería muy agradecido. Una carta dirigida a la Mesa de Supervisores por su organizacion ayudaría mucho para resolver los problemas. Un representante en la junta de 3 Feb. a las 10:30 a.m. ayudaria aún mas.

a pile of rubble .....
then cleared ground .....
and a church rises .....
San Ignacio is back !

The men nail and saw
while the women cook
and the heart of a village
comes to new life .....

JUNTA GENERAL DE MAYO

PRIMER MIERCOLES DE CADA MES EN

RICHEY SCHOOL

7:30 P.M.   TODOS INVITADOS

Recently there was a meeting called for the people of the pueblo to see whether they wanted to hold their Easter ceremonies here.

When it was decided that they did want them here, plans were laid for immediate re-construction of the church. They collected any material they could get hold of, both within the village and through donations from outside.

Capable hands quickly brought the results seen in the above photos. Many ornaments have also been added, and a bell and other necessities are expected to be on hand soon.

It was also decided that the following people would be those in charge: Juan Easbrol, Francisco F. Ochoa, Manuel F. Valencia, Teresa P. Ochoa, Marcelina Robles, and Secundina A. Acuña.

When the first Mass was celebrated the afternoon of January 28, Felipe Olivas reminded all to see to it that the church and the plaza be given due respect.

All of us look with pride to the work that the people have done here with their hands and their hearts. And we all look forward to the return this year of the ceremonies of Lent and Holy Week.

R. J.

35% of School District No. 1's labor force is minority. All of these people are found in the lower half in responsibility and salary. 42% of these are janitorial.

Tucson School District No. 1, 1968: 66% of children in retarded classes were minority children. Mexican-Americans, being 25% of the District, were 47% of the retarded classes. Blacks, being 5.1% of the District, were 15% of the retarded classes. But Anglos, being 67% of the District, were only 34% of the retarded classes.

NO HAY ??? DISCRIMINACION

You hear things like this do not happen any more. But they do.

The following remarks came from a California Superior Court Judge, Gerald S. Chargin, speaking while sitting in Santa Clara County Juvenile Court.

In passing sentence on a 17 year old Mexican-American youth, Judge Chargin said (according to court transcript:

"Mexican people, after 13 years of age, it's perfectly all right to go out and act like an animal. We ought to send you out of the country ---send you back to Mexico. You belong in prison for the rest of your life for doing things of this kind. You ought to commit suicide. That's what I think of people of this kind. You are lower than animals and haven't the right to live in organized society---just miserable, lousy, rotten people. Maybe Hitler was right. The animals in our society probably ought to be destroyed because they have no right to live among human beings."

LA VOZ has heard that Chargin has been removed. He had just better be.

Well, Lent Season is almost here. I have news for our people. I am happy to announce that this year we are going to have the Easter ceremonies here in the village. I know the people who live here in the village are more than happy to have them here rather than have them at the new village. It was quite a problem when they were having them at the new village. There were problems like transportation, and no place to stay, especially for people who did not have relatives living over there. Or if they did, other people were staying there too, etc.

I do not know how the people from the new village feel towards this. I can only guess. But the majority of people who have taken part or take part in the ceremonies live here.

And also, in the first place, why did the men demolish the church without consulting or letting the people know about what they had in store as far as the church was concerned. I am speaking about the men who took part in this, or for that matter anybody who took part in it. Do you think it was really worth it? Do you think you will gain something out of it?

You could not wait, could you, right after my grandfather passed away. My grandfather taught all the second generation about the ceremonies and our culture. He was the head of the church. When he died in 1967, you could not even wait six months to start tearing the church down. I know some of you people disliked my grandfather very much, what he said and believed in. He taught almost every one of you except the elders to take part in the ceremonies, or a little something that you know now. You do it the way he taught you, and the thanks you gave him was destroying the church after he passed away.

These words have been directed to those who destroyed the church.

I know that my grandfather will be happy that the church has been built again. May he rest in peace.

Teddy Acuña

YMAA COMES TO END

Frank Gonzalez Wood brought us the following letter just before we went to press. It tells of the end of the Young Mexican American Association.

YMAA was founded over two years ago for the purpose of tying together crime prevention and rehabilitation. For the first time in Tucson, there was a group of ex-Fort Grant and ex-Florence young men ready to work for the betterment of all of Tucson.

Their main method was to get changed hardened criminals to advise youngsters to go straight, and at the same time to keep the members busy through brotherhood.

To get quicker results YMAA also attacked bad police policy. So for more than two years we asked, pleaded and begged for citizens in power to give money and equipment.

But we have seen the light. Therefore we are calling it quits. We thank the few who did help us.

YMAA will keep its club house open, which is called EL QUINTO PATIO. Here members will keep to themselves, and they will read books, play checkers and cards, watch TV, listen to radio, play records, talk and drink coffee.

As a group we will play our softball team, the "Tu Sabes", and have our annual carne asada, never forgetting to be carnales. Anyone is welcome to visit, but to ask us to attend meetings, etc. is taboo, and will only bring displeasure.

****

(Editor's note: Just in case any of our readers missed it in the press and on radio and TV, charges against Frank G. Wood regarding the UA-BYU incident were dropped on January 26. Wood and his witnesses gave assurance that he was nowhere near the University gym before, during or after the incident.)

PEÑA HOME BURNS

The burning of their house on Calle Sahuaro on January 26 was a disaster for the Valentin Peña family. But we thank God that the family escaped unharmed. And we give thanks to all those who came to the aid of the family.

BEAUTY

Beauty is
the first rays of sunlight touching the clear blue sky with its bright golden fingers.

Beauty is
a dove soaring over a blue lake spreading peace to all who are watching.

Beauty is
our flag flying free in the air Promising love and freedom to all mankind.

Gloria Jimenez
Richey School

FIESTA

CARTAS

Esta es una comunicación para enterar a su público de una organización nuevo que se acaba de formar. Creo es de suma importancia a la gente los barrios de habla española. Esta organización lleva el nombre de P.A.D.R.E.S. (Padres Asociados para Derechos Religiosos, Educativos, y Sociales) Es una organización de Padres Mexicano-Americanos y otros sacerdotes que han dedicado sus vidas y sus talentos a la gente de habla española en los Estados Unidos.

Esta organizacion se originó en San Antonio, Texas, en Octubre del año pasado, y ahora se ha extendido por todo el Sud Oeste y el resto de los EE. UU. donde existe el pueblo Mexicano, Cubano, Puertoriqueño, o en general gente de habla hispana.

La razón de esta organización es el hecho que en los EE. UU. hay doce millones de gente Catolica que habla español. Esto encompasa a un cuarta de la población católica total en los EE. UU. o en palabras mas sencillas....uno de cada cuatro católicos en los EE, UU, habla español. Sin embargo, aunque hay tantos de habla hispana, no hay ningún obispo Mexicano, Cubano, o Puertoriqueño. En el nivel legislativo de la iglesia catolica no existe ninguna representacion de la gente de habla español.

De entre esos 12 millones de Católicos de habla hispana proporcionalmente hay muy pocos sacerdotes y monjitas. No podemos aceptar que Dios no ofrece vocaciones en abundancia al pueblo de habla hispana. Es lógico entonces que el problema existe dentro de la misma estructura de la Iglesia en el sistema de seminarios que no han apoyado al jóven de origen latino. En tantas parroquias mexicanas o de habla hispana no hay sacerdotes que hablan el español o entienden a la gente en suficiente para instruir y hacer el mensaje de Cristo aplicable a los tiempos de hoy.

Esta organización no está en contra de nadie o de nada. Esta POR nuestra raza. Por mas efectivo envolvimiento de la Iglesia en las necesidades y problemas de nuestra gente. POR visible dirección de parte de la iglesia a nuestra gente. POR cosas que no se han hecho y necesitan hacerse entre nuestra gente de parte de la Iglesia Catolica. POR los derechos religiosos, educativos y sociales de nuestra gente.

El día dos de Febrero se juntarán aquí en Tucson más de 300 sacerdotes de todas partes de los EE. UU. en conferencia nacional. No tanto para discutir problemas pero para hacer resoluciones y demandas a la iglesia. Para levantar una voz fuerte y un frente sólido de Padres hablando por los derechos de la gente.

P. Vicente Soriano
Director Regional
P.A.D.R.E.S.

And East-West comparison:
Catalina High cost $4,200,000.
Pueblo High cost $2,700,000.00

EDITORIAL: YOUTH EDITOR SPEAKS OUT

Schools are trying too hard to make children believe that people in positions of authority are always right. In a classroom the teacher is the authority and whatever she says is right because she is the teacher, even if it does not make sense to the child. If a child thinks about a question in a different way, a way that seems right to him, he is usually told that is the wrong answer. That is why too many of our children today are afraid to speak up, because they are not given the chance to speak for themselves. That is why many of us are finding out that the only way people will listen to us and treat us like human beings is by standing up and fighting for our rights. This also makes children worry about saying things the teacher will like, instead of figuring things out themselves. So children learn not to think for themselves just because of what the teacher says.

In poor communities especially, schools make children afraid --- afraid to act different, afraid of arguing with the teacher, afraid of getting the wrong answer. Schools indoctrinate children not only the way they teach, but also by what they teach them.

Schools try to give children a middle class picture of what life is really like. Books that are used to teach children to read tell about white people who live in suburbs with nice houses.

Sometimes I think that children from slum neighborhoods learn their lessons so well that when they are asked to draw pictures of the houses they live in, they draw pictures of the houses they see in their readers. And other children, who are not that stupid or are not fooled that easily, see that this is just the opposite of what they learn from their own lives. So they stop trying to learn, and when they get older, they drop out. So the only other choice for them now is to decide that the school is right about life and they are wrong, so they begin to mistrust their own judgment and consider themselves inferior. A lot has to be said about us Mexicans. People might consider us lazy, but this cannot make us forget our pride and tradition. We have a beautiful culture which we are proud of, and we do not want to suppress it.

Cecilia Valencia

REDACCION - EDITORIAL BOARD

Redactores:

Ramon Jaurigue
Pete Lopez
Teddy Acuña

Youth Editor:

Cecilia Valencia

LA VOZ DE MAYO is published each month by the Mexican American Yaqui Organization of Tucson, Arizona.

MAYO GOES TO PIONEER

January 20, 1970, was a beautiful night. Because we are supposed to be living in what is called a democracy, the people's opinion was asked about the proposed Tucson freeway system. That night the people gave their opinion...a loud, four-hour, unmistakable NO!

There were all kinds of people at the Pioneer Hotel Ballroom, rich and poor and all the in-between people. But nothing was more impressive than the turnout of MAYO people. It is too bad the TATPA men could not see our people gathering at the plaza of San Ignacio and the church of Santa Rosa, while the church bell kept on ringing. We wish they could have seen the people first fill the bus and then the cars that lined up behind. We wish they could have seen everyone pinning on the "no freeways" buttons, made by MAYO young people.

But the TATPA men did see the people of MAYO when we got to the Ballroom. The message came through loud and clear. It was the message printed on the front page of last month's LA VOZ:

Do not tear down our homes. Do not destroy our barrios. Do not wall us in with great barriers of cement. Do not waste the money that is so badly needed by the people for real necessities. Listen to the wisdom of other men who propose practical and sensible solutions to the transportation problem.

The people have spoken....the people of MAYO and the people of all Tucson. The people have spoken in a direct and orderly way because they believe in democracy. Now it is up to the men in the tall buildings downtown to listen. They are there to serve the needs of the people. The people know what they need, and they know what they do not need. And they have made themselves heard.

Gentlemen, no freeways. Period.

Y MAS

Importante! Importante! Aunque dimos un NO absoluto a los propositores de los freeways la noche de 20 Enero, ellos siguen tratando de ser dictadores. La noche de 26 Enero, ellos trataron de dar un plan nuevo al mayor y el concilio de la ciudad - dejando atrás el plan para el freeway este-oeste, pero proponiendo otra vez el Butterfield Freeway (sin usar la palabra Freeway....si, señor...) Afortunadamente unos de nosotros aprendimos de esta trampa una hora antes de la junta, y fuimos a la junta del concilio. En vez de aprobar este freeway (que sería un desastre para los barrios al sur de la catedral y para el nuevo Centro de Salud) el concilio nos dió un Public Hearing la noche de 24 Febrero. Vamos, MAYO, hay poder en la unidad!

AROUND MAYO

No hay un articulo con noticias de Ciudad Modelo en esta edicion porque el proyecto C. M. ya tiene su propio periodico en español y ingles: se llama CHANGING TUCSON. Considerando los editoriales en la primera edicion parece que CHANGING TUCSON será una otra verdadera voz de la gente de los barrios. Buena suerte a la redaccion y personal!

******

Gracias a todos que han ayudado en la resureccion de iglesia de San Ignacio. Hay un articulo entero que habla de los organizadores y los trabajadores en estas paginas; aquí nomas queremos mencionar y darles gracias a los siguientes: Padre Ricardo Cantrell por su regalo de la ramada que formó la primera parte de la nueva estructura....Padres Jose Gorsuch y Arsenio Carrillo por los candeleros y otros ornamentos....todas las personas que nos dieron materiales para extender la iglesia a su tamaño actual.

******

Miraron ustedes el programa FIESTA en el canal 6 cuando nuestros estudiantes en la educacion para adultos aparecieron? Doctor Eiselein de Canal 6 nos dice que esta interesado en la filmación de mas eventos alrededor de MAYO.

******

Muchísimas gracias a la PIMA DEMO-CRATIC COALITION por su ayuda en transportacion la noche de la junta en el Pioneer Hotel. Felipe Mendez y sus tropas ya son una vista familiar en todas las juntas en que luchamos por los derechos de nuestros barrios.

LOS ANIMADOS

LOS ANIMADOS DE MAYO now have a new president. He is Sammy Tapia, and we are all looking forward to working with him in the future. Thanks again to past president Richard Flores for his time in office.

Plans are now being made for a St. Valentine's party for the little children. It will be on February 15th, from one to four, at Santa Rosa Hall. The party will be given by three groups: Los Animados, the Newman Club teachers who work with our kids every Sunday, and the Spanish Club of Salpointe High School.

It was great to have so many members present for the Freeway Hearing at the Pioneer January 20th! By the way, those "No freeways" buttons were an ANIMADOS product.

Rosie Jimenez

******

In School District No. 1, 1968-69 25.7% of the students were Spanish surnamed, yet only 3.5% of the faculty were Spanish surnamed.

LA VOZ DE MAYO

THE VOICE OF MEXICANS, AMERICANS, YAQUIS AND OTHERS, ORGANIZED IN THE BARRIOS OF
PASCUA, ADELANTO, AND BLUE MOON (ORACLE PARK), TUCSON, AZ. VOL. 2 NO. 1 FEB. 1971

Despues de muchos meses de
planear por nuestra iglesia,
el trabajo se comenzó a los
principios de Diciembre 1970.
La plaza había sido destruida
y entonces había sido tempor-
almente reconstruido. Ahora,
finalmente, una iglesia per-
manente ha sido comenzada.

La iglesia de San Ignacio es
para la comunidad como el cubo
es para la rueda. No tenemos
que decir muchas palabras a-
qui - la iglesia hablará por
si misma.

Pero mientras los cimientos
se están instalando, queremos
darles gracias a todos que
han ayudado y seguirán ayudando. Gente de afuera del barrio como Fred Palafox, Roberto
Ruiz y todos los demas, y gente del barrio, que han hecho
las excavaciones y tendrán que
poner los bloques y todo. Y
tambien el departamento de
recreo de la ciudad bajo Gene
Reid que ha cooperado.

Trabajemos en conjunto con
todo nuestro esfuerzo, para
que la Plaza Ceremonial Yaqui
sea una señal de unidad y
orgullo cultural que todos
podemos apreciar.

Pues cooperemos todos a par-
ticipar en la construccion de
la iglesia.

Donde hay unidad, hay poder.
¡Que viva MAYO!

JIBASU JITA YANE

Por Manuel V. Alvarez

Itepo ca coche sime taehua
tequipanua levela tucari tahti.
Qo seenu taca ama gosnaiki abril
mecaci batte sime batora im ho
acame aman te yahak tutuli sime
yaura a tuturiawak besa itom
utteata vempo avichak. Hunuk
tucapo seenu o ou pusimpo opoak
ileni nokac; im ussim emchim
ussimmac aman yaahan Richey
School hunuk o ou osowam nake
tua am nake; eme kechi enchim
ussim tua nake; emeu nokac am
mahtane, ini tui ini ca tui
eme iñaca ussim kaybu govi-
ernota tequil makne; enchim
ussim sua. Govierno vetchivo
ca oviachi ussita buisbaeteco
abuiste jiba tua. Catem emo
baitatta.

Ca sime teguil sepsu natena, ta
wa bat huelle na tebahua; besa
batnataka ne emou nokac ini
tequil vetana.

Juevena itom ussim inim hoomen
tequipanuan haibu sime ussim
vetchivo tequil auk.

After many months of planning
for our church, the work was
begun early in December, 1970.
The plaza had been destroyed;
then it had been temporarily
rebuilt. Now, at last, a permanent church has been begun.

The church of San Ignacio is
to the community like the hub
to the wheel. We do not have
to say many words here - the
church will speak for itself.

But as the foundations go in,
we do want to thank all those
who have helped and will continue helping. People from
outside the barrio like Fred
Palafox, Robert Ruiz and all
the others, and people from
the barrio, who have done the
digging and will have to lay
the blocks and all. And also
the City Recreation Department
under Gene Reid who has cooper-
ated.

Let's work together as hard as
we possibly can, so that the
Yaqui Ceremonial Plaza will be
a sign of unity and cultural
pride that we all can be proud
of.

So let's all join in, and participate in the construction
of the church.

Donde hay unidad, hay poder.
Que viva MAYO!

Ramon Jaurigue and
Teddy Acuña, editors

Continúa en la pagina 2

AROUND MAYO

At a Mayo Board of Directors meeting at Richey School, it was decided that the by-laws be enforced on the Board members who are absent and are not coming to the Board meetings. Also there was discussion of incorporating the organization. Every member that was present approved and passed that the organization be incorporated. It was presented to the residents at a Model Cities Unit meeting Dec. 8, 1970 for approval. There was some discussion and a motion for incorporation was made and passed by the whole body. The paper work on the Articles of Incorporation is now being done and will be discussed at the next Board of Directors meeting for final approval.

+ + + + +

We're really late with this issue, but not too late to thank all who helped and shared in the talent show at Richey and the Christmas Posadas -- also those who decorated the church for Christmas.

+ + + + +

Most everyone must know by now, but we're glad Rafael Gomez is once again our MAYO Model Cities Community Aide.

+ + + + + +

We hear Padre Memo's clases biblicas are getting much enthusiasm. Anyone else interested can talk to Ralph Gomez.

+ + + + +

We of MAYO are overjoyed that the two El Rio groups are now one united Coalition. We believe with all our heart in the motto of the MAYO Organization: HAY PODER en UNIDAD.

+ + + + +

You may have heard the good news already....soon the hall next to Santa Rosa will become a child Day Care Center. More news on this later.

By R.H.J.

NEW DRUG PROGRAM

by Rosie Jimenez

A new drug treatment program, under Tucson-Southern Counties Mental Health, has begun. Twelve barrio counselors will soon work directly with hardcore drug users in the Model Cities area. Two supervisors, both ex-addicts, supervise the counselors. Several of the counselors are also ex-addicts. To learn how to communicate with drug addicts and to be a group therapist is the main purpose of the training program. The training program consists of encounter groups, field training, classroom discussions, and role-playing. When the training is completed the counselors will be out in the streets and working from six storefront centers located in the area.

The counselor is to communicate with the hard-core user and to give help to him if he wants it, through counseling, group therapy, and referral to agencies. A follow-up will be done. The person will also be helped in receiving Methadone. Methadone can be obtained through the treatment program.

Methadone, a synthetic drug, is used to maintain a hard-core addict. The craving for stuff (heroin) is blocked by this drug which is taken orally. The person will be able to feel productive. His life style will begin to change. Methadone will not give him a rush (high), but can be addictive.

Also working with the program are three nurses, an administrator, a social worker, a training coordinator, and a research director.

We hope the drug treatment program will be an effective one.

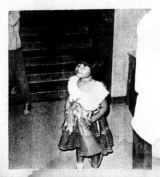

"Backstage at the Richey School talent show......"

JIBASU JITA YANE
por
Manuel Alvarez

(continuacion de la pagina uno.)

Ili teopo buttawacame veme ayana uchia into watem car oficina, sami joona, sisig joona, cari restorant. Je jabesa ili giosti yak opo usyoisi noka, hunuk ili te vetana, ussim aturec tuisi buicri amac yabae, junensu cuasmapo loria pascapo ven teopo te hipuene Lios Iton achay licencia itom mikne.

Ussim tuisi machi ane, nar mekka tuca apo ileni limet carimbo hamta, tomovipo ll nosontene; bempo caita hik ta itapo ahikkaha batora vetana.

Chicti tucapo escuela etap goobusanimpo caita juneiya aman ructine hibba, ca nah tria tarune, yueme caita caita vetchivo tuine: Uss evetchivo tequipanua jabes nabuitine empo hibua baete jabesa buanne empo buantai jabesa ca cotne empo cokoe jabasa encho toboctana emp ahuemateco into jabesa em enchi mahta? Junuk jamut kaybu vevesito en aeway ju o ou empo ca ioiore into a ania.

Ussi: En yohuem nake, am ioiore, am ania, am hinneu vempo junen awatateco: In yac Dios aman tecato enchi naikiane, cat am suale wat ussim vempo caita yari evetchivo.

Into goi Lomingo vemela wa te natebay bu u tequil bee naue tequipanuane o owian, hamuchim ussi hiohuia, sim maloka yeu tahti, o ou jit waatateco tequipanuane ae vetchivo.

(Editor's Note: Don Manu Alvarez, who has authored the Yaqui language articl since LA VOZ DE MAYO bega is professor of the Yaqui classes at Richey Communi School. His classes are 7 to 9 p.m. each Wednesda and Friday. These classe just as all Community Sch Classes, are open to all.

+ + + + +

LA VOZ de MAYO -- The Voice Mexicans, Americans, Yaquis and Others Organized in Barrios Pascua, Adelanto, a Blue Moon -- is published monthly (more or less) at Tucson, Az.

Mailing address: 802 W Adel.

Editors: Ramon Jaurigue
          Pete Lopez
          Ceci Valencia
          Teodora Acuña

Art & Lay-out: Rosie Jimen

SCHOLAR-SHIPS

All young people of our Model Cities Unit who are interested in scholarships to further their education whether at the University of Arizona, Pima College, or other places, should contact the Unit Chairman as soon as possible. See him at our next MAYO general meeting on Feb. 9th, or even better, before then.

DREAMS

I'm flying high and home free.
My feelings find their
possibilities.

I see,
yet my eyes are blind.
I watch the spiral pattern
of my mind.

The dark slowly fades away.
My mind is filled with
light of the coming day.

Gloria Jimenez
Seventh grade
Richey School

La nueva iglesia de San Ignacio

Community School Director R. Jaurigue signs up the first student for the Adult Education program, Gene Preciado.

CATECHISM

There are now catechism classes for all children from grades 1 to 8 at Holy Family Church each Saturday. We encourage all parents to send their children. The bus leaves from in front of Santa Rosa church each Saturday morning at 8:45. The classes last until 10 a.m.

DOCTRINA EN SAGRADA FAMILIA

Ahora hay clases de doctrina para todos los niños de los grados uno a ocho en Sagrada Familia todos los sabados.

Animamos a los padres para que manden sus niños. El bus irá de en frente de la iglesia de Santa Rosa cada sabado a las 8:45 a.m. Las clases duran hasta las 10 a.m.

CARTAS

Señor Editor:

Porque hay muchos lectores de LA VOZ DE MAYO en el area del Barrio Libre, yo quisiera usar sus paginas para anunciar algo:

Estamos dando la Misa cada Martes y Sabado a las 6:30 de la noche en la Capilla de San Martin de Porres (Calle 39 y Avenida 10.)

Muchas gracias,

Padre J. Shaughnessy
El Apostolado de los
Barrios de Tucson

\+ + +

Readers of LA VOZ:

The HELPMOBILE is coming to the MAYO Area again. It is parked across the street from Santa Rosa church every Tuesday morning from 10 o'clock untill 12 o'clock.

Would you like to make a patchwork quilt, like the one Matilda Ybañez is making? Henrietta Womack is making a yarn picture. Concha Ruiz made a warm poncho. And the Christmas decorations for the church were beautiful.

We make cookies some mornings and Fred serves coffee. Bring your young children. They can have juice and cookies while they play and watch Television together. Remember, that's on Tuesdays, at 10 a.m.

Sue Druckman, Barbara
Soble, Fred Bayne

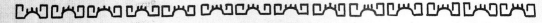

VENGAN TODOS A LA ESCUELA DE LA COMUNIDAD! ESTAS CLASES SON GRATUITAS.
EN LA ESCUELA RICHEY...... LAS CLASES SON DE LUNES A VIERNES.

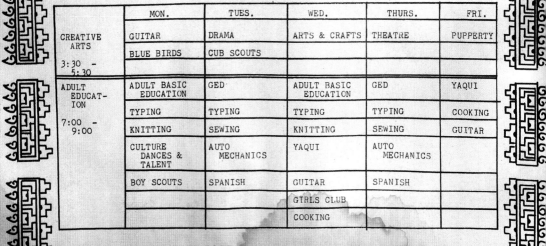

	MON.	TUES.	WED.	THURS.	FRI.
CREATIVE ARTS 3:30 - 5:30	GUITAR	DRAMA	ARTS & CRAFTS	THEATRE	PUPPERTY
	BLUE BIRDS	CUB SCOUTS			
ADULT EDUCATION 7:00 - 9:00	ADULT BASIC EDUCATION	GED	ADULT BASIC EDUCATION	GED	YAQUI
	TYPING	TYPING	TYPING	TYPING	COOKING
	KNITTING	SEWING	KNITTING	SEWING	GUITAR
	CULTURE DANCES & TALENT	AUTO MECHANICS	YAQUI	AUTO MECHANICS	
	BOY SCOUTS	SPANISH	GUITAR	SPANISH	
			GIRLS CLUB		
			COOKING		

COME ONE - COME ALL - TO RICHEY COMMUNITY SCHOOL PROGRAM FOR CREATIVE ARTS AND ADULT EDUCATION. THERE IS NO CHARGE. CLASSES FROM MONDAY THROUGH FRIDAY.

Newspaper Clippings

When I started working on this project, I needed a place to start and double-check my sources. My family Ralph, Crystal, Erin, Francine, and Adelina Jaurigue gave me newspaper clippings and published interviews featuring Ramon Jaurigue. Thankfully, Ramon was aware of the responsibility he had to talk to the press. Here's the proof that Ramon facilitated the purchase of Old Pascua, thereby cementing the tribe on their land, and helped the community gain jobs, along with co-founding the low-cost clinic meant to serve the impoverished community.

From left to right: Don Manuel Alvarez, Ramon Jaurigue, Rosie Jimenez, Teodora Acuna

6-13-70

Participation Is The 'Gut

By TOM DUDDLESTON JR.
Citizen Staff Writer

"Citizen participation . . . is a nebulous term," two Model Cities workers agree, but it's the "whole guts" of the program and the key to its success, they say.

And as the program moves into a "year of action," participation is an indispensable requisite and the biggest problem the Model Cities program faces, contend Ramon Jaurigue and Fred G. Acosta.

Jaurigue is acting director of a $75,000 federal Training and Technical Assistance grant (T&TA) approved for Tucson's Model Cities program last September.

The money is used specifically to provide the residents an opportunity to extend, increase and improve the quality of their participation in Model Cities planning processes.

Jaurigue said the program financed by the grant provides residents with the knowledge to cope with the Model Cities program. . . building their capacity to respond quickly and effectively to the requirements of each Model Cities function.

The special program offers training from resident consultants in the field and specialists on anything related to Model Cities — "as a vehicle for residents to express themselves and their hopes and goals while the planning is going on," Jaurigue said.

Funds are used to supplement Model Cities planning by the City Demonstration Agency (the city), and to be responsive to the city by providing a director as a link between the residents, the CDA and the fiscal agent for the project, the Committee for Economic Opportunity.

The Model Neighborhood Council of Model Cities last year requested the grant together with the city and the CEO.

The Office of Economic Opportunity awarded the grant on terms that the ideas of neighborhood residents would be incorporated into the working program and T&TA activities would be coordinated with other agen-

Ramon Jaurigue

cies operating in the Model Cities area.

Jaurigue serves as the coordinator, minimizing any lack of communication between the city, the fiscal agent and the 24,000 residents of the six-square-mile midtown Model Cities area.

He and Acosta maintain t biggest problem in Model Citi is to give the people it aims serve an understanding of t program so they can join in a help on a meaningful level them.

"People don't think much Model Cities because they do know much about it," Jaurig said. "And they've been slight in the past and are sick of pla ning and projections and wa action now."

Under the training and ass tance program, consultants a sent to the model neighborhoo to talk and "communicate w the residents on a person-to-pe son basis," Jaurigue said.

He said the consultar frequently knock on doors a talk, telling of Model Cities r lated meetings, what is agendas and how important attendance and participation are

Visual aids such as films Model Neighborhood Coun meetings or of the Model Citi area also are used, he sa Acosta said the University Arizona KUAT-TV already ha filmed five half-hour program related to Model Cities.

Newspaper clipping from The Tucson Citizen on June 13th, 1970 with Ramon Jaurigue and Fred G. Acosta.

The first M.A.Y.O. meeting on April 28, 1969

Of Model Cities Program

...ta and Jaurigue say the ...Cities program "has not ...e anything" for the resi-...a problem they largely ...e to poor resident coop-

...ta is the deputy director ...odel neighborhood coor-...for the Model Cities pro-...nd works with Jaurigue in ...stering the training

...nd Jaurigue contend in-...te income, 25 per cent ...loyment rate, a below-av-...ducational level and poor ...se from help agencies all ...esident cooperation in the

...del cities wants residents ...ation and not resident ...ation," Acosta said. Jau-...admitted pacification oc-...a both sides, manifested ...r a "silent majority" of ...ultants or residents.

...grant, budgeted through ...d of this month, gives ...tive services" to Model ...rea residents, as in pro-...stipends to involved citi-

...poor are always asked to ...er," Acosta complained.

so stipends are offered to defray the costs of meeting such expenses as use of autos, in order to support the participation of the near, or acutely, impoverished.

An extension of the official ending date for T&TA — June 30 — has been requested because a work program has been planned, Acosta said, and additional months until Aug. 31 would enable its implementation.

"Understanding the concepts of Model Cities is a complicated thing," Acosta says, and the training program offers orientation of residents by actual "doing" instead of in sessions of a classroom nature.

Jaurigue said the Model Cities program gives use of all federal and other resources available to a central agency to coordinate rehabilitation and improvement of social and economic conditions in a given area.

At the end of the six years Model Cities will be federally budgeted, he says the areas should be "demonstration models illustrating what can be done by coordinated federal and local action and resources."

Fred G. Acosta

The training grant money for Tucson's Model Cities program was accumulated with $60,000 from the OEO, and $7,500 each from the City of Tucson and the local CEO, representing Santa Cruz and Pima counties.

Jaurigue is the first Model Cities worker whose salary is paid by a private agency, an advantage in that there is an appreciable increase in manpower hours for the project, but no drain of budget money.

The Catholic Social Service "made a commitment" May 15 and loaned him to Model Cities, agreeing to continue paying his salary, Jaurigue said. He and Acosta advise other such commitments by concerned agencies.

As far as success of the grant and Model Cities is concerned, "basically we cannot promise anything . . . there has only been about 5 per cent implementation of programs against problems," Jaurigue said.

Acosta, as the bridge between the city and Model Cities residents — "when blunders occur, I try to keep the flow going," said Model Cities is always concerned with people and money.

"If you've got the money, you need people . . . if you've got the people, you need money. . ."

"Now," with the money, stress Jaurigue and Acosta, "We want some relevant participation by residents . . . we want the talking people.

WITH $55,000 GRANT FROM CATHOLICS

Yaquis To Buy Pascua Village Land

A $55,000 grant from the Catholic Church Development Program will give Yaqui Indians at Old Pascua Village ownership of the land on which they have squatted for more than 50 years.

The grant is one of five made by the Catholic Church to Arizona community groups.

Of a total state grant of $154,650, $40,000 was given to the Valle del Sol Organization in Phoenix; $20,000 to Chicanos Por La Causa, Phoenix; $15,000 to the Pima County Welfare Rights Organization, Tucson; $24,650 to the Dine-Bi-Naa-Yei, Cooperative of Pinon, Chinle, and $55,000 to the Mexican American Yaqui and Others Organization, who will handle the land purchase negotiations for the Yaquis.

The land at Old Pascua Village, consisting of 130 lots, is now owned by the Marshall Foundation, a Tucson charitable foundation which receives its revenue from rent on the property it owns adjacent to the University of Arizona.

According to Ramon Jaurigue, president of MAYO, negotiations have been going on with the Marshall Foundation on the purchase of the Pascua land and a figure of $55,000 had been agreed upon.

Jaurigue said that the Catholic Social Service had been designated as the delegate agency by MAYO to handle the transaction.

He said "the Yaquis have been trying hard to help themselves but have been limited because financing for housing and repairs has been contingent on the ownership of their land."

Oct. 6, 1971 p. 35

Candlemaking — Yaqui Style

Placing wicks in small vigil lights manufactured by the Yaqui Indians at their 1117 N. Main Ave. factory are, from left, Bonnie Elenes, Lupe Garcia and Mrs. Dora Tona. What began as a neighborhood project seven months ago has become a lucrative business.

Yaqui Indians Expanding Candlemaking Business

By LAWSON ALLEN
Citizen Business Writer

The Yaqui Indians are floating a $25,000 loan and hope to corner the candle market in Southern Arizona.

What is now an expanding business venture did not begin that way less than a year ago, however.

"Our original idea was to give the young people something to do, some form of useful activity to keep them occupied and off the streets," explained the Rev. Anthony Sanchez.

Father Sanchez has worked closely with the project since its modest beginning with a $500 grant from the Catholic Social Service here.

Candlemaking, it turns out, has done more than keep some Yaqui youngsters busy. They discovered there is a market — and money — for their product. The loan from the Great Western Bank will give them the working capital to expand and provide more employment to meet the increasing demand.

"The company will continue to operate in the rented five-room factory, but with the loan we will be able to buy the materials we need to fill all the orders that are coming in," Father Sanchez said.

The sudden influx of orders is due in large measure to the Yaquis' recent decision to make candles in jars and sell them to restaurants.

They are now producing about as many restaurant candles as they are small eight-hour vigil lights for churches and decorative candles to be used on festivals and holidays.

There is more to candlemaking than pouring wax in a mold. It is a business, and the Yaquis are learning a little about free enterprise.

Last October they set up the Yaqui Corp., and all the workers in the factory are shareholders. The company's secretary, Natalia Cocio, has enrolled in the University of Arizona where she is specializing in business administration. Studying bookkeeping in a night course at the university is company president Ramon H. Jaurigue.

"It is the workers' company, and they are taking it seriously, and doing a good job," said Father Sanchez.

"Of course they received some help in the beginning. They didn't know how to make candles, and the federal government paid all the expenses of having a candlemaker come here for three or four weeks to teach them.

"Also, business people here have been helpful and encouraging, and their cooperation has made many things a lot easier," he added.

Six persons are employed at the factory, but Father Sanchez expects this to increase to 10 within the next few months.

"Now that they can buy new jars and not be forced to take so much time and labor cleaning used jars, production at the factory will increase tremendously," he predicted.

"In fact, we are going to cover Tucson and Phoenix first and then expand to all the towns in Southern Arizona. There is a market for good candles and we hope all Southern Arizona will be buying candles from the Yaquis instead of New York or Los Angeles," he said.

In The Light Business

Yaqui Corp. President Ramon Jaurigue and Mrs. Jaurigue pour wax for an order of offering candles for a local church. Similar candles in jars for restaurants can be produced at a rate of 3,600 a day.

Leonor & Ramon Jaurigue ran a candle making factory to help give members of their neighborhood work.

Jay Facing Fight On Hospital Board

By DENNIS ESKOW
Citizen Staff Writer

Attempting to reverse a move by Thomas Jay, chairman of the Board of Supervisors, to name businessmen to a proposed County Hospital advisory board, the Mexican-American Youth Organization will meet May 15 to determine new courses of action.

"Some people are angry and others are anxious to see more changes made in the hospital," said Ramon Jaurigue, president of the group, who contends all members of the committee should be users of the hospital.

The supervisors Monday tabled for further investigation the recommended list of committeemen, submitted by Dr. Frederick Brady, head of the County Health Department. Names on the list were not made public.

Jay said the list "did not contain any representatives of the business community." He told Jaurigue and others representing the Mexican-American group that he wanted "people who carry the burden of financing the hospital" on the advisory board.

"The board should consist of people who use the facility," Jaurigue said today, adding that the county's board of health, to which the advisory board would answer, already is composed of businessmen.

Supervisor Jim Murphy says he supports appointment of users to the board. Supervisor Dennis Weaver has not commented on the issue.

The MAYO leader said users are more knowledgeable about problems of those who must use the hospital.

"Just for an example, people who come for 8 o'clock appointments usually don't get in to see a doctor til 3."

Several organizations are seeking appointment of users to the board, including the Citizens Coalition for Social Action and the Catholic Social Service organization.

Naming of the board had been tabled once earlier by the supervisors.

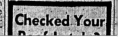

Ramon quoted in Tucson Citizen for healthcare refo

TUCSON, ARIZONA, FRIDAY, DECEMBER 13, 1974

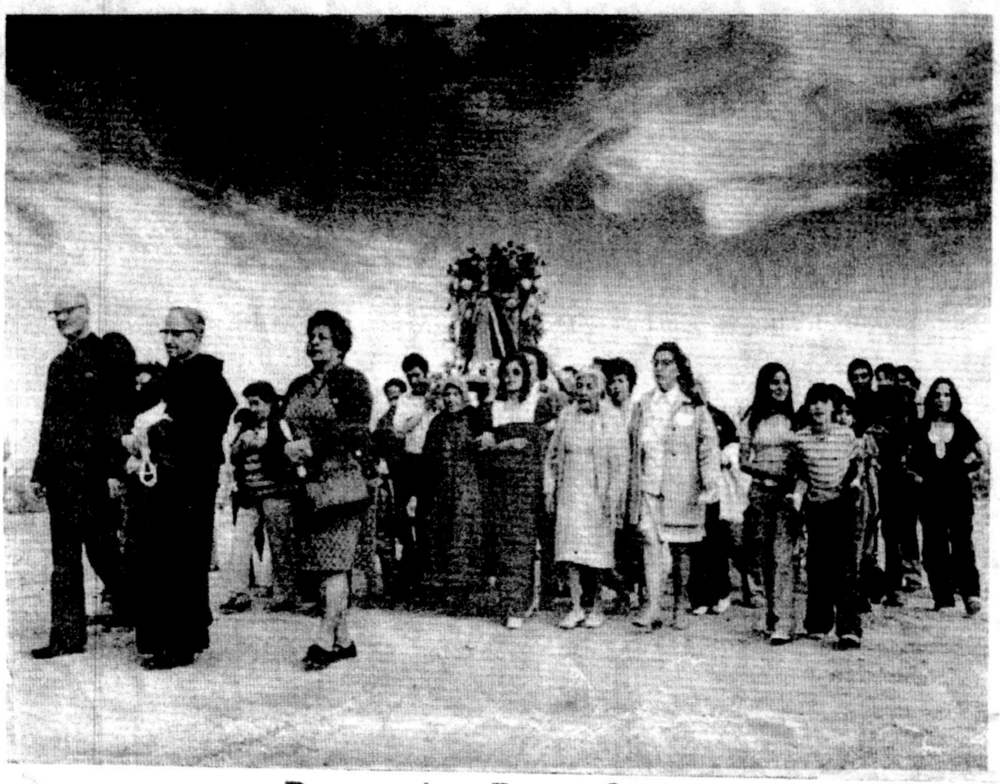

Procession Bears Statue

A procession of Mexican-Americans bearing a statue of Our Lady of Guadalupe on her feast day, Dec. 12, approaches a historic site at the foot of "A" Mountain where community leaders yesterday dedicated the future location of the Mexican-American Cultural Center. The procession wound across desert brush from the Santa Cruz River to the dedication site and a primitive ramada, where Mass was celebrated. The bottomland area is considered by many to be the birthplace of Tucson and was the home of Indian tribes who settled there about 1,100 years ago. (Star Photo by Art Grasberger)

Site At Foot Of 'A' Mountain Dedicated For Culture Center

By JUDY DONOVAN
Star Staff Writer

The Mexican-American Unity Council yesterday dedicated a historic site at the foot of "A" Mountain as the future location of a Mexican-American Cultural Center, amid mariachi music and solemn religious observance.

Now a small city park, the 6.1-acre site on S. Mission Rd. between the mountain and the Santa Cruz River was donated to the council more than two years ago. Since then, plans have developed for the construction of a center to include a job-training facility, community activity center, day care facility, library, museum and theater. Open to the public, the center would include all aspects of the Mexican and Hispanic culture.

Attending the ceremonies before approximately 250 persons were Mayor Lew Murphy, City Council and state Legislature members and leaders of the Mexican-American community, historical organizations, educational fields and governmental agencies.

"This is something that is long overdue," Murphy told the crowd. Referring to the historic significance of the site which is near the first European settlement of Spanish missionary priests begun in 1699, the mayor said the future center could be a melding of the past and future at a place that probably is the birthplace of Tucson.

"In reality, it is a return to us of the land where our ancestors made history," said Jennie Morales of the unity council.

Tom Peterson of the Tucson-Pima County Historical Commission and the Arizona Historical Society said Tucson is the first community in the state to officially use bilingual site markers. He unveiled a metal plaque which describes in Spanish the history of the cultural center site and surrounding area.

Since Indian tribes first settled the rich Santa Cruz bottomland in about 800 A.D., the area at the base of the mountain has been continuously occupied, making the community approximately 1,200 years old, Peterson said.

Following the dedication, a procession of Mexican-Americans bearing a statue of Our Lady of Guadalupe, the patroness of Mexico, arrived from the riverside to the park. The Rev. Narciso Santesmases of Santa Cruz Church celebrated mass outdoors under a picturesque ramada, on an altar bearing the statue. The mass was in honor of Our Lady of Guadalupe whose feast day it was.

Ramon carrying the cross up 'A' Mountain

Consumer Unit Meets Friday

Pima County Hospital's Consumer Council will meet for the first time next Friday for an orientation session with the County Board of Health.

Dr. Frederick Brady, county health administrator, and Joseph Herrick, county hospital administrator, also will take part in the meeting, designed as an education session on how the hospital system works.

"I am anxious to get together if only to meet the other members," said Mrs. Refugio Yabes, one of five persons appointed to the advisory body last week by the Board of Supervisors.

None of the members would speculate what the advisory board will be doing until after the first meeting.

"We'll have time to decide what we're going to accomplish after we've gotten together," said Oscar Duarte, a new council member, and South Tucson Police sergeant.

Other council members include Ramon Jaurigue, of the Tucson Model Cities program; Mrs. Tommie Thomas, "A" Mountain area Council director, and Mrs. Jaunita Bean, who uses the county hospital along with her seven children.

The consumer council will advise the county hospital and the health department on complaints coming from hospital users and will also propose ways to alleviate problems at the hospital.

Ramon's work with the Pima County Hospital Council.

Hospital's New Panel Criticized

Appointment of a new five-member Pima County Hospital Consumer Council — announced by the Board of Supervisors today — already has been criticized by one of the council's members.

Ramon Jaurigue, a Model Cities policy board member who accepted appointment to the council, said the unit "still is not representative enough and will have to be expanded."

Jaurigue said the Coalition for Social Action, which represents several minority group organizations, will meet next week to determine "what needs to be done to balance the council to include more consumers and not just people who live near the hospital." The coalition's steering committee last week asked that an additional three members of the council be appointed.

Others besides Jaurique appointed to the council are Mrs. Rugugia Yabez, Mrs. Tommie Thomas, Oscar Duarte and Mrs. Juanita Bean.

The appointments came after a year-long battle within the Board of Supervisors over whether there should be a users-only council or one that included businessmen as well as users.

Mrs. Yabez, of 502 N. Riverside Ave., was honored last year as woman of the year by the Tucson Council on the Aging. She also is active on the Mexican-American Cancer Society.

Mrs. Thomas, 846 W. San Juan Trail mother of nine, is director of the "A" Mountain Area Council.

Jaurigue identified Duarte, a South Tucson police sergeant and bailiff, as a member of the council not using the hospital. Duarte is former station manager of KXEW radio.

Mrs. Bean, 220 W. Veteran's Blvd., and her 11 children are users of the hospital facilities.

Ramon wanted more representation within the Pima County Hospital Council.

Southard will head housing unit

M. James Southard is the new president of the Tucson Housing Corporation Board.

Other officers elected at the board's annual meeting were Hugh Holub, vice president; Mrs. Lorraine Harsch, secretary, and Mrs. Quincie Douglas, treasurer.

Executive committee members are Doris Rush, Harlan Agnew, Ramon Jaurigue, Richard Martinez and Jimmie Walker.

The corporation is aimed at finding housing for low-income and middle-income people in the downtown area. It is funded by Model Cities.

Proof that Ramon worked with the Tucson Housing Corporation Board to help low-income families find affordable housing.

Additional Materials

My mother, Francine, gave me a five-page document written by Ramon. It felt like a final letter from him after his death. It's unclear when this was written, but it read like a speech making the argument that the Yaqui people were here first, and highlighting the importance of keeping them in Old Pascua.

PASCUA

The City of Tucson is presently developing a Land Use Plan which is intended to assure orderly growth, permanency and stability for many areas of this city. Same areas have been identified for residential use. One of these is Pascua Area where 3,000 people live west of Miracle Mile and south of Grant Rd.

The area gets its name from Pascua Village, the settlement of Yaqui Indians, which is at its heart.

This year, to support the permanent development of Pascua, the city through the Model Cities program will put in sewers and lights where none exist today. Planned for the near future is rehabilitation of housing along with the improvement of streets and other such facilities.

In its design of a long range land use plan, the City is interested in Cultural values along with economic and the others. And it is to this theme that we are talking most directly today.

For Pascua Village holds one of the greater treasures belonging to Tucson. The Easter Ceremony of the Yaqui Indians is unusual for the entire country and at the moment it deserves the attention of the wider community which it enriches.

There is perhaps nothing else quite like it in the entire nation. For in this ceremony, the rich life of the North American Indian of pre-Spanish days is complexly blended with the western Christian religion tradition.

In the past, the Yaquis have made their ceremony available to Tucsonians and tourists as spectators. Now they need your help.

The Yaquis were originally hunters whose homeland was primarily the valley of the Yaqui River in southern Sonora. There they were "discovered" by the Spanish explorer Cabeza de Vaca in the 16th century.

The Easter Ceremony in a sense is almost timeless in that the heritage of the Yaqui Indian religious tradition fades into the dark distant past.

In another sense, the ceremony began in 1617 when the Jesuit priest Father Perez de Ribas went among the Yaquis, carrying with him the Catholic tradition of dramatizing the Passion of Our Lord.

The ceremony that Tucsonians see today is a living memory of those two traditions.

After the arrival of Perez de Ribas, the Yaquis continued their lives peacefully for a century. But then came a time of war as the Yaquis fought for their independence against an effort to subjugate them and take their lands.

Eventually, the Yaquis were decisively defeated in 1886. Many of them were transported to the Yucatan Peninsula. But some crossed the border at the turn of the century and found new homes in Tucson and Phoenix.

Here, the Yaquis settled near the Santa Cruz River, earning their living as farm helpers. The community became known as Pascua Village, taking its name from the Indian word for Easter.

Then in 1909, the Indians revived their Easter Ceremony at Pascua, using a simple ramada as a chapel. The Ceremony has lived there since.

The ramada is the architectural ancestor of all the southwestern chapels. And so it was at Pascua where the Indians eventually built a permanent chapel named San Ignacio de Loyola after their patron saint.

The Easter Ceremony is actually more than a moment on the calendar. It is so interwoven into the lives of the people that it runs through the entire year.

The Yaquis look upon their participation in the ceremony as a religious devotion which they denote to their community. The dancers such as the Matachinis and other participants are members of religious societies which transmit the rituals down through the generations.

Catholic tradition is represented musically by western instruments such as the violin and the guitar or the harp. During the ceremony, the people move through the Stations of the Cross as they do in the European Passion Plays.

The prehistoric music is represented by the drum, the flute and the rasp. Ancient Indian tradition still appears in Tucson today also in the complicated role of the Deer Dancer. As the economic source of the ancient Yaqui way of life, the deer still holds meaning — as friend as well as food.

The ceremony is very complex, involving for example deep meaning in the use of flowers. Yaquis hold close the legend that the blood of Christ on the Cross was miraculously converted into flowers as it fell to the ground. In the Easter Ceremony, flowers symbolizing divine grace, the good and the beautiful, overcame evil.

In 1968, the chapel of San Ignacio de Loyola was torn down. This was part of the episode in which some Yaquis moved to New Pascua Village offered the Indians west of Tucson.

Many Yaquis, however, did not move — because of feelings about roots in Old Pascua or financial inhibitions. And they naturally had a desire to carry on the ceremony which is the heart of their life.

Within the Pascua Area with a purpose to develop its resources there is the Mayo Organisation. Its voting members are the residents of the area — Yaqui, Mexican and others. But participants are invited to join from all of Tucson.

Early this year, Mayo went to the Mayor and Council requesting permission to put up temporary facilities for the 1969 Easter Ceremony and beyond that to be allowed to rebuild a permanent plaza.

A simple ramada-chapel was erected to permit the Easter celebration. But beyond that, the City Community Development Department has taken an interest in the permanent project.

The people themselves through Mayo went to the Design Center — an organisation of the local chapter of the American Institute of Architects, intended to help those unable to afford architectural services.

And in response, a group of four Design Center members has now designed a new Plaza based on the Yaqui directions. The group included three professional architects — Fred Palafox, James Kelly and Dan Harrington — along with University of Arizona student Douglas Eddy and the consultation of another architect, Mike Lugo, who is active in Model Cities affairs.

The design of the chapel is consisten with photographs of the original San Ignacio de Loyola chapel, including bell towers.

Construction material is to be of concrete block (instead of mud adobe) with a white plaster surface.

The chapel itself — called the Capia — is a 30 by 40 feet structure with a 10-feet high opening along with a wing on each side. The two wings will not only serve the Easter Ceremony but act as a center for year around recreational and other purposes. One wing, known as the reception room, is used by participants to prepare themselves for the Easter Ceremony.

The other wing will include an office and toilet facilities.

At the entrance to the Plaza, the architects have designed an enclosed kitchen (built of concrete block) 30 by 25 feet and similarly a 30 by 45 feet ramada which is used in the Easter Ceremony.

On each side of the Plaza are to be eight 8 by 10 feet stalls which will serve to serve food and other things during the Fiesta.

The Plaza ground is to be unpaved in line with Yaqui tradition.

The entire facility will be available for a multitude of purposes, fitting in with the Yaqui tradition where religion is a daily, year around part of life.

The Plaza is considered by the Yaquis "public land" having been deeded as such by former owners.

The Marshall Foundation owns 132 lots which are occupied by Yaqui families without payment of rent. Also, 24 Yaqui families own their own lots.

The Yaqui population of Old Pascua Village has been variously estimated at between 600 and 900 persons.   Every indication is that while some will move to New Pascua, a substantial number and probably the majority will permanently make Old Pascua their home.

Labor Unions have volunteered supervisory service for the Plaza construction project. All labor will be voluntary.

Since the culture of the Yaqui people, as particularly symbolized in the Easter Ceremony, is such a rich part of the life in this entire valley, it is reasonable that the city generally be concerned that it continue to live with the permanent development of the Plaza

HENRY BARAJAS is a Latinx author from Tucson, AZ. He is best known for his graphic memoir about his great-grandfather Ramon Jaurigue, titled *La Voz De M.A.Y.O.: Tata Rambo*. He has contributed to anthologies benefiting mass shooting survivors and The Southern Poverty Law Center such as *Where We Live* and *The Good Fight*. Currently, Barajas is the Director of Operations at Top Cow Productions— and he lives with his roommate's cats Ophelia & Morticia in Los Angeles, CA.

J. GONZO is a Chicano artist, born and raised in Cypress, CA., who resides in Phoenix, AZ. He attended the Orange County High School of the Arts' Visual Arts Program and went to a terrible trade school for a degree in Graphic Design. He also apprenticed and tattooed professionally for a number of years before entering the world of advertising and design. Gonzo has spent the past 20-plus years using his creative skills at ad agencies, toy and comic companies, design studios, and freelancing as well as creating his own comic book title—*La Mano del Destino*.

CLAIRE NAPIER is a freelance editor and cartoonist. She was a features editor at Women Write About Comics for six years, and Editor in Chief 2017-2018. She still writes for WWAC, as well as at ComicsMNT and Shelfdust. Among others, Claire edits Hari Connor's award-winning *Finding Home*, the activist memoir *La Voz De M.A.Y.O.: Tata Rambo*, and is currently editing the story comics magazine *BUN & TEA*. She can be found at @illusclaire and will be delighted to work with you.

BERNARDO BRICE is a Chilean letterer based in Santiago, Chile. On par with collaborating on *La Voz De M.A.Y.O.: Tata Rambo*, his lettering credits include *Artifact* (Valve Corporation), the benefit anthologies *Where We Live* (Image Comics) and *The Good Fight*, the independent graphic novels *The Bawdy Tales of Lazlo Cale* (Grenade Fight), and *Savage Empire* (Likes to Fight), among others.

The Top Cow essentials checklist:

For more ISBN and ordering information on our latest collections go to:

topcow.com

Ask your retailer about our catalogue of collected editions,
digests, and hard covers or check the listings at:
Barnes and Noble, Amazon.com,
and other fine retailers.

To find your nearest comic shop go to:
www.comicshoplocator.com